ALLEZ ALLEZ ALLEZ

www.penguin.co.uk

Also by Simon Hughes

SECRET DIARY OF A LIVERPOOL SCOUT
RED MACHINE
MEN IN WHITE SUITS
RING OF FIRE
ON THE BRINK

ALLEZ ALLEZ ALLEZ

THE INSIDE STORY OF THE RESURGENCE OF LIVERPOOL FC, CHAMPIONS OF EUROPE 2019

SIMON HUGHES

BANTAM PRESS

TRANSWORLD PUBLISHERS
61–63 Uxbridge Road, London W5 5SA
www.penguin.co.uk

Transworld is part of the Penguin Random House group of companies
whose addresses can be found at global.penguinrandomhouse.com

First published in Great Britain in 2019 by Bantam Press
an imprint of Transworld Publishers

A CIP catalogue record for this book
is available from the British Library.

ISBNs 9781787632707 (cased)
9781787632714 (tpb)

Typeset in 11.5/14.5pt Sabon by Jouve (UK), Milton Keynes
Printed and bound in Great Britain by Clays Ltd, Elcograf S.p.A.

Penguin Random House is committed to a sustainable
future for our business, our readers and our planet. This book
is made from Forest Stewardship Council® certified paper.

1 3 5 7 9 10 8 6 4 2

In memory of the 96
and those who have
suffered ever since

CONTENTS

CONTENTS

REALITY

INTRODUCTION: NEVER GIVE UP

Divock Origi had not played for Liverpool in a league game for nearly sixteen months and he'd not scored for the club in nineteen months. While Liverpool surged towards the Champions League final in 2017–18 he was on loan at Wolfsburg, where just six goals in 34 appearances were indicative of a torturous campaign. The team only remained in the Bundesliga through a relegation play-off and he was once substituted in the first half of a game against Hoffenheim. When he came back to Melwood in the summer of 2018, Liverpool fielded offers from Wolverhampton Wanderers and Huddersfield Town. Jürgen Klopp, Liverpool's manager, tried to encourage him to try the latter, where his friend David Wagner was in charge. Another loan might just have reignited his career but Origi did not believe another fight against relegation was in his best interests. Then, right at the end of the summer transfer window, Everton came in: a permanent deal to cross Stanley Park. At the right price, Origi might have gone. But he stayed and decided to fight for his place.

Origi, whose parents came from Kenya to Belgium in 1992 when his father, also a centre-forward, signed for KV Oostende, was considering his options again by the start of December. In the intervening three months he'd made just one Liverpool appearance – as a substitute in the humbling defeat at Red Star Belgrade in the Champions League, a result which complicated Liverpool's qualification for the knock-out stages. The winter transfer window posed possibilities of routes out of Merseyside altogether and possibly back to France where Marseille as well as AS Monaco were monitoring his situation. Origi, though, did not want it to end like this for him in England, where his career had seemed so promising following Klopp's appointment in October 2015 – a manager who had wanted to sign him in his previous role at Borussia Dortmund. In early 2016 Origi had become Liverpool's first-choice centre-forward and he was scoring goals, many of them important. Then, wham! A red-card tackle in the Merseyside derby from Ramiro Funes Mori ended his season early. While he missed the Europa League final through a serious ankle injury, Liverpool missed him too. His form then had been 'outstanding' according to Klopp; form he was unable to rediscover, which explained why Wolfsburg – a club usually in Germany's top six – seemed a sensible temporary solution.

Origi is intelligent, speaking four languages including Swahili, French and Flemish. He is also introspective and he was hurting. He assessed himself – what could he do better to get himself back into Klopp's thinking? He'd have been a psychologist if he wasn't a footballer. He is a keen observer of people's reactions to situations good and bad – his teammates' reactions, even his own. He'd encouraged his friends to do personality tests and watched a lot of TED TV. He came to realize that as much as he could talk through his concerns with Klopp – a manager he related to because of their shared emotional intelligence – the only way of getting back in the team was to train hard.

The opening months of Liverpool's season had been a slog: winning regularly in the league but hardly impressively. An optimist would say they were grinding results out; a realist would say they needed a shot of adrenaline to get the players moving faster, more convincingly.

On Sunday, 2 December the Merseyside derby was heading towards a draw. Everton's supporters in the Anfield Road end had sent a blue flare onto the pitch in celebration. Though it meant Everton's record at Anfield included no victories in twenty years, their joy, to some extent, was understandable. The result would have sent Liverpool four points behind Manchester City at the top of the Premier League table. A small victory.

With ten minutes to go Klopp turned back to his assistant Peter Krawietz. He was becoming desperate. They talked for ninety seconds and then the call came for Origi, who was warming up near the Kop. There was hardly a sense of anticipation that something remarkable was going to happen when he went on at Roberto Firmino's expense, the team's first-choice centre-forward. The groan that followed was enormous. Virgil van Dijk – the world's most expensive defender – ballooned a volley high into the night. It was the 96th minute and Liverpool's last chance of a goal had been spurned. The sound of plastic seats being tipped up and left was audible. The Evertonians in the distance cheered. But then, something outrageous happened. The ball plummeted from the sky. Everton's England international goalkeeper Jordan Pickford was watching it all the way. It came down fast, through the glare of the floodlights. It seemed like it might tip the top of the crossbar and bounce into the Kop. But Pickford couldn't be sure. His fingertips touched the ball and it rolled down the woodwork. Everton's defenders had stopped. Origi had not. Pandemonium.

Six months later Mohamed Salah entered the Anfield pitch wearing a dark t-shirt emblazoned with the words: NEVER GIVE UP. He had missed Liverpool's 4–0 victory over Barcelona which sent them through to their second Champions League final in as many seasons because of a head injury sustained at Newcastle, where Divock Origi's headed goal in injury time kept Liverpool's domestic title ambitions alive. Three nights after that Origi would score twice against the Spanish champions to help overturn a three-goal first-leg deficit. Salah – and certainly Origi – had never given up, but neither had any of their teammates, spurred on by their inspirational leader, Jürgen Klopp, whose own life story and career path had been underpinned by struggle, glory, disappointment and recovery.

Klopp had begun the 2018–19 season with questions still to answer. He had built Liverpool up during his two and a half seasons at the club but was yet to win a trophy. He had promised to bring silverware by his fourth year at the very latest, and those doubting him claimed he was the world's greatest cheerleader – all he really did was hug his players and make them feel better. Would that translate into palpable football success?

By June 2019 he was hugging his players again. He was hugging Andy Robertson, the Scottish left-back who was told he was too small to play for Celtic and had begun his amateur career on the dole just six years previously. He was hugging Virgil van Dijk, the Dutch national team captain who was not fancied by any of the established clubs in his homeland. He was hugging Joël Matip, the free-transfer defender from Cameroon who the author of this book once likened to 'a caribou trying to control an ice cube'. He was hugging Trent Alexander-Arnold, the 'normal lad from Liverpool whose dreams have come true'. He was hugging Jordan Henderson, the team captain who'd been heckled by some inside Anfield a few months earlier when Klopp asked him to help out at right-back in a 1–1 draw with Leicester City. He was hugging Georginio Wijnaldum, whose 84-year-old grandmother was watching in the stands – she had raised him in Rotterdam, walking the forty-five minutes to the training ground every day to make sure her grandson was safe. He was hugging James Milner, the 33-year-old 'grandad' according to Van Dijk who Klopp believes can play until he's forty. He was hugging Alisson Becker, Fabinho and Firmino, the club's Brazilian triumvirate who believed in Klopp when Philippe Coutinho did not. He was hugging Salah, whose 25-yard larrup against Chelsea in April was the goal of the season. He hugged Sadio Mané, whose route, like Salah's, had started in rural Africa and had taken both of them to this: Liverpool's waterfront with a quarter of a million people in attendance, welcoming the champions of Europe home after a magical weekend in Madrid.

At the back of the bus, Origi separated himself from the celebrations temporarily and looked at his medal. Klopp saw him and leaned over. 'Everything OK, Divock?' Klopp asked him, holding a beer bottle in both hands, knowing, of course, that it absolutely was. 'I am fine, boss,' Origi told him. 'But I can't believe we've done it.' His goal in the final had helped Liverpool cross the line in Madrid less than twenty-four hours earlier. 'You have done it, Divock,' Klopp corrected him. 'You had to believe in yourself first. Then we helped each other.'

Brendan Rodgers had almost guided Liverpool to their first league title in twenty-four years. Fifteen months later, though, he was on the verge of the sack. Having written a 2,000-word article in the *Independent on Sunday* about where it had all gone wrong for Rodgers at Anfield, I discussed who his replacement as manager might be, should he depart. Three reliable sources had told me that though Jürgen Klopp was available after leaving Borussia Dortmund in the summer – where he had won two Bundesliga titles – Liverpool's ownership group, Fenway Sports Group, were more likely to look elsewhere for a new manager. Klopp had been an ambition out of reach in 2012 when Rodgers was appointed, but the structure at Anfield had evolved since, with Michael Edwards' rise towards sporting director and the belief that any potential new manager must be willing to operate within this framework. Rodgers didn't want to initially but went along with the idea, though eventually turned against it when the pressure on him began to rise. While José Mourinho's position at Chelsea was under review and their more recent culture of success as well as their financial reach had the potential to send Klopp there, Fenway would need to make Klopp the most expensive manager in the club's history to bring him to Anfield.

These factors boiled down to a fifteen-word line at the very end of a piece which suggested those clamouring for a Klopp appointment might be disappointed. The article, I thought, had far more interesting details relating to the fall of Rodgers. And yet, perhaps it proved to be the detail with the most consequences – I will never know for absolute certainty. Other journalists had published similar commentaries. Maybe they were having similar conversations. Maybe, even, Liverpool had set it up to appear this way and had decided to wait for Klopp while he took a sabbatical, making it look like Rodgers had their full support – the sort of thing done by owners who care about perception.

The following morning my mobile phone started ringing. It was a contact who had a direct line to one of the three key figures at Fenway. He quickly told me that the article had stimulated dialogue between John W. Henry, Tom Werner and Mike Gordon, the ownership group's leaders who lived in different parts of the United States. Crucially, I thought, he did not seem interested in contesting any of the parts about the shortcomings of Rodgers: how his relationships with players had cracked, how the trust of staff at Melwood that were meant to support him had been lost. Instead, he was focused on finding out how I had established the role of Klopp in all of this. It's a well-trotted-out line but nevertheless a truism: any journalist worth his or her corn never reveals their sources. I fired back with a series of questions myself and it became clear that Fenway had recognized that Klopp's personality had the capacity to overwhelm. 'That is exactly what this club needs,' I said.

In the past Fenway, who openly admitted they knew little about the game of football but emphasized their success in running other sports franchises across the US, had listened to and followed the advice of what they called 'pre-eminent soccer advisors'. On this occasion, however, I was informed that they were considering following different advice, and while it was true there were some doubts about Klopp – including Fenway's own pulling power – they would seriously consider him if he was still available should they decide to change manager.

Rodgers' position had been unstable across the summer and it was well known that he needed to start the new season positively. After Liverpool concluded the month of August by losing 3–0 at Anfield to West Ham (which also happened to be my wedding day), in September it got worse: a comprehensive 3–1 defeat at Manchester United was followed by draws in Bordeaux then with recently promoted Norwich City, a side that would finish the campaign in the relegation zone. For a full-strength team, extra-time and penalties were required to beat League Two side Carlisle United despite having home advantage.

With Rodgers drowning I had in the meantime contacted Klopp's agent, Marc Kosicke, and we spoke for nearly an hour about Liverpool. Though the agent would not commit to any sort of interest in a position already taken by another manager, it became clear that Liverpool was intriguing. The discussion centred on the club's history and culture but also its current operation. One of the questions related to Ian Ayre, the chief executive. On reflection, I painted a rosier picture of the environment than was accurate.

Soon there was another call. 'What is Klopp's agent's number?' I thought, 'This is ridiculous – surely at least someone at Liverpool should have the mobile number for Jürgen Klopp's agent.' It was clear that the story was moving on but I was asked to keep the conversations in strictest confidence. Liverpool's next game was the Merseyside derby, and then there was an international break the following week. 'They must be planning a change,' I thought.

A few hours later, another call. 'Can you speak to Klopp's man and get him to contact us?' I knew that Fenway operated around potentially sensitive situations using middlemen, affording themselves an opportunity to claim a plausible deniability argument if a story ever became public, particularly relating to takeovers. I was not surprised to be told by Klopp's team that the first call must come instead from Liverpool. They seemed like fair people but we had only ever spoken over the phone before. As far as they were concerned, I could have been part of a British newspaper sting.

In the impasse I reached my own solution. Two calls were then made. Fenway would have Klopp's number. Klopp would have Fenway's number. 'Sort it out between yourselves but if anything happens, I want to know first.' Again, I wondered whether this was all part of a ruse, a delaying tactic to try to deflect what was already a reality: that Klopp had long agreed to become Liverpool's manager.

Ultimately, the subsequent silence was a sign that discussions were moving along. The lines to both parties went dead for a week. In the meantime Rodgers was indeed sacked, during a meeting with Ayre at Melwood immediately after a 1–1 draw with Everton.

It transpired that at another meeting in Manhattan a couple of days before that game Fenway had met with Carlo Ancelotti, the urbane Italian who was manager of Napoli in 2018–19 when

Liverpool squeezed past them to reach the second round of the Champions League, setting Klopp and his players on the path to Madrid. It was Klopp, of course, who proved to be the manager who impressed most in Manhattan. He had blown Fenway's leaders away with his charisma and appetite to manage a club which a decade before had won its last Champions League title and was a quarter of a century away from its last domestic championship.

Mike Gordon, whose relationship with Klopp became the strongest amongst Fenway's leaders, recognized quickly that Klopp was an extraordinary personality who was willing to stake his own reputation on the future of a club starved of success. Like many of his players Klopp's path to this point had been unusual: a boy from the rural heartlands of Germany's Black Forest becoming an icon of the urban masses, firstly in the industrial Ruhr Valley with Dortmund then on Merseyside, where the culture was formed on the docks.

By June 2019 Liverpool was undeniably Klopp's team. Each of his players had something to prove even if some of them were pricy, but they had all bought into the *gegenpress*, a tactic which means that after surrendering the ball Klopp's team immediately tries to win it back rather than falling back to regroup. That is at the basis of everything Liverpool have become; a symbol of response which has translated to the fans as a show of guts and resistance – to recover from the disappointment of losing – the ball in this case – by having the courage to go again and immediately rectify a wrong. Three weeks after the final league game, where Liverpool had taken the most expensively assembled squad in Premier League history all of the way, another opportunity presented itself in Madrid. Typically, Tottenham Hotspur were not going to be allowed out of that corner.

HOPE

1. YOU ARE FUCKING SHITE

THE SIGNIFICANT OPENING WORDS OF THE NEW FOOTBALL SEASON were delivered by Ben Tollitt, a Liverpool-supporting Tranmere Rovers winger who three years earlier had been playing in the eleventh tier of English football at Widnes, the rugby league town with a power station.

Having moved up three levels in one move by signing for Skelmersdale United, Tollitt was spotted by the Portsmouth manager Paul Cook. Like Tollitt, Cook began his playing career amidst Merseyside's uncertain non-league circuit where all clubs fall deep into the shadow of Liverpool and Everton. Though he would finish the 2018–19 campaign pushing for another return to the Football League at what seemed his natural level in the National League with Wrexham, Tollitt had originally joined Tranmere to be closer to home.

Tranmere were a league club again for the first time in four years, having been promoted in a dramatic play-off final where their left-back Liam Ridehalgh was sent off after just 48 seconds at Wembley against Boreham Wood, whose average attendance of 600 would have easily made them the smallest club in the top four divisions had they prevailed at Tranmere's expense.

Having nearly reached the Premier League at the start of the 1990s, Tranmere had a reputation as cup specialists under John Aldridge, the former Liverpool forward, and in 2000 they lost in the League Cup final to Leicester City. Successive relegations in 2014 and 2015 brought fear the club might go under altogether but the guidance of Mark Palios, the one-time FA chief executive, helped them return to where they felt they belonged.

Tollitt was in the sort of mood to put Loris Karius in his place. He had travelled to Kiev where, six weeks earlier, Karius made two mistakes which led to Real Madrid goals in the Champions League final, the most-watched televised game in club football. The first involved Karius not seeming to recognize the hardly inconspicuous presence of a 6 foot 1 inch centre-forward in Karim Benzema as he tried to roll the ball out, and with that Real took the lead. His second mistake involved Gareth Bale's 25-yard shot sliding through Karius' fingers. The final score was 3–1 to Real Madrid. With a better goalkeeper, Liverpool may have become European champions for a sixth time.

Liverpool doctors would claim Karius had sustained concussion after Sergio Ramos barged into him from a corner, sneakily and dangerously applying his left elbow at the German's temple. Ramos had earlier ended Mohamed Salah's night, the player in the Liverpool team who carried the hopes and dreams of the club on his shoulders after a record-breaking season during which he scored 44 times.

In the flab of immediate disappointment, however, the significant detail about brain injuries was not available and the focus of Ramos' role was absolutely on Salah, so everything else he did that night seemed to melt away. Karius was already viewed as the weak link in this team. His Liverpool career had started eighteen months earlier by conceding a corner from his own goal-kick in a game against Sunderland. He had been bought to replace Simon Mignolet but it took Karius a long time to convince the manager who had bought him that he was ready to play instead of the Belgian. When it was decided that Mignolet's time was up after mistakes in a 3–3 draw with Arsenal, Karius was given six months to prove he could replace him but, as the 2017–18 season wore on, there were signs that Karius was feeling the pressure – though it never became the absolute focus of discussion because the Liverpool machine kept on rumbling through Europe. In the Champions League semi-final second leg in Rome, Karius had let two goals race past him with all of the agility of a slip fielder with creaking limbs in a veterans' cricket match.

On the long and expensive journey home from Kiev, thousands of supporters like Tollitt arrived at the conclusion that, although they had sympathy for Karius on what had been a harrowing experience that will ultimately define his career, Liverpool really needed a replacement.

Karius did not help himself by misjudging the mood when he released a promotional video towards the end of the next month, showing him running across a Californian beach like David Hasselhoff, ready to save the day even though he'd not long ruined it for so many people just a few weeks earlier. He was a good-looking blond-haired 24-year-old with modelling contracts who gave an outward perception of himself as being extraordinarily confident. At Manchester City, where he had spent his youth before returning to the womb of the Bundesliga with Mainz, the coaches there – as well as some teammates – were intrigued by his Lehmannesque sense of place, which translated as a healthy arrogance to those who believed in him, and borderline delusion to those who did not. It is fair to say that it did not surprise any of those coaches from the early days that Karius had become so active across social media. 'Always showing off as a kid,' said one coach. 'But I do wonder whether he's actually trying to disguise his own insecurities,' said another.

Liverpool's first pre-season friendly went by without incident, an easy 7–0 victory at Chester. There were more people watching at Tranmere, however: a bigger crowd, more journalists present and a sharper focus – an enormous Kop stand behind Karius at Prenton Park. The World Cup was only at its semi-final stage and the domestic season was already under way in terms of preparation. It did not feel like there had been a comfortable distance between what happened to Karius in Kiev and his next public appearance. The smell of cleanly cut abundant green turf can bring optimism to footballers: a new season, a fresh start. Yet it felt like Karius was never going to be able to escape his past: he would forever be remembered as the goalkeeper who lost Liverpool the trophy which had made legends out of even average players.

He would stand there alone with his hands on his hips and his head bowed, looking at the floor after he had failed to handle Oliver Norburn's ferocious free-kick, allowing Tranmere to pull a goal back and make it 3–1. He would have five touches in total, and another two picking the ball out of the net because Tranmere later scored again. Behind him, Prenton Park's Kop roared with laughter. In front of him, Tollitt simultaneously worshipped and cursed his presence.

Karius would never be able to win.

The tears inside Kiev's Olympic Stadium did not flow only onto the already sodden shirts of those on the pitch. Near the halfway line behind Jürgen Klopp's dugout sat two family members who had travelled to Ukraine to support Loris Karius. The sight of his mother staring into the middle distance, looking away from the game while it was still going on as she held his sobbing girlfriend, prompted Klopp's wife Ulla to move a few rows and try to offer some reassurance. At the final whistle, while Karius lay on the floor, the three women – all of them connected by the desperation of it all, each of them from the same region of southern Germany – stood there, wrapped in each other's arms.

Klopp reacted the only way he knows how to disappointment. He returned to the hotel. He turned his cap back to front and, in getting drunk, ended up singing with a man wearing a Liverpool shirt whose nickname might make you think first of cabaret.

Andreas Frege – or Campino, as he is known – was born in Düsseldorf but his mother was English. He had fallen in love with the club Klopp now managed after Liverpool had beaten Borussia Mönchengladbach in the Uefa Cup final of 1973. Football was Campino's passion but his talent was in music, and Klopp became a fan of his group Die Toten Hosen – translated directly as 'The Dead Trousers'. He and Klopp had become close friends. They shared similar social and political views, which went a long way towards explaining why Klopp was Liverpool's manager rather than Bayern Munich's. Campino believed in punk rather than floorshows. His band did not exist solely to promote causes but were prepared to go that way. The Dead Trousers had made stands against xenophobia and racism, they supported Greenpeace in a campaign to end nuclear testing, and though Klopp had also worked with PETA he had not gone quite as far as Campino who once posed without wearing any clothes to promote the causes of the animal rights group. Amongst their later initiatives related to Bayern's domination of German football, Die Toten Hosen released a song in 2000 spiked with antipathy. In 'Bayern' Campino would yell: '*Many things can happen/Many things can come to pass/One thing I know for sure. Never in my life would I go to Bayern! (Never go to the f**king Bayern!)*'

Despite two opportunities to follow the path nearly every other German manager dreams of, Klopp had seen things differently. He wanted to build something truly memorable rather than just be another coach coldly steering the Bayern wheel only to get fired when the players turned on him and directors conspired to save themselves.

For Klopp, Kiev had felt like another opportunity lost to really mark all of his work at Liverpool with a first trophy, the most lucrative of them all. In two and a half seasons at Liverpool he had lost three finals but had returned the club twice to the Champions League, a competition which had been qualified for only once in the seven seasons before his appointment.

At Melwood, a few days after the Tranmere friendly where Karius dropped his latest clanger, Klopp did not possess the demeanour of someone who was cut up by the recent past, nor did he give the impression that he did not know what he had to do to move Liverpool forward. Klopp had spent the summer in Ibiza. He was tanned, bearded, lean and refreshed. He had not watched the latest final back in too much detail. When your team loses its most outstanding player after a quarter of the game in Salah; when your team concedes from an overhead kick delivered by a substitute introduced only 90 seconds beforehand; when your team – or your goalkeeper – throws in another two in concussion, or not, you sympathize with Klopp and realize why there is little point in agonizing over what else could really have happened: what else could have gone wrong? 'Only scenes . . . there is no reason for that, to be honest,' he said when asked about the depth of his reflection.

Klopp had sympathy with Karius because he recognized that concussion may have played a role in the event that will forever define him as a footballer. Klopp was compassionate. Yet he remained a football manager with consistent views and, even before Kiev, other goalkeeping targets were being identified. Even a Liverpool victory in Ukraine would not have saved Karius, with or without him being at the centre of a dreadful plot – just as Jerzy Dudek's crucial role in the miracle of Istanbul thirteen years earlier had not saved his Liverpool career, with Pepe Reina soon brought in to replace him.

As he spoke, Klopp knew that in a Sardinian villa, Alisson Becker was preparing to travel to Merseyside. The AS Roma goalkeeper had let in seven goals across two legs against the team that wanted to sign him just a few months before, as Liverpool reached the final of the Champions League with a 7–6 victory on aggregate. Chelsea were interested in the Brazilian too – as were Napoli – but Klopp's determination was emphasized by the world-record fee he was prepared to pay. Whereas Karius had cost Liverpool £4.75 million just two years earlier Becker – who was eighteen months older – cost nearly fifteen times as much and this represented a world record which stood for only two weeks until Chelsea realized Liverpool had changed the going rate for a position that Klopp appreciated all too well could define how moments in history are recalled.

Liverpool had choreographed the announcement of another signing with the sort of stealth not expected from a club which had, for so long, got so much wrong in the transfer market – not least the summer before when it emerged Virgil van Dijk, then of Southampton, had met Klopp in a Blackpool hotel and the revelation contributed towards the breakdown of any deal for six months.

This time, though, before the conclusions of many journeys back from Kiev, Liverpool had signed a new midfielder without any build-up of speculation or even prior mention.

Fabinho was another footballer in his early mid-twenties; not too young so there would be a long wait to see him emerge as a key figure in the team, but with enough experience to expect an impact in his first season. He had played once for Real Madrid as a teenager before shifting positions at Monaco, where he was recycled from right-back to a more central role, his height and energy adding power and thrust at the base of a creative midfield. In 2017 he became a surprise Ligue 1 winner as well as the Monaco's chief penalty-taker, while also earning his first caps for the Brazilian national side. He was offered to Manchester United twice, who only wanted him the second time around after preferring Nemanja Matić initially because of José Mourinho's history with the Serbian at Chelsea. When the opportunity came to go to Old Trafford again, Fabinho had already been persuaded by Klopp that Liverpool was the place he wanted to be. Instead, United would sign another Brazilian in Fred, who was selected in the Brazilian World Cup 2018 squad ahead of Fabinho.

He was quietly spoken but his long limbs, as he stretched out of a leather seat in an Anfield executive suite in mid-July, offered a sense of Fabinho's presence. It had been harder for him to establish himself in the national team because he had never played a minute of first-team football in Brazil, leaving Fluminense for Portugal's Rio Ave on a six-year deal brokered by GestiFute, the organization owned by the world's most famous sports agent, Jorge Mendes. Three of those years would be spent on loan elsewhere, firstly in Madrid where he played mainly for the second team and then Monaco, where he was given more responsibilities. 'In Brazil,' Fabinho said, 'it helps if you have played for one of the big clubs first, because then you have the local and national media talking more about you and a lot earlier.'

Fred, from one big city in Belo Horizonte, had moved to Porto Alegre as a 16-year-old, and had won two state championships with Internacional at the expense of city rivals Grêmio. Fabinho, meanwhile, had spent his youth in the subtropical sprawl of northern São Paulo State and, on moving to Rio de Janeiro from Campinas, had made it onto the substitutes' bench only once before choosing to leave for Europe. 'I was not a well-known player in Brazil,' Fabinho admitted.

In the heat of Kiev, the dearth of midfield options for Klopp was exposed. For the last five weeks of the 2017–18 season it had been the same players filling the same three roles and by the end of May – against the highest-quality opposition – a midfield which required high energy to ensure the team's structure is supported both in defence and attack began to clank. Klopp had sold Philippe Coutinho for a British record fee to Barcelona in January, he knew Emre Can was leaving for Juventus and he also knew in Kiev (unlike anyone outside the club) that Alex Oxlade-Chamberlain, who had been bought in anticipation of Coutinho's departure, was injured for at least ten months with no date marked for his return. This led to him wanting to sign Nabil Fekir from Lyon but Liverpool's staff were unhappy with the results from his medical. The process of the transfer of Fekir had been problematic because of the high demands of Lyon's notoriously confrontational president Jean-Michel Aulas. While Liverpool earned points for the way Fabinho was handled a few weeks earlier, the sense of frustration at the collapse of the Fekir deal was exacerbated by the embarrassment of the accidental release of an interview with him wearing the same Liverpool training kit as Fabinho, after the club's media staff were sent to Paris to meet him.

Though Liverpool had two new midfielders in Fabinho and Naby Keïta, who agreed to join in the summer of 2017, perceptions about what Klopp had at his disposal were skewed by the end to the Fekir saga and the uncertainty around Oxlade-Chamberlain. It had been to Klopp's credit that he made the departure of Coutinho feel like it wasn't actually a loss, though undoubtedly Liverpool could have done with him in Kiev. In terms of numbers, though it seemed like Liverpool had more midfielders than they started the season with, they actually had fewer, and this was an issue for Klopp to deal with because perception did not meet reality.

Klopp anticipated that it would take Fabinho time to adjust to English football. While the focus at Tranmere had been on the torment of Loris Karius, Fabinho's talent had shone brighter than Keïta's, with his physical capacity to eat up space and retrieve possession using those long legs. Yet Klopp believed Fabinho had a tendency to drop too deep, making Liverpool's defence a back three too often – as he'd been instructed in France. Klopp wanted him higher up the pitch because that is where Liverpool are more destructive, winning possession back quickly much closer to the opponent's goal.

'We do it differently to Monaco,' Klopp stressed. 'You can push him into position but because it's natural for him moments later he's again deep . . .' In front of Fabinho was Jordan Henderson, who it is fair to say was not the most popular Liverpool captain in Liverpool's history, but he consistently did the job Klopp expected of him: his alertness and intensity setting the pace and crucial to the framework of the entire team.

Given Klopp's warning, it should not have been a surprise that Fabinho had to wait until October to start a league game – sometimes he was not even a part of the match-day squad. It was during this period that the encouragement of Klopp's first-team coach Pep Lijnders became important. The Dutchman spoke Portuguese, having worked at FC Porto from the age of 23 where he coached at the academy for seven years. Lijnders recognized Fabinho was finding training tough because the responsibilities in his position were different and the intensity was greater. Whereas at Monaco he was expected to run up and down the pitch, the job at Liverpool involved moving from side to side to fill in the gaps when others around him took calculated pressing risks. Klopp would temporarily change Liverpool's formation from 4–3–3 to 4–4–2 to help Fabinho's integration, and this allowed him, for a short period of time, to develop his confidence by playing what was more of a natural game. 'Then you saw the real Fabinho,' Lijnders said, describing him amidst the 'organized chaos' of Liverpool's play as a 'lighthouse', which reflected his emergence as a consistently reassuring figure. 'His timing, his vision, his calmness, it gives another dimension to our midfield play,' Lijnders believed.

Fabinho described his introduction to English football as 'really horrible'. He was backed by a solid family and small but close circle of friends who had supported him throughout his career. Unlike other Brazilian footballers, he had not emerged from the favelas and had lived in an apartment block as a child, without growing up with many of the self-worth issues that are associated with poverty. This did not make him any less driven, however, because he was hardly wealthy. Fabinho explained how his father took on a variety of jobs simultaneously to support his family, which included three children. While he had worked as a school caretaker, a security guard, a bricklayer and at a railway station, Fabinho's mother was employed by a utilities company, and his sisters were teaching assistants. Through the help of his closest friend, Ricardo – now his brother-in-law – Fabinho was able to travel to youth games by car rather than by bus. After struggling with homesickness in his first year in Europe, Ricardo moved for two years to live with him in Monaco and this helped him adjust.

England fascinated him because he had seen how Brazilian footballers with his characteristics had succeeded there. It would be too narrow to describe him as a classic Brazilian number 5 – a Gilberto Silva or a Dunga – because, with time, his influence would be felt across more space on the pitch. Bernardo Silva, a very different sort of midfielder, who had left Monaco for Manchester City twelve months earlier, had promised Fabinho that he would 'love' the English style of football, telling him too that a record-breaking City's most difficult opponent had been Liverpool – a team that had beaten City three times in four games during 2017–18.

One of the first people to congratulate Fabinho on his move to Liverpool was Kylian Mbappé – another former teammate at Monaco who has since become a World Cup winner with France; the new Pelé. It was difficult to tell whether what Fabinho said next about the teenager was a joke or a genuine statement, but it did feel like more of a joke.

'He has already said for the next season he will remain at PSG, but I will try slowly to convince him to come to Liverpool,' Fabinho pledged, revealing a grin that few would see – certainly on a football pitch – for a few months, at least.

2. STANDING FOR SOMETHING ELSE

RUEDI ZBINDEN WAS A SQUAT FIGURE WITH LIGHT BLUE EYES AND cropped grey hair in military style who, according to German colleagues, spoke with a strong Swiss accent and operated in a classic Swiss need-to-know style. He told you just enough information to be impressed by his work but never to the point you'd be able to figure him out entirely. He was 59 years old and he wore a half-length brown leather jacket reminiscent of a detective. In basic terms, detective work was a big part of his job: a figure in the shadows – always in search of something hidden.

Zbinden had captained FC Basel before becoming assistant to Christian Gross when Gross returned to Switzerland after being sacked by Tottenham Hotspur in 1999. But his talent was in scouting – or 'watching' as he put it – rather than coaching. Zbinden did not even miss the warm-up before matches. He would never answer a call or talk to the person sitting next to him. 'I want to absorb everything and form my own judgements,' he said. 'Questions come later.' Sometimes he watched a single player. Sometimes he looked at all 22. 'I watch every movement of each.' He would almost fall asleep, he became so focused. He described his condition as a kind of trance. And sometimes it happens: 'Suddenly I see something different in one.'

Zbinden and Basel were pioneers in Swiss football, becoming the first club to implement a professional scouting structure. Zbinden started in 2001 and eighteen years later only three other clubs across Switzerland had one or more full-time scouts, with most managing a part-time system based on very specific instructions.

'Many clubs feel they can buy new players from video,' said Zbinden. 'I say, "That's not possible. Never."'

He had led Basel's recruitment team with distinction; his signings delivering the most successful period in the club's history while also earning nearly £70 million in sales. Yet because Basel had emerged as the wealthiest club in the country, Zbinden felt a tariff on domestic targets and this explains why he soon started looking further afield for new signings. His first full-time foreign scout was based in Buenos Aires and his second, in Prague. Had it not been for the 'guy in Buenos Aires', as he called him, withholding his name with a sense of mystery, 'we might have not gone for Mohamed Salah.'

A trip made by Zbinden to Argentina in 2002 ultimately led to Salah ending up in Switzerland a decade later. Back then Zbinden was having a lunch with Enzo Trossero and Néstor Clausen, the head coach of Independiente and his assistant, when he mentioned that he was going to spend his afternoon watching Chacarita Juniors, a club based in a rundown neighbourhood of the capital city.

Trossero knew Zbinden because he had coached in Switzerland with FC Sion. 'Are you crazy?' Trossero asked. 'Never in your life are you going to watch a game of Juniors. That's too dangerous.' Zbinden ignored his friend and that is where he saw a 19-year-old playmaker for the first time called Matías Delgado. His simple act of heavily disguising a pass to the striker in front of him made the scout rise from his seat. Zbinden established contact with the Juniors president via a Swiss acquaintance whose command of Spanish was better than his. 'No chance,' the message came back. What happened next taught Zbinden a lesson that he would carry with him and play a part in his signing of Salah because sometimes, a stroke of luck is needed to get what you want.

When an Israeli agent asked him months later which player he really wanted to sign and he told him about Delgado, the agent put him in direct contact with the player's father who realized his son had a chance of succeeding in Europe and subsequently put pressure on the president. Suddenly, a way opened and Delgado became Zbinden's first transfer of an Argentine from South America to Switzerland.

Across two spells, where he also made Basel money through a transfer to Beşiktaş, Delgado would play nearly 400 games, scoring more than 100 goals. Over the next ten years Zbinden had contact with 'the guy in Buenos Aires – our most valuable signing' almost every day and that is why a 17-year-old Ecuadorian striker who had not made his professional debut for a second division team called Rocafuerte came onto Basel's radar before anyone else's. Within two years of Felipe Caicedo becoming a £200,000 signing he had been turned into a £7 million profit after Manchester City – enriched by their Abu Dhabi takeover – made him one of the first purchases of the Sheikh Mansour era.

In 2011 the scout from Buenos Aires was dispatched to Colombia for the Under-20 World Cup when Egypt's number 12 impressed on the opening day of the competition in a game held in the tropical city of Barranquilla. Philippe Coutinho, Casemiro and Oscar would all soon play for top European clubs but Mohamed Salah's talent shone the most.

Egypt would draw with Brazil before beating Panama 1–0, then filleting Austria 4–0 to make it out of their group. It was then that the man from Buenos Aires sent a note back to Switzerland which described Salah as a winger who 'certainly belonged to one of the top five players in the tournament'. Egypt's journey would end in the last sixteen where Argentina – inspired by Erik Lamela, who later joined Spurs from AS Roma – won narrowly, but only after Salah had scored his country's penalty.

'We wanted to see him play in Egypt,' Zbinden remembered. 'But there was a problem – the stadium catastrophe with multiple fatalities. The league was suspended for three or four months and we couldn't watch him live.'

Basel had focused on other targets when a German agent with good contacts in Egypt approached the Swiss club's sporting director Georg Heitz and essentially asked him for a trial for Salah or, as Zbinden put it, 'a training period'.

'He (the sporting director) didn't know Salah but he asked me about him. I looked through the notes and saw that our scouts had produced a glowing report from the tournament in Colombia and I said, "Definitely. If we can see him in training, we'd love that." That's how it happened. He came for five days. I'd say it was more of a coincidence than a discovery.'

Had Egypt qualified for the Under-17 World Cup which they hosted in 2009, then maybe Salah would have appeared on Basel's radar even sooner because Zbinden based himself in Cairo for that tournament. Egypt had not been a country where Zbinden thought he had a chance attracting new players.

'Or Africa generally, really,' he admitted. 'Africans tend to go to France or Belgium, it's very difficult for us to get players from there to join us. There weren't many Egyptians at all in Europe at that time. Neuchâtel Xamax had one, but across Switzerland . . . I don't remember many Egyptians in the Swiss league throughout the competition's history. Salah was just a lucky break.'

Zbinden eventually got to see Salah play in his homeland three years later, but only after signing him: 'We saw international games, to show the player we were there for him. Times were quite troubled – once, I pulled down my windows in the car to greet all the fans but the police fired tear gas and I suddenly couldn't see anything at all. I just said: "Drive, drive! It's getting dangerous!" '

During the initial trial period, Zbinden had been concerned about Salah's final pass, final cross and final shot. Could he deliver when it mattered? At that point, he had only watched him on video where 'you could see his pace, his dynamism and skill, which made him very interesting'. Georg Heitz had done most of his research online, looking at newspaper reports, and he did not find anything negative.

'In his five days of training he only really convinced us on the fifth day,' Zbinden remembered. 'I had doubts because he had technical deficits; he couldn't cross the ball with his right foot and his crosses from the left and his shots weren't very good either. We thought: "That's not the same guy from the videos!" He was still young, had problems with the language, and going from Cairo to Basel was like going to another world for him. We had to be patient. We had to wait for him to show his qualities. It would have been better to see him playing at [his] home, where he was comfortable and knew his teammates. He would have been able to show his class more quickly there, I'm sure. With us, it took him a few days.

'But in the very last training session, a five-a-side, he exploded! He dribbled, he scored goals. Heiko Vogel – the Basel coach – and I just looked at each other and said, "Ah, he is the guy from the videos, after all, the guy we wanted." I was worried he didn't have what it takes. I was nervous about telling him a story he did not want to hear. But he showed his quality and then I couldn't say no.'

Heitz spent 3 million Swiss francs on Salah (£1.5 million) and he would sell him eighteen months later for ten times that amount. Salah was 20 years old and marked as Xherdan Shaqiri's replacement, who'd signed for Bayern Munich – the winger he would later keep out of the Liverpool side. In 2012, though, Zbinden saw lots of room for improvement. 'His technique wasn't quite there yet, especially his finishing,' he stressed. 'Someone [in the Swiss press] wrote that his shots were so far off target that they're hitting the pyramids. He was not the most gifted technically either and I think this is where he worked on his game the hardest.'

Salah surprised Zbinden by how quickly he integrated into a new culture: 'He's a smart guy and a little devious. In the team hotel, he always pulled pranks. He's like that on the pitch, where he radiates joy. Football is not work for him, it's a game. He laughs on the pitch. For me, these are the best players, the ones who look as if they're having fun. Others are very serious for 90 minutes, it's hard work for them, but Salah is a player who enjoys the game.'

Zbinden says in Switzerland 'nobody would have expected' his achievements at Liverpool even though he was outstanding for Basel, particularly in European games against Chelsea and Tottenham Hotspur. He would help Basel to their seventh Swiss Super League championship, scoring five goals in 29 games before starting the next season in even better form, which led to interest in him gathering. Though Michael Edwards, Liverpool's sporting director, wanted to sign him then he believes Edwards got a better player when he was three and a half years older. 'If you sign a player at the wrong time, his career as well as the history of the club can turn out differently,' Zbinden warned.

Cairo, Basel, London, Florence, Rome and then Liverpool. In London, with Chelsea, he was viewed as an expensive flop, a winger who could not finish. In Florence he rediscovered his confidence and that led to a move to Roma, who still thought they were making a handsome profit when they sold him to Liverpool, which eventually looked like a knockdown fee. The direction of Mohamed Salah's career, though, was arguably shaped most by what happened in Port Said when he was not even there – an event which had a profound effect on his path, the feeling around him as well as the unique pressure he was facing by the summer of 2018.

Initially, his chances of moving to Switzerland became slimmer because of what happened in the Mediterranean city just around the time Ruedi Zbinden was making his travel arrangements to go to Egypt. In February 2012, moments after Al-Masry beat Al-Ahly 3–1, floods of men dressed in black jackets spilled onto Al-Masry's pitch armed with knives, broken glass bottles and rocks. The outcome was horrifying. Amidst stabbings and dark-age scenes where some Al-Ahly supporters were lifted and thrown from the stands to their deaths, the youngest victim – aged 13 – was crushed like many others as he tried to escape at an exit tunnel that had been closed off by the police, who but for switching the stadium's floodlights off did not intervene. When the terrible noises stopped and the lights were turned back on, the reality was revealed: seventy-two people had been killed and more than 500 were injured.

Though twenty-one Masry ultras were sentenced to death for their part in the carnage, across Egypt it was believed ideology and politics had contributed to an awful conclusion. During the Arab Spring just ten months earlier, Ahly ultras had been linked to the uprising against Hosni Mubarak, the former president who was ousted after a thirty-year dictatorship.

What was much clearer was Mohamed Aboutrika's role in the

aftermath of Port Said, the player regarded as the greatest in Egypt's history. He was an Ahly midfielder and one of those who fled the field in fear of his life. As fans bled to death on the dressing-room floor, he cradled one of them, whose last words were, 'Captain, I've always wanted to meet you.' In the days that followed, Aboutrika and two of his Egypt teammates, Emad Moteab and Mohamed Barakat, retired from football before being persuaded back. 'I decided that I needed to play on for the people who died that night,' said Aboutrika, whose decision to visit the family of every victim saw him transition from being a supremely talented footballer into a symbol for hope.

'Every athlete,' said Aboutrika, who studied for a bachelor's degree in philosophy, 'has a humanitarian role in society. He doesn't live solely for himself, but for others, too.' Before Ahly he had represented Tersana in his home city of Giza and there his intelligent performances soon resulted in the offer of a pay rise that he rejected, insisting that each of his teammates should earn the same money for helping him flourish. His words and actions led to him becoming the face of hope to millions of Egyptians and this was reflected in Tahrir Square, the site of the rising against Mubarak in 2011, where his mural was painted to include a beard. He was viewed on a religious level. Aboutrika became an emblem of the revolution, but the country's transition towards democracy proved tempestuous and his endorsement in 2012 elections for the Muslim Brotherhood leader Mohamed Morsi would not be forgotten by the new president Abdel Fattah al-Sisi when he seized control from Morsi twelve months later.

Sisi, the former head of the armed forces, subsequently ushered in the most severe clampdown on dissent in Egypt's history, and one of his first acts was to place all members and associates of the Brotherhood on the terrorist watch list. In 2015 the holiday company Aboutrika co-owned was accused of 'committing hostile acts against the state'. Aboutrika himself was playing in Qatar for Baniyas, where he wore the number 72 shirt in honour of the Ahly supporters who died in Port Said. After having his assets frozen Aboutrika was warned that he faced arrest if he ever returned to Egypt.

Until April 2018 Salah's Twitter handle @MoSalah22 was a mark of respect to Aboutrika, whose shirt number had been 22 – the same as Salah's at Basel – when he finally moved out of Egypt six months after Port Said, which led to the closure of the league for the rest of the season. At the time of its suspension Salah had sometimes played as a left-back and his team El Mokawloon were third from bottom in the table. He and Aboutrika became team-mates in the national team under the American coach Bob Bradley who said, 'the big player for us was Aboutrika . . . Salah looked up to him as a player and a man. You could tell he wanted to learn from [him] and do things the right way.'

Aboutrika's fame and subsequent exile stood as a warning to every Egyptian that nobody was immune from the country's politics. Having filled the space left behind by Aboutrika Salah knew about the potential consequences of half-truths and perception around beliefs. While Liverpool supporters came to love Salah for his exploits on Merseyside, Egypt defines him. He would join Liverpool from AS Roma ahead of the 2017–18 season for £38.5 million and what followed was sensational: a haul of 44 goals in 52 games. All sorts of records were broken and he wasn't even playing as a centre-forward. And yet, it was what happened in Cairo right at the start of the campaign that really changed his life for ever.

Egypt were on their way towards qualifying for their first World Cup in twenty-eight years when, with four minutes to go, Congo scored to seemingly shatter the dreams of 95 million people – including Salah's. The following minutes were the most dramatic of Salah's career, as he collapsed to the floor in reaction to Congo's equalizer, beating his hands into the turf. He managed to raise himself, screaming into the night as he tried to stimulate the crowd by waving his hands. Then, when Egypt were awarded a penalty in the third minute of injury time, he stepped forward and it became 2–1. Egypt were going to the World Cup. The country had a new national hero.

While Mohamed Aboutrika grew up playing football in the arid alleyways of Giza, Mohamed Salah was raised in the Nile Delta in the dusty village of Nagrig, about eighty miles north of Cairo, surrounded by onion fields and jasmine. The stories about him travelling to and from the capital five days a week just for training sessions are the stuff of legend across Egypt, where the numbers go up depending on who you listen to: the average journey time stretching from two hours to a whopping nine, with the total of microbuses involved ranging between just the one or, instead, five.

Nagrig is the sort of place where chickens and cows roam the unpaved streets and doors are left ajar, with neighbours always welcome. When Salah married his wife Magi in Nagrig there was open invitation to all villagers. Though it was remembered as *the* social event of 2013 in Nagrig, his wider fame at this point had not been realized.

By 2019 Salah's immediate family had relocated to London. The demand on him had become exhausting, while it was also safer considering the potential consequences of political unrest. Sisi's men, after all, were unable to knock at his door in England. Salah had since paid for the construction of a religious school in Nagrig as well as an ambulance station and a charity food market.

Aboutrika's fate had made him realize that Egyptian football and footballers had often been caught up in politics. Salah's popularity had risen not only because of his ability and his achievements but also because he'd managed to steer well clear of it.

As he topped the Premier League's goalscoring charts in early 2018 and his new team blew opponents away in the Champions League, there had been some uncomfortable developments at home. After the year started with the Egyptian Football Association announcing its support for Sisi, once ballots were actually cast in the presidential elections in March, Salah was revealed as the surprise runner-up. Ahead of the election, five other major candidates had been either suspended or jailed while tens of thousands of Egyptians were detained. This led to more than one million spoiling their ballot papers by removing the names of Sisi and his single opponent – included as a sham to suggest 'democracy' was in place. In protest, they voted instead for Salah.

He had become a rare figure for whom all Egyptians, regardless of class or politics, could unite. In 2019 Salah was included in *Time* magazine's top 100 most influential people in the world and he used this status to promote change, though not in politics. It was incredibly brave of him to speak out instead about the treatment of women, cutting through all societies and religions with his message. This indicated he was becoming more confident in himself and truly did realize the difference he could make, not only in Egypt.

According to Ahmed El Ghoul, who played with Salah at El Mokawloon, it was beneficial that he never played for either of the Cairo giants, Al Ahly or Zamalek, though that could have been different had it not been for Mamdouh Abbas, a wealthy businessman who built his fortune on property and petroleum before becoming chairman of Zamalek. In 2011 he said in an interview: 'Salah needs much more work.'

That decision by Zamalek, according to El Ghoul, has probably helped him in the long term. 'It's the first time an Egyptian player has got to this level,' he said. 'He belongs to Egypt and only Egypt.' Though Salah was criticized in some quarters for giving money to a social fund created by Sisi, El Ghoul was one of many who saw it as 'a donation for Egypt – not to a political party. That will go to the poor.'

Salah is cautious with his words and he rarely grants interviews, removing opportunities for creating controversy over his statements or opinions. After scoring his 40th goal for Liverpool in a 3–0 victory over Bournemouth in April 2018, he was convinced by a persuasive media officer at Anfield to speak publicly for the first time as he tried to scuttle through the mixed zone, the area where players and journalists meet. Though he was friendly and clearly a warm character, Salah would offer only short answers to simple questions about his amazing feats.

Ian Rush, Liverpool's all-time leading goalscorer, holds the record for the number of goals in a season at 47. To equal that total, Salah would have needed a hat-trick in the Champions League final against Real Madrid and, as unlikely as the target may have been as the game kicked off in sweltering heat, he was denied that opportunity by the actions of Sergio Ramos. Salah would leave the field after less than half an hour's play in agony, after being dragged and twisted to the ground by the Spanish defender.

A dream year ended in nightmare. While Liverpool lost 3–1, Salah was left racing to be fit for Egypt's first World Cup in decades. Across social media in Egypt, the Arabic hashtags for 'Ramos the Dog' and 'Son of a Whore' were soon trending on Twitter, while an Egyptian lawyer threatened to file a lawsuit against Ramos, equivalent to £874 million, for causing Egyptians 'physical and psychological harm'. The mood was summed up by a headline the next morning in the *al-Masry al-Youm* newspaper: 'The Night Egyptians Cried: Ramos the Butcher Dislocated Abu Salah's Shoulder.'

Though Salah scored twice for his country in Russia, he would miss the vital opening game against Uruguay and ultimately, Egypt left the competition at the group stage without recording a single point.

Salah was dismayed by what he experienced in Russia, where Egypt based themselves in Chechnya. He was forced into receiving an honorary citizenship from the region's warlord leader Ramzan Kadyrov before being asked to pose for photographs in a PR stunt sanctioned by the Egyptian Football Association who had yielded easily to Sisi's demands.

Preparations for Egypt's crucial second game with Russia in St Petersburg were then disrupted by Egyptian celebrities and other notables being permitted into the team hotel late at night and early into the morning. Later in the summer, Salah took to social media to vent his frustration at the lack of institutional professionalism. He wrote on his Facebook page: 'When you have a player or players who get to sleep at 6 a.m., there is a problem.' A mixture of well-wishers and partygoers were still arriving at Salah's room at 4 a.m. despite his pleas for the introductions to stop. When Salah's frustration became public, however, he believed it was 'painted to make me appear like I am acting arrogant, but I am not'. It did not seem like a good time to be considered one of the greatest footballers in the history of a country that had tilted back towards authoritarian rule – one which required heroes to project credibility and stability, not only amongst foreign powers but to its own people.

No sooner was the 2018–19 Premier League season underway – with his goal the first of Liverpool's campaign in an easy 4–0 victory over West Ham United – than Salah was back in Egypt for national team duty. But this time he went with a list of requests, not least a guarantee of his own safety due to the amount of attention on him.

For Salah, football had always offered an escape from realities, but it was becoming an extension of his problems. All of this was well hidden from the public in Liverpool, who were nevertheless patient with him as well as supportive as he took time to reach the performance levels and create the impact of the previous year.

Mohamed Salah was topless. In front of him, thousands of fully grown men were clambering over themselves, trying to get closer to him. In the madness, one of the men snapped his Achilles and spent the night in a Southampton hospital where he was told he would watch the rest of Liverpool's title race wearing a plaster cast. The previous eight seconds had felt like ten minutes. The frustration of two months without a goal for Salah vanished in an instant.

'Pass it, pass it . . .' the Liverpool end at Southampton screamed – and those not screaming were thinking it. Roberto Firmino had galloped 70 yards to help Salah and the Brazilian was now in space, running ahead of him and towards Southampton's goal. But Salah was not passing.

The score was Southampton 1, Liverpool 1. Shane Long was a hard-working Irish centre-forward. Those who tried to stop him regarded him as a pest. Jamie Carragher, the legendary Liverpool defender, hated playing against him because of his pace and his perseverance. He had scored crucially against Liverpool before – once for Reading, knocking Liverpool out of the FA Cup in 2010, and then for the club he was currently representing seven years later in injury time at Anfield to seal Southampton's progression to the League Cup final. Long, though, was not a prolific scorer of goals. Across twelve Premier League seasons and 333 games, he had scored just 49 times, an average of one in seven games – or around five or six a season. His 50th would come against Liverpool, giving Southampton the lead at St Mary's after nine minutes. His new manager Ralph Hasenhüttl wondered whether the goal had come too early. 'Eighty minutes against Liverpool is a long time,' said the Austrian, who twenty years earlier, then in his early thirties, had developed a friendship with Jürgen Klopp as their playing careers in Germany wound down and the pair enrolled on the same coaching course in Cologne.

Both were now 51 – men born seven weeks apart but back then Klopp had taken temporary charge at FSV Mainz, the club he had played for for eleven years – the majority of his professional career. While Klopp was popular and Mainz turned to him in a crisis, Hasenhüttl had moved around a lot – eight clubs across three different countries in nineteen years. He was contracted to Greuther Fürth in the German second division and he would have one more stop with Bayern Munich's reserve team before embarking on a coaching career which took him to Red Bull Leipzig where he managed Liverpool's Naby Keïta before the call came from Southampton, whose fortunes he transformed by hauling the team out of the relegation zone. As Liverpool arrived only Cardiff could send them down, but Hasenhüttl did not think the five-point gap was comfortable enough. To secure their Premier League status, Hasenhüttl believed Southampton needed to play a perfect game because, he said, 'Liverpool are now one of the best teams in Europe and they give you so much to think about.'

Hasenhüttl's first season in Leipzig – the club's first in the German top flight – had finished with Champions League qualification for the first time in the club's history, and that achievement was thanks, in part, to the midfield running of Keïta, whose 14 goals helped secure second place in the Bundesliga. After it was announced Keïta was moving to Liverpool ahead of Hasenhüttl's second campaign in charge, however, performances dropped and Keïta did not quite reproduce the energetic form which prompted Liverpool to spend £48 million on him. 'If there's one player who can make it at every club in the world, then that's Naby,'

Hasenhüttl had said after the Guinean departed for Anfield, where he struggled for game time in the one area of the pitch where it felt like something was missing at Liverpool.

When Keïta met Trent Alexander-Arnold's cross at the far post at St Mary's to equalize for Liverpool, it was indeed his first goal in England. There was an unusual moment in the celebration where he looked behind him to check whether he was offside then instantly held his head in his hands – suggesting to anyone watching through the keyhole of a television camera that he might have been. Instead, Keïta was simply relieved: relieved that his personal drought was over and relieved that Liverpool were no longer behind in a game where they could not afford to drop points.

Liverpool and Manchester City had exchanged places at the summit of the Premier League table twenty-one times, though that was partly explained by the pattern of games – rarely did either play at the same time. A Liverpool victory on the south coast would put them two points ahead of City again, who had a game in hand but a tougher run of fixtures to follow. Aside from facing Tottenham three times in the space of ten days, with two of those games in the Champions League, there was also a trip to Crystal Palace as well as the Manchester derby at Old Trafford.

Like Shane Long, Mohamed Salah was chasing his 50th Premier League goal, but unlike Shane Long this record only applied to his time at Liverpool, the club he had represented for just twenty months. He had been stuck at this point for nine games, knowing he could become the fastest player in Liverpool's Premier League history to reach a landmark met by Robbie Fowler after 88 league games, Luis Suárez after 86 and Fernando Torres after just 72. Southampton was Salah's 69th game. Eight hundred and twenty-nine minutes had passed since his last goal and Liverpool desperately needed to find a winner. A tap-in would have done nicely, a scuffed shot that bobbled in off the post would have been fine. Time was running out on Liverpool's title campaign. A 1–1 draw was simply not enough for Liverpool considering the quality of the team they were chasing at the summit of the table.

Fortune had fallen Liverpool's way in the injury-time defeat of Tottenham five days before when Salah's header forced a mistake by Hugo Lloris who parried the ball onto Toby Alderweireld for an own goal. What happened here was different. A moment of individual brilliance from Salah made possible by the collective effort of his teammates, chasing him and making opponents think about his options – freeing up the space. When previewing Liverpool's Champions League home tie with FC Porto a few days later, Virgil van Dijk would simplify the reasons behind Liverpool's capacity for late goals: 'We have strikers who keep working and midfielders who keep running,' he said.

In the 80th minute at Southampton, it started with a block on the edge of Liverpool's eighteen-yard box by Andy Robertson, which made the ball spin to the right and towards Sadio Mané where the Senegalese launched into another tackle with such ferocity that the noise that followed was like a crack of lightning. Suddenly, an electric current charged through the Liverpool team. Jordan Henderson's header became an assist because of its accuracy and depth but mainly because of what Salah did next after he received possession 70 yards away from his target.

Liverpool were playing in purple but their players were like the Red Arrows, supporting Salah in neat formation as he scuttled his way up the pitch. Six of them went with him but after 50 yards three disappeared from view, such was Salah's pace. Roberto Firmino's gallop had seemed to gain momentum, he was getting faster – he had gone the furthest and even beyond Salah – but that was because Salah was slowing down, he was preparing something. With that, his left-foot shot swept past Angus Gunn and into the net.

In just eight seconds, the world appeared different. Salah tore off his shirt in front of the Liverpool fans, while ripping up the record book. It was the most sensational way to become the fastest Liverpool player to 50 Premier League goals. While Ruud van Nistelrooy had done it in 68 games for Manchester United, Alan Shearer needed just 66 at Blackburn Rovers. Both of those players were the regular penalty-takers at their clubs and Salah was not. Both players would also earn a league winners' medal for their efforts. Would it be the same for Salah?

Robertson and Jordan Henderson had both tried to hug Salah

in the celebrations but Salah's trickery – even in moments of passion – meant he ducked as Robertson tried to embrace him which led Robertson and Henderson to end up hugging each other.

Liverpool's intensity had increased when Klopp brought on Henderson as well as James Milner. Klopp had wanted Henderson's 'verbal aggressiveness', but he also got a goal six minutes after Salah's, having been pushed into a more advanced midfield role following discussions with the manager. Again Firmino had been the architect, the Brazilian delivering one of the best understated performances of the season considering the number of headers he cleared when defending set-pieces. His pass towards Henderson meant the finish was simple and while Firmino celebrated the assist as if he'd scored himself by coolly folding his arms, Henderson's emotion was raw and uncontrolled. Liverpool's defiance had been embodied by the identity of their goalscorers, each of whom had endured difficulties throughout the course of a season where doubts were never far away.

Liverpool had now endured setbacks in each of their last five games: Burnley taking the lead at Anfield, Bayern equalizing in Munich, Fulham equalizing late at Craven Cottage, Tottenham equalizing at Anfield and now Southampton taking the lead away from home. Liverpool had shown grit and could not be accused of flaking. They were able to grind out victory after victory.

When Salah received possession, even though he was so far away from goal and not in scoring form, Southampton's defence immediately looked like it was in trouble. Salah could have been a 100-metre sprinter. His pace was expected but the calmness of the finish was not. The shirt off in the celebration showed what it meant to him. The chaos of Liverpool had taken him for one moment at least. The possibilities seemed endless.

3. COOKIE MONSTER

THE FOOTHILLS OF THE ALPS, MID-SUMMER. THE SUN WAS LOWERING and dusk would soon envelop Évian-les-Bains, a place associated with spring water and golf rather than football. Liverpool's players were gathered in the outdoor dining area of a five-star hotel where the cost of rooms started at £700 a night. There were glorious views of Lake Geneva behind them and the soothing sound of water crashing into rocks. But the players, on their tables of threes and fours, were looking forward at the sound system and the screens set up by Jürgen Klopp.

When the Liverpool squad had traipsed across America at the start of July playing exhibition games, Klopp had described Évian as 'my week'. Two summers earlier, he'd held a meeting with Fenway Sports Group, telling them that the team's preparations would come first during any pre-season schedule. Fenway, having already awarded him a new contract just six months into the job, listened and without any further discussion agreed straight away.

For Liverpool the US presented commercial opportunities and Klopp liked the country having backpacked around California in his late teens. For him, though, Évian brought an opportunity for sharp focus after a fortnight Stateside. This meant cycling to the training field, traversing steep hills – which merely formed part of the warm-up. The gruelling sessions that followed would prepare Liverpool's players for the endurance that was needed to carry them through the next ten months. 'I really love the sessions,' Klopp said enthusiastically. 'There should be a 100 per cent difference between the first day of pre-season and the last day. We really want to see big, big progress.'

Evenings provided down-time. There were the usual options: spa facilities, including massage options and Jacuzzis. The night, though, ultimately belonged also to Klopp. He saw it as an opportunity to bring the players closer together. There was wine and beer for those who needed Dutch courage, soft drinks for those who didn't. Karaoke beckoned.

Whereas each of the previous five summers had been disrupted by big-name stars angling to move away from Anfield, the sight of five new signings lining up to sing was a reminder of the change at Liverpool. Emre Can had left but Fabinho was his replacement, supposedly a more mobile and athletic midfielder. He was the first up to sing – Brazilian hip-hop that nobody had heard of – and he seemed the most uncomfortable of the new boys, though he was still learning English. It did not help him that Virgil van Dijk was next, who is so calm and confident. He went for Tamia's 1998 R&B hit, 'So into You'. Xherdan Shaqiri followed him, performing Bob Marley's 'Three Little Birds' – though not particularly well, according to Daniel Sturridge, who filmed the performance before directing the camera towards his own face, where his expression provided illustration in the absence of words. Sturridge preferred Naby Keïta's mysterious Guinean hip-hop, dancing with him on the wooden decking.

Alisson Becker, meanwhile, had only joined the squad forty-eight hours earlier having flown in from Paris after signing from AS Roma, but his personality was already beginning to shine through. Sturridge, who knew the music industry well enough to form a label called Dudley Road Records, suggested he might sign the Brazilian following his acoustic version of 'Don't Look Back in Anger' by Oasis. Very rarely does a player adapt to his surroundings immediately but the goalkeeper was already making new friends in the squad. 'A cool dude,' Sturridge called him. 'I like this guy's vibe.'

He had been the spotty kid who suffered from weight problems because he liked fizzy drinks and cookies. His grandmother

Antonia had described him as a 'glutton' and could remember him coming home from school or football training, heading straight to the kitchen where he'd eat loaves of sweet cinnamon bread. He loved fried food, especially cheese. During holidays, Antonia recalled taking him to the market where he'd gorge on chocolate and beg his grandmother not to tell his mum. His weight was getting out of control and Alisson cried whenever one of his uncles tried to warn him that it might stop him becoming a professional footballer. They had to use threats in the end, telling him that if he didn't lose pounds, he wouldn't be allowed to play football ever again.

Becker translates from Brazilian into English as Baker. He was born into German stock in the south of Brazil; gaucho country. Novo Hamburgo, in the region of Rio Grande do Sul, is famous for its colourful horsemen and their lively cowhands, its grilled meats as well as its music. It was not famous for its goalkeepers but thanks to Alisson's perseverance, the tactics of his family as well as the guidance of coaches, that would change. The fat kid – for two weeks in 2018 – became the most expensive goalkeeper in the world.

Alisson's great-grandfather Gustavo and his father José had been goalkeepers. His mother Magali was a handball player and a goalkeeper too. The Beckers appreciated the art of goalkeeping and recognized the most talented in the family had not been Alisson but his brother Muriel, who became Internacional's number 1 six years before Alisson made it into the first team. Muriel believed that his brother was, in fact, better suited to a defensive midfield role due to his technical ability and anticipation, skills he'd later demonstrate in goal. Alisson described goalkeeping, however, as his 'calling – it is in the blood of the family'.

In addition to concerns about his weight, there was a feeling at Internacional that he wasn't quite tall enough. The Beckers had pinned all of their hopes on a professional career for Muriel, and this led to discussions about alternative paths for his brother. Though the family would be considered a part of Brazil's emerging middle class, with his mum working as an estate agent and his dad supplying footwear to retailers, José Becker had lost his job when Alisson was a teenager and that sharpened their belief that he should focus on his studies. It became an issue that 40 miles separated Novo Hamburgo from Porto Alegre, the city where Internacional were based, and the training times for both Alisson and Muriel were different, which placed a considerable financial strain on the Becker parents given the number of trips they'd have to make.

Before he signed for Internacional Alisson had travelled to Porto Alegre with his brother to watch him train. Daniel Pavan, his coach of eight years, believed this sight had been his inspiration: seeing his brother in a professional environment and realizing what could happen if he really focused. Pavan would have fierce debates with Alisson's parents, telling them he should continue even though they thought it might be better if he stopped. He was not always the first-choice goalkeeper in the youth teams but Pavan bet on his growth into a man because he'd seen the size of other members of his family. His instincts were proven correct as inside eighteen months Alisson grew by four inches to become taller than all of the other goalkeepers at Internacional – a development that soon led to his integration into the Brazilian national set-up. By 2009, when the World Cup was held in Nigeria, he was the country's number 1 at Under-17 level. Philippe Coutinho had been a teammate and he was chosen Brazil's number 10 in the squad – along with Neymar, the number 11. Disappointment followed, however, with a group-stage elimination after defeats to Mexico and Switzerland.

Pavan remembered Alisson's reaction to the setback, viewing Brazil's performances in the tournament with personal shame. Yet Pavan also knew that he'd done enough to bring interest from European clubs, one of which was Liverpool, a club then deep in financial trouble and looking for cheaper solutions in the transfer market. Spaniard Eduardo Macià was Liverpool's chief scout back then and he'd attended Brazil's only victory in Lagos, where Japan were beaten 3–2. Pavan believed Internacional would have sold Alisson there and then for £1 million had an offer been made, but Liverpool – with Rafael Benítez in his last season in charge – did not have the funds to meet Internacional's asking price.

Alisson's professional first-team debut was still five seasons away and Jorge Andrade, Internacional's academy director, saw him develop over those years while Brazilian goalkeepers in the age groups above him emerged as amongst the best in the world. There is a word in Brazilian Portuguese that reflects those of the past, the keepers who would make impossible saves but also outrageous mistakes. According to Andrade, Alisson was not a 'flying goalkeeper' or a *'voador'* – he was not eccentric or theatrical. Instead, his presence and consistency made him stand out. His size had once been a weakness but now it was a strength. Thanks to his strong positional sense he was able to cover a large portion of the goal. Pavan believed he was not a risk-taker. Looking at him as a 25-year-old representing Liverpool, it was difficult for Pavan to mark a weak point. 'He dominates the fundamentals of the position and combines this with a strong personality,' he said.

Alisson's first task at Internacional was to become the undisputed number 1, and when Muriel was sold to Belenenses in Portugal a gap opened up. Muriel had recognized his brother's progress and had admitted to Pavan that he was merely minding the position until Alisson was ready. Manager Abel Braga thought slightly differently, though, and in 2014 decided that AC Milan legend Dida should be the team's new goalkeeper, making Alisson wait another season before truly making his mark, once Dida had retired twelve months later.

In 2015 Alisson finally established himself at both club and national level. His status with the latter had largely been thanks to a conversation between 1994 World Cup winners in former goalkeeper Taffarel and Dunga, the captain turned manager. Chile had beaten Brazil in the opening round of qualifying for the 2018 World Cup in Russia, and Dunga's number 1 Jefferson had not convinced. Though Alisson had fewer than 50 club games under his belt, Dunga decided to make a change after speaking to Taffarel, who saw something of himself in the 22-year-old. 'The length of his arms,' said Taffarel, 'allowed him to make saves that other goalkeepers could not make.' He identified also with Alisson's calm nature, telling Dunga as well as his successor, Tite, that Brazil had found a player who would represent the country for the next fifteen years. Before signing for Liverpool, Alisson's international record was spectacularly good: across 31 games, he had conceded just 15 goals, keeping 19 clean sheets. Brazil had been beaten just twice in that period and the first of those defeats was against Peru in Boston during the 2016 Copa America when Raúl Ruidíaz's goal came off the striker's arm.

Dunga trusted Taffarel implicitly but the area of Alisson's game that surprised the most was the ability with his feet. After his first couple of training sessions, Dunga was confident enough in what he saw to tell the media that whenever Alisson meets the ball, 'He thinks like a striker – where he will shoot, what else he might do.'

His transformation from the fat, spotty teenager that even his parents had doubts about had been dramatic, yet there remained some cynics. Though he still suffered from acne and he joked about still being in puberty during interviews, he was now heavily bearded with long, dark hair. Some of his managers had called him 'goleiro gato' or 'handsome goalkeeper', with Argel Fucks, Braga's successor as Internacional coach, using the nickname 'muso' [the muse] to get his attention. He was offered modelling deals but refused them because he feared negative headlines which might impact the way people viewed him. It did not help that he had replaced Jefferson, a veteran from Botafogo, who was a popular figure amongst the leading reporters and broadcasters from Rio de Janeiro, a city that is far more influential than Porto Alegre when it comes to football.

One pundit even suggested that his sharp blue eyes had set some of his coaches into a trance from which they could not escape, affecting their judgement. Alisson, though, earned respect for the intelligent way he defended himself during interviews – without inciting further headlines, and all the time maintaining consistency on the pitch. While he and Taffarel discussed the challenges ahead at a series of barbecues back in Porto Alegre, Pavan believed Alisson would have been treated differently had he played for a more distinguished club from Rio or São Paulo, even though he'd already given strong indication of his potential before making it into the national team by featuring prominently in Internacional's run to the semi-finals of the 2015 Copa Libertadores, where they lost narrowly to UANL of Mexico.

Respect across Brazil only really came after Alisson moved to Italy. Juventus had wanted to sign him and offered the same money as AS Roma, promising to make him the successor of Gianluigi Buffon. Alisson loved Buffon and was attracted to the idea of replacing him but he wondered what as much as two seasons on the sidelines might do to his own development. In Rome, a former Arsenal goalkeeper was in his way and, though Wojciech Szczęsny would play ahead of him for most of his first season in Italy, Roma did not make much of an effort to stop the Pole when Juventus made him an offer to take him to Turin in the summer of 2017.

When Alisson stopped Bologna from scoring against Roma, pundits in Italy compared the save to that made by Gordon Banks against Brazil from Pelé at the 1970 World Cup in Mexico. This resonated with the media back in Brazil, who listened even more attentively when his manager Eusebio Di Francesco reacted to a back-heel pass made by Alisson in a game against SPAL by describing him as 'the goalkeeper of the future' having been 'stunned by his presence and the calmness he brought to the entire team'. Roma had spent £8 million on taking him from under the noses of Juventus and, at the time, club captain Daniele De Rossi admitted inwardly questioning the wisdom of spending so much on a goalkeeper who, for a while at least, would probably be back-up to Szczęsny.

Two years later De Rossi understood why. 'He is the No.1 of No.1s,' Roberto Negrisolo thought. 'He is the Messi of goalkeepers, because he has the same mentality as Messi. He is a goalkeeper who can define an era.' Negrisolo was Roma's former goalkeeping coach and Alisson reminded him of a cross between Dino Zoff and the Belgian, Michel Preud'homme, encouraging him at Roma's training ground in Trigoria by telling him that he was 'born for this'.

Alisson's record in Serie A was outrageously good for a debutant, keeping 17 clean sheets – his impact reflected in the fact that the same Roma defence recorded just one during the season after he left for Liverpool. In 2017–18 Roma also had the second-best defensive record in the league, only behind champions Juventus. Alisson had the second-highest save success rate across the top European divisions. A measure of his contribution towards Roma's 2017–18 campaign was the number of saves he actually made, finishing only behind another Brazilian in Nícolas Andrade from Verona, a club who were relegated from Serie A.

It was believed in the Italian media that without Alisson Roma would not have been able to reach the semi-finals of the Champions League, where they met Liverpool, who blasted seven goals past him across two legs. Michael Edwards, Liverpool's sporting director, had already held discussions with his opposite number in the Italian capital by then, and it became immediately clear that Roma wanted a premium considering the criticism that came their way after selling Mohamed Salah for what was made to feel like loose change a year earlier, before he proceeded to define Liverpool's season by scoring 44 goals.

It was noted as significant by Edwards that Alisson's distribution was statistically almost the best in European football, considering his success rate stood at 78.9 per cent, only behind Gianluigi Donnarumma, the great hope of AC Milan. It was more significant, though, that while Alisson had made 155 saves in 49 appearances, Loris Karius – the goalkeeper he was replacing at Liverpool – had made just 58 saves across 32 games.

While Real Madrid thought about taking Alisson to Spain but were not willing to meet Roma's asking price, Chelsea were – but Alisson's representatives recognized the progression being made at Anfield and were taken by the enthusiasm of Jürgen Klopp when they met him. Klopp told Alisson, 'Do what you do,' though it did help that Liverpool were also willing to pay the financial demands of his agent – just as they had with Virgil van Dijk six months earlier, before he rejected Manchester City to move to Merseyside.

The only club prepared to match Liverpool's offer had been Napoli, Roma's Serie A rivals, though their firebrand film producer owner Aurelio De Laurentiis was told that he had come too late. That did not matter to a man who was unused to being told no, and as Alisson stood at his holiday villa staring out across the settled blue waters of the Tyrrhenian Sea, he knew that in a few hours a hydrofoil could have taken him across to the Gulf of Naples. Behind him, his agent Ze Maria Neis was taking a call from De Laurentiis who was telling him he'd give him whatever his client wanted if he chose to stay in Italy.

Alisson had taken the advice of Roberto Firmino about the lifestyle in England during their time together at the World Cup, where he was told that Firmino's happiness was reflected in the agreement of a new five-year contract. Though Philippe Coutinho had since departed for Barcelona, he too suggested that Liverpool was a calm place for any family to live, comparing the privacy afforded there with the madness of Barcelona or, indeed, the Italian capital where he had spent the previous two seasons.

Klopp had joked with him that had he not been Roma's goalkeeper in the semi-final just a few months earlier, Liverpool would have put fourteen past him rather than seven across the two legs. For £66.8 million, Klopp would sign the most expensive goalkeeper in the world instead of Napoli, who Liverpool would draw in the Champions League group stages, along with Paris Saint-Germain and Red Star Belgrade.

Liverpool's efforts to get Alisson would directly be rewarded several months later when, in December, they needed to beat Napoli in the last group game of the Champions League at Anfield without conceding. At the final whistle Klopp used exaggeration as a tool, telling Jamie Carragher in a pitch-side interview, 'If I knew Alisson was this good – I would have paid double.' Behind him the crowd, whirling their red and white scarves, celebrated Liverpool's progress at the expense of the club he could have gone to. 'Alisson, Alisson, Alisson,' they chanted repeatedly, as though he was a gladiator.

In the main stand was also De Laurentiis who stood there with his arms folded surely contemplating what might have happened had Alisson been representing his team rather than David Ospina, a goalkeeper who wasted his peak years at Arsenal trying unsuccessfully to displace a fading Petr Čech. It was a night which underlined that football is largely defined by the stealth of recruitment, an area which Liverpool had so often failed in over the previous decade. Michael Edwards' tentacles were already wrapped around Alisson and his advisory team by the time Napoli made their approach. And the Brazilian's injury-time save from Arkadiusz Milik when the score was 1–0 seemed to go on for ever. There was the length of the cross, the distance it travelled from José Callejón's left foot. There was Milik stumbling and the sense of the moment slipping away from him, though nobody knew for certain. Somehow, Alisson got in the way. And somehow, Liverpool were through.

His shirt number was 13 and the title on the back of it was A. Becker rather than Alisson, as is the common practice of most Brazilians who carry their first name or nicknames with them into their football careers. Alisson was different because of what happened on his honeymoon in Florida when he and his wife Natalia went to Disney World and he was addressed as 'Princess Alisson' as he waited to go on a Cinderella-themed ride with his wife because it was assumed, when he'd booked, the reservation was for a woman. From that moment he joked that if he ever left Brazil he'd play it safe rather than give encouragement to crowds – especially those who didn't want him to do well.

There were plenty of those, particularly after the impressive way he started his Liverpool career, recording three clean sheets in his first three games. There was nothing for him to do on the opening day against West Ham but he saved spectacularly from a free-kick at Crystal Palace when Liverpool's lead was narrow, before provoking gasps and then cheers from the Anfield crowd as he chipped the ball over the onrushing Anthony Knockaert despite the slender margin of Liverpool's 1–0 advantage over Brighton.

Klopp's message to Alisson was clear: be brave, but don't try anything stupid, 'I don't like the chip' – but Liverpool's supporters' faith in their new goalkeeper was absolute, with many taking to social media to express their delight that the team finally had a goalkeeper with the sort of attitude and ability that causes confidence rather than dread to spread.

In the next game at Leicester, however, Alisson went too far.

He was on schedule to record another clean sheet when he tried to dribble past Kelechi Iheanacho before turning back into trouble. The Nigerian substitute forward then dispossessed him and helped Rachid Ghezzal reduce the margin of Liverpool's lead. Though they held on, Alisson's mistake became the focus of post-match discussion.

Late in September, once he'd had time to reflect on what had happened, Alisson sat down at Anfield to preview Liverpool's game with Chelsea – the other Premier League club that had been interested in signing him before they reacted to Liverpool's determination by breaking the world record for a second time in as many weeks themselves, recruiting Kepa Arrizabalaga for £71 million from Athletic Bilbao.

Alisson spoke in long sentences and I felt sympathy with the interpreter who was helping him, even though his English was already supposedly excellent. He was asked about how he dealt with the Leicester mistake and he admitted that in the past, he had locked himself away wanting to be alone whenever he'd done something wrong, but not now. He was keen to stress that his professional history was not decked by many errors. 'My game is characterized by consistency and that is what has brought me to Liverpool and helped me grow and develop,' he said. 'I like to make simple saves. If the ball is in front of me I won't dive. If it's to the side of me I will dive to the side. I like to keep it simple. My saves are not to show off, or Hollywood saves for the camera.

'I am working on playing with my feet, so I take risks,' he continued. 'I am waiting for options. I am waiting for the centre-backs to produce an option. I'm waiting for the full-backs to appear as well; hoping that a space for a pass will appear at the last moment. That's what happened in the Leicester game. I was waiting for that option of a pass, leaving it very late for the option to appear. It was at a time of the game when we were under pressure and I do know now that I should have taken the option of kicking the ball into the stands.

'The ball,' he reasoned, 'held up in the grass. I think otherwise it would have been a successful dribble. I was pushed from behind as well, and that was a real learning curve for me about the

Premier League. Here the referees maybe don't call the fouls that you would expect to get in other leagues. Things are different here to other countries and I've learned that I can't wait for the referee or expect the referee to call the foul.'

He vowed to take fewer risks when options do not appear. Then he stretched out his long arms, wrapped his knuckles and spoke like a religious man or a philosopher. 'The secret of the wise man is to learn from the errors of others,' he concluded. 'However, unfortunately in the Leicester game it was my error. I do take some risks and leave it late to play the ball, but I'll stop taking these risks in the Premier League because of the different style of play, the physicality and the different refereeing styles.'

John Achterberg, Liverpool's Dutch goalkeeping coach, had suggested to Jürgen Klopp that it would be a good idea to make Alisson train with rugby bags in preparation for the Premier League's physical demands. In the past when Simon Mignolet was the first choice, or when Loris Karius replaced him, Klopp had insisted on a defender standing between any striker and the goalkeeper from corners. By the time Liverpool met Napoli in the Champions League – in the same fortnight Alisson flung himself across the goal in his yellow kit like Bananaman to stop Everton from taking the lead in the Merseyside derby at Anfield – the Brazilian was dealing with opponents himself at corners without needing the assistance of a teammate.

Alisson genuinely did not seem to care about the amount of money that had brought him to Liverpool, though he did describe it as 'crazy and absurd'. Instead, he seemed to relish the challenge of justifying the price tag, insisting it was about time a goalkeeper's value to any team was recognized as being as important as a striker's. 'Any error that we make can potentially be fatal for the team,' he admitted. Seven games into his Liverpool career, he already appreciated this reality better than anyone.

GRIND AND REWARD

4. THE HIGH ROAD FROM GIFFNOCK

Life at this age is rubbish with no money #needajob
9.12 p.m., 18 August 2012

ANDREW ROBERTSON HAD BEEN AN UNEMPLOYED TEENAGER FOR whom gloom had nearly overtaken hope. The sandstone quarries of Giffnock in south-west Greater Glasgow had long stopped providing jobs for the town's young men, and when Robertson was told by Celtic – the club he loved the most – that he was too small, as a 15-year-old, there were few options for him to turn to. That is why he joined the closest Scottish League football club to Giffnock as a junior, a club whose amateur status was reflected by their motto *Ludere Causa Ludendi* – 'to play for the sake of playing'.

The patrons of Victorian Glasgow had taken open green spaces seriously and one of those built in 1857 was Queen's Park. Its designer, Sir Joseph Paxton, was also responsible for planning vast public areas in Birkenhead as well as in Liverpool. Without Paxton delivering Queen's Park, perhaps a football team would not have formed ten years later – the first in Scotland. Perhaps then there would have been no football team for Robertson to learn his trade – and no reasonable starting point for a journey that would ultimately take him all the way to Anfield.

Queen's Park had been in the bottom tier of Scottish football for four seasons by the time Robertson looked at his Twitter feed and sent out a message which generated more traction in a couple of seconds six years later, when he reached the Champions League final with Liverpool, than it did in all of the years in between. He was not an academy footballer who envisaged a future in the professional game. His school picture at St Ninian's shows a boy with an uneven knot in his tie and an oversized claret blazer. He was otherwise a smart student who at sixth form gained good grades in history, business management and physical education. In the months before he made his Queen's Park first-team debut he promised his parents that if he did not earn a full-time contract at a football club within twelve months he'd focus instead on a path towards university. Nobody then envisaged him becoming the most recognizable Scottish sportsman behind Andy Murray.

Joe Fuchs was his PE teacher at St Ninian's and he saw his pupil as intelligent but more passionate about football than anything else: his crushing experience with Celtic had not dampened his spirit, certainly not for sport, where he was really competitive and always wanted to win. Fuchs would play him at table tennis, and whenever Robertson lost he would want a re-match straight away. As well as football, he represented St Ninian's at cross country, athletics and golf. He was pushed on by competition with two schoolmates who became professional footballers as well. Though Calum Gallagher scored on his debut for Rangers against Dunfermline Athletic he would play only five times for the Ibrox club before moving on to St Mirren then Dumbarton. Liam Lindsay, meanwhile, came up through the system at Partick Thistle and spent the 2018–19 season earning promotion from League One into the Championship playing for another German manager in Daniel Stendel at Barnsley. Robertson was the school football team's captain and Fuchs was proud when the left-back led a league and cup Double in 2011, not long before he emerged in Queen's Park's first team. 'There was certainly something about his character and confidence at an early age that marked him out for success,' Fuchs told the *Daily Record* after Robertson became national team captain in 2018. 'He was different from the rest of the boys.' Fuchs could not initially put his finger on precisely what that difference was but when pressed he identified a natural enthusiasm in Robertson in everything he did – there were no half-measures. He did not take himself seriously but he took sport very seriously, and this made him balanced: determined yet humble. Fuchs believed fame had not changed him one bit. Whenever he needed help with school events, whether they were awards evenings or charity fundraisers, Robertson would help out. 'That's just the sort of person he is,' he thought.

In the research of any footballer, a reporter or author will usually come across at least one person who is jealous of the player's achievements. Maybe it is due to the nature of Robertson's unlikely ascent that in this case that's proved impossible. Nobody foresaw his rise. He was not a big head. According to Fuchs there were more talented footballers at St Ninian's but none had the love of the game like Robertson.

His release from Celtic coincided with that of Bernard Coll's, who then joined him at Queen's Park, where Coll was initially considered a better prospect in youth teams and was selected ahead of Robertson at left-back. When Robertson signed for Liverpool in the summer of 2017, Coll joined East Kilbride in the Lowland Football League.

Coll believed Robertson benefited from full-time training. He quickly became fitter and stronger. Having already played competitive football, he went to Dundee United with an appreciation of the value of three points and a better understanding than the academy players at Celtic regarding what it took to win football matches.

Another of his teammates in the juniors at Queen's Park was Ryan McGeever, who was picked up by Falkirk before reaching Queen's Park's first team. It was, according to McGeever, Robertson's capacity to learn quicker than others that set him apart – and this was illustrated by the fact he passed his driving test aged 17 before anyone else. 'He wouldn't shut up about it,' recalled McGeever, whose career has been restricted to Scotland having returned to Queen's Park from Falkirk before moving on again to Brechin City. McGeever said Robertson was the sort of lad to be quiet at first but as soon as he felt comfortable with people, his personality shone through. 'A genuinely lovely, funny guy,' McGeever called him. 'A lovely family as well.' He had met with Robertson for a coffee on a couple of occasions since his fellow defender joined Liverpool and noted he was exactly the same person as he was at Queen's Park. When he reached the Champions League final by knocking out Roma in May 2018 McGeever sent him a message and Robertson replied straight away, saying how much he appreciated it. 'Just small things like that, when you consider how many folk must have been congratulating him, shows what a top man he is.'

Like Coll, McGeever would not have picked Robertson out as the one player in his team capable of playing for Liverpool in a Champions League final. Lawrence Shankland, a centre-forward, would break all sorts of records as a professional but found his level at Ayr United. Robertson and Shankland entered Queen's Park's first-team environment at the same time, along with Aidan Connolly and Blair Spittal who both joined Robertson at Dundee United. Shankland's ability stood out more, though – everyone talked about him. 'There were guys who were maybe more naturally talented that aren't even playing football today,' McGeever said. 'But Robbo was always technically sound, never shirked a challenge and worked his socks off every single day. He loved football so much.'

Autumn into winter had been a slog for Liverpool, winning regularly in the league but rarely spectacularly. Sometimes they lost – but only in the cups. Though only one defeat was totally unexpected – at Red Star Belgrade in the Champions League – it had been the performance in Naples which Jürgen Klopp thought about the most and, later in the season, he'd describe the loss as the worst in his time as Liverpool's manager. 'We did not – we could not – run,' he reflected. 'A bad night; a bad, bad night.'

It had been the away games in Europe, indeed, where Liverpool struggled. The results were deserved: that 1–0 injury-time defeat in Naples should have been settled a lot earlier; the 2–0 chastening in Serbia was uncharacteristic of a Klopp side, outrun and outfought. They then fell to Paris Saint-Germain where Neymar – the most expensive player in the world – delivered a hypnotic first-half display that was enough to give his team an advantage to get them over the line as Liverpool pushed for an equalizer towards the end, though they were never convincing. The only encouraging element from that night was the way in which the Paris players celebrated. It became clear that beating Liverpool was now treated as a scalp.

The league was a different matter. Following Alisson's mistake at Leicester Liverpool had gone to Wembley, defeating Tottenham Hotspur 2–1 in a game where Georginio Wijnaldum broke a duck which had lasted two seasons. His early header was his first away goal for the club since signing from Newcastle. PSG were then beaten 3–2 at Anfield on a memorable night, sealed by Roberto Firmino's late winner. The Brazilian had been introduced as a substitute having had his eye gouged at Spurs a few days earlier. He celebrated, pretending to be a pirate.

After Southampton conceded three on Merseyside, there were four games without a win: Chelsea progressed at Liverpool's expense in the League Cup before a 1–1 draw that felt like a victory in the league at Stamford Bridge because of another late goal, this time a spectacular equalizer from Daniel Sturridge. Liverpool's players danced in the Stamford Bridge dressing room that night.

There was late drama too the following week when Manchester City missed an injury-time penalty at Anfield, Riyad Mahrez clearing the crossbar. It was another stroke of luck for Liverpool in the latter stages of a game. Spurs, in injury time, should also have had a penalty and the chance of an equalizer following a clumsy challenge in the box by Sadio Mané as he chased back, helping out in defence.

Huddersfield Town away (1–0) then Red Star and Cardiff City at home (4–0 and 4–1) all came easily before a draw at Arsenal. There were comfortable wins against Fulham and Watford. Then came Paris, which left Liverpool needing a victory against Napoli in their last Champions League group fixture a fortnight later.

Thanks to Alisson's intervention, that would happen. Yet there had been a series of morale-boosting moments before that. Everton came to Anfield first – who would ever be able to forget how that finished? Certainly not Jordan Pickford. Burnley were dispatched confidently on a freezing December night at Turf Moor, then Mohamed Salah dazzled at Bournemouth the following weekend, where he scored a hat-trick in a 4–0 win. The debate about Salah's perceived prior struggles had stretched well into the campaign where he'd scored just nine goals by the start of December, compared to 19 the previous year. Was he actually a one-season wonder or was it even fair to judge him on the standards he'd set himself in 2017–18? On the south coast two weeks before Christmas his mood was encapsulated by his third goal where he resisted two fouls from the trailing Bournemouth defenders before leaving a vapour trail in his wake.

Salah's goal then secured the passage through to the Champions League knock-out stages and Liverpool should really have beaten Napoli by more even if they were nearly caught out in the seconds before the final whistle.

There was a bounce at Anfield as Manchester United arrived already eight points behind Liverpool. In his previous two encounters as United's manager, José Mourinho's extreme tactical conservatism prevented Liverpool from developing any momentum but this occasion felt different inside the opening 30 minutes as Liverpool surged forward in search of a goal.

Klopp would describe this period as amongst the best of his reign. Sadio Mané had the opportunity to join United when he left Southampton in 2016 but signed for Liverpool because of Klopp, 'the coach who believed in me'. Though the Senegalese had given Liverpool the lead, Alisson's mistake was punished by Jesse Lingard – a former Liverpool academy player. From there Liverpool dominated and, although Xherdan Shaqiri scored twice via deflected goals to seal a deserved three points, it was the drive of left-back Andy Robertson that stood out the most. The following day Mourinho would be sacked as United's manager. Some of his last words in the position were in praise of a Liverpool team whose qualities contrasted with his own, but more particularly in the competitiveness of Robertson.

Mourinho undoubtedly was making a cryptic point to United's players as well as the board, yet his assessment of Liverpool was accurate. 'They are fast, they are intense, they are aggressive, they are physical, they are objective,' he said, which contrasted with the levels of his team. 'They play 200 miles per hour with and without the ball.

'I am still tired just looking at Robertson,' Mourinho concluded. 'He makes 100-metre sprints every minute. Absolutely incredible.'

'The season he broke into the first team, Rangers were in the Third Division,' remembered David McCallum, then Queen's Park head of youth development, who later took on a similar role at Ibrox. 'This brought plenty of interest. There wasn't any one particular game or moment, but he played four times against them and every chance he was presented with, he met it full on.'

All eyes in 2012–13 were on Rangers, the fallen champions whose financial demise led to a reformation in the same league as Queen's Park. This was a stroke of fortune for Robertson because it meant there was more focus on the competition than there ordinarily would be. When Rangers went to Hampden Park for what was their local derby on 29 December, more than 30,000 supporters showed up – over thirty times more than Queen's Park's average attendance that season.

Robertson was leading a double life: a teenager desperate for a job by day, a left-back challenging the might of Rangers by night. He spent a year working at Hampden for a pittance – much like the apprentices of old used to do: sweeping the terraces, mopping the floors and scrubbing the showers. With the money earned, he bought his first car, a Renault Clio – which Ryan McGeever remembered so well.

One of Robertson's tasks in early 2013 was to operate the ticket office and help out with hospitality when the stadium held international football matches and rock concerts. Belgium played Scotland at Hampden, Robertson showed Vincent Kompany to his seat and gave him a programme. Less than five years later he would play for a Liverpool team that defeated Manchester City and Kompany three times in the season where City achieved a record points total in the Premier League.

Willie Neil was kit manager for the Scottish Football Association and he saw Robertson's transformation from handyman to Scotland's captain. Another one of Robertson's duties at Hampden was to wash the kits, fold them neatly and place them in the changing rooms. Neil believed it 'stuck in the throat of the people at Celtic that they let him go'. He thought Queen's Park played a crucial role in rebuilding any broken confidence and deserved credit for putting him back in the shop window. 'It has all happened in an amazingly short space of time – from Queen's Park to the Scotland team to Liverpool,' Neil told the *Scotsman*. 'He is not the type of boy player who goes overboard with his celebrations and gets involved in silliness. I think that comes with family. His family are really well grounded and they have been a big influence on him – his big brother and his mum and dad. Andy is just a level-headed guy and was very well mannered, right from day one. He still has not lost that. He still has that civility. I do not think, however big he gets, that he will ever lose that because I do not think his family will allow him.'

Robertson played 43 times in a season where Queen's Park narrowly missed out on promotion, finishing third behind the champions Rangers. In that team, managed by Gardner Speirs, was Aidan Connolly whose emergence as a teenage prospect, like Robertson's, alerted the professional clubs. In the summer of 2013 both players signed for Dundee United. From there, Connolly's progression would not match Robertson's and five years later he was playing for Dunfermline Athletic. The winger considered Robertson's determination to prove people wrong his greatest asset. His story, he thought, was inspirational for all boys in Scotland who have been told they are missing something. 'It just seems with Andy, whenever somebody says he's not good enough, he's not physical enough, he always seems to shut them up,' Connolly said. 'Everyone looks at Andy as an inspiration.'

It helped Robertson that Dundee United had looked towards Queen's Park for new recruits before. In 2010 Barry Douglas – another left-back – had transferred between the clubs, though the manner of United's approach had angered those at Queen's Park after their status as an amateur institution was taken advantage of when it came to financial settlements. United were not obliged to pay Queen's Park a penny and they avoided any compensation fees.

Three years later, when Douglas decided to move to Poland

and sign for Lech Poznań, United approached Robertson – though this time, it was agreed that Queen's Park would get ten per cent of any future transfer deal. It meant Robertson cost nothing in the first transfer of his life – though he would later earn Queen's Park £300,000 when he signed for Hull City.

His youth-team coach in Glasgow, McCallum, thought he went to Dundee United not expecting to play, that he'd spend some time finding his feet before gradually building himself into the team. But Douglas's departure had left a big space. Like Robertson, Douglas emerged as a fine player in the Championship where he was nominated in the team of the year in 2017–18, having helped Wolverhampton Wanderers reach the Premier League, before moving to Leeds United where he also shone under the legendary Argentine coach, Marcelo Bielsa.

'Great lad, great player, Barry,' thought Jackie McNamara, the Dundee United manager. 'But Andy had something else. His will to succeed was unbelievable.' Like Robertson, McNamara had been let go as a youth when Hibernian told him he was not tall enough to make the grade, a measure of the prehistoric thinking that once permeated British coaching circles. Yet he went on to play for Celtic and represent Scotland, captaining both. For McNamara, Dunfermline was the club that, like Dundee United with Robertson, 'took a chance'. He could relate to what he called 'the lost boys of football' and he saw a bit of himself in Robertson – though he never envisaged him becoming Scotland's captain. 'What we saw was potential,' McNamara said. 'The thing with Andy was that he was always on the front foot with his defending and attacking. He was slight, but he was very hungry to learn and to do well. Together with his attitude that made me feel he always had a chance.'

He did not anticipate how quickly Robertson would adjust to professionalism and a jump of three levels. According to McNamara one of the first English clubs to make their interest known in his development was Everton, with Roberto Martínez visiting Tannadice around Christmas time in 2013. 'We fielded a few enquiries,' McNamara remembered. 'His development was sensational; he just suited being a professional footballer. There were times when I had to pull him away from the training pitch. It seemed like he didn't want to be anywhere else. He'd felt let down by the Celtic experience and did not want to let this opportunity go.'

Dundee United were playing at Hibernian in the Scottish Premier League. Having driven three and a half hours to Edinburgh from his home in Lancashire, Stan Ternent decided to leave early. Just twenty-five minutes had been needed to make his mind up on the visiting team's left-back. Ternent had seen Andy Robertson play for the first time a few weeks earlier in another away game at Kilmarnock, where 'he stood out by a mile'. On the second scouting trip, he called Steve Bruce as soon as he could get a signal on his mobile phone. ' "Are you sure?" Bruce asked. "Of course, I'm sure." And that was that.'

Ternent was a Gateshead-born Sunderland supporter before his emergence as a legendary lower league manager at Bury and Burnley, the club he came to be associated with the most. In 1990, when Liverpool lost 4–3 to Crystal Palace in the FA Cup semi-final, he'd been Steve Coppell's assistant at Villa Park – 'A day we did Liverpool because of our determination to prove a few people wrong,' he remembered. Seven months earlier Ternent had been on the bench at Anfield where Palace had lost 9–0.

He'd originally seen Robertson in his role as head scout of Hull City after hearing about the talents of Stuart Armstrong, a midfielder who embedded himself in Brendan Rodgers' treble-winning Celtic side of 2016–17 before he moved to Southampton in 2018 for £7 million. There was something more about Robertson, though: the intensity of his play, his concentration, his pace and his power. Full-time training had turned him into an athlete as well as a footballer, and Ternent liked his backstory, how he'd been let go and let down by Celtic – it said to him that he was able to recover from setbacks. 'Robbo was more of a no-brainer,' Ternent believed.

When he was Sunderland's manager Bruce liked what he saw in Jordan Henderson, even though the future Liverpool captain was still a teenager. At Hull he trusted Ternent and made an offer for Robertson straight away. Bruce was a former Manchester United captain but he was from the north-east and trusted Ternent's opinion as if his life depended on it. Robertson became a £3-million signing. Roberto Martínez had been looking for a long-term replacement for Leighton Baines and was considering using the left-back's experience in midfield. Bruce, though, moved the quickest and he was persuasive, telling Robertson that within six months to a year he envisaged him becoming the team's first-choice number 3.

Initially, Bruce planned to use him sparingly, though. This changed when Robertson made his first appearance in a friendly against VfB Stuttgart – the club Jürgen Klopp supported as a boy. Robertson scored inside 12 minutes following a marauding run from left-back. He'd feature in the rest of the pre-season games before appearing in Hull's starting XI on the opening day of 2014–15 at Queens Park Rangers. There were a further sixteen league appearances in a campaign where Hull ended up getting relegated, but Robertson played in Europe and largely acquitted himself well at the higher level. Phil Buckingham, the respected football reporter at the *Hull Daily Mail*, liked the spring in Robertson's game, the way he was always on the front foot trying to make something happen. Though he would find it hard to rise above the mess at a club in financial turmoil, and his performances suffered later, Buckingham wondered what Robertson would be like in a better team of players where the environment was more secure. There was, after all, only so much a left-back could do in a struggling side.

Mike Phelan was Bruce's assistant – and another staff member with links to Manchester United, the club he'd return to after José Mourinho was sacked in December 2018 and Ole Gunnar Solskjær was installed as his replacement. He could remember Bruce telling him about Robertson, a player who would not 'say boo to a goose'. Inside six months, he'd established himself amongst the rest of the squad to the point where he was unrecognizable from the person who'd joined from Dundee United. 'Once he'd got into the first team you couldn't shut him up,' Phelan recalled. 'There was a huge character change, like he'd been waiting for his moment – he just needed that stage to express himself.'

Keith Bertschin was Bruce's first-team coach: 'Andy was a young, quiet lad, almost sheepish, to be perfectly honest. That's understandable when you're new to a club, but the lads helped to bring him out of his shell and he soon became a part of the group. Over the course of that first season I saw him develop and grow in confidence. He made a few mistakes, as youngsters do, but he learned in each game he played. He worked on the weaknesses but he also reinforced what he was good at: the way he'd travel up the pitch, get in behind and use that beautiful left foot of his. By no means was he the finished article but he learned fast and learned from the people he respected.'

Bertschin believed Hull's relegation helped Robertson's development in the long term by giving him the chance to shine more regularly: 'In the Championship you have to work hard because it's always going to be a scrap to get out of that division. Without being willing to roll up your sleeves and fight, you'll not get very far. When you've been in that scrap you learn things about yourself that you might not have done by playing in the Premier League. You have to be mentally strong. You find yourself tested more in the Premier League, because giving the ball away might lead straight to a goal. But, as a stage to learn, the Championship can be very beneficial. That will have toughened him up and now he's got that never-say-die attitude.'

Alex Bruce was Steve's son and a regular in the side. He saw a teammate whose determination shone above all of his other qualities: 'There was always something about Robbo. He might have been quiet when he first came to Hull but you couldn't shut him up at the end. He'd hold his own and you can see that in his character now. He's taken to Liverpool like a duck to water. He was always an unbelievable athlete. He could run all day. He had all the makings of being a great full-back but there's always going to be a question mark over a young lad coming into English football for the first time. He's done well with Dundee United but the Premier League is a very different level. He had all the attributes for the modern full-back but you'll never know how they handle it on the big stage until they're there. It wasn't always easy, he'd tell you that. He knew he had to work on his positional play as a defender when he first came, but he's done that to such a point where you'd have to say he's one of the best left-backs in the country. Arguably the best.'

Liam Rosenior, Hull's right-back, liked Robertson's bravery and his willingness to receive possession, as well as his belief that he could make something happen. His crossing ability, he believed, was outstanding. Rosenior, whose father Leroy had a long career as a professional footballer, used to stay behind with Robertson after training at the left-back's request because he wanted to learn more about angles and positioning. 'He really wanted to work and become better, he was always asking me questions, especially about one-on-one defending and the defensive principles of being a full-back,' Rosenior remembered. There was something about Robertson that made him different. At the start of his time at Hull, Rosenior thought he looked like a student arriving for work experience. 'He was a bit of a geek, to be honest.'

Much later into the 2018–19 season, before Liverpool went to Southampton and won with two goals in the final ten minutes, Jürgen Klopp was asked about Virgil van Dijk and his impact on the Liverpool team after joining for a world-record fee from the club he was preparing to face. Klopp believed it counted for something that his squad was made up of backstories which involved different paths as well as different sums of money. 'Having different characters always helps,' Klopp said.

You could never describe Klopp as mainstream but it was a word he used here – 'mainstream players', i.e. players that cost a lot of money, those who have always been ranked highly from their days at academy level. 'Well, that can cause problems,' the manager believed. He saw Van Dijk in a similar light to Andy Robertson, even though one cost nearly £70 million more than the other. 'Not everyone thought they were always *that* good.' He thought Liverpool's defence was now 'a proper one', and that although his team featured a few players who took more of the headlines, they were humble enough to recognize that without the supreme efforts of those beside them, individual acclaim would have been a lot more difficult to achieve, if not impossible. Robertson, for example, had supplied so many goals for Mohamed Salah. It became a regular sight, the Scottish full-back raiding down the left before Salah made a diagonal run into the box. There was a sense that Klopp took great satisfaction in seeing the development of players like Robertson. Life at 18 with no money may have been rubbish but by 25 he was an elite footballer who seemed more than comfortable with his status as one of the best left-backs in the European game.

5. BIG BROTHER

IT WAS LATE ON A FRIDAY NIGHT AND NEIL LENNON WAS SITTING BEHIND his desk at Celtic's Lennoxtown Training Centre, way out to the north of Glasgow, where the Campsie Fells loom and the colour of the sky merges with the earth. He was a fortnight into his second spell in charge of a club he had helped to five league titles as a player and then three more as manager, the last of which came in the season after he signed Virgil van Dijk.

As a well-known Catholic leading Celtic in a city where the sectarian divide with Rangers reaches poisonous levels, he recognizes how paranoia can ruin a person, and because of this he believes trust became one of his greatest strengths. The challenge at Celtic, 'a juggernaut of a football club', has been distorted by the presence south of the border of the English Premier League, where the worst top-flight club receives a minimum of £100 million a year through broadcast rights just for participating, while Celtic could win everything in sight domestically and receive just £2 million in television revenues.

When Lennon thinks about making a signing, he first has to consider the limitations around fee, but then there are other criteria: does the player have the ability and character to compete against clubs like Barcelona and AC Milan? Does he also have the potential to be sold at a huge profit? Virgil van Dijk became Lennon's record signing but he cost less than Kelvin Wilson was sold for in the summer of 2013, when Wilson went back to Nottingham Forest – the club Lennon had originally signed the defender from for nothing. That Van Dijk stands 27th on the list of Celtic's all-time record signings shows not only what Lennon was competing against but what amazing value Van Dijk proved to be. Inside two years Celtic would make a £9.5 million profit by selling him to Southampton. Lennon knew that Wilson was going so he asked John Park, Celtic's chief scout, to source possible replacements. Park had started his career as an IT manager at Glasgow Caledonian University before working in recruitment in the youth system at Hibernian in Edinburgh. During José Mourinho's first spell at Chelsea Frank Arnesen, the sporting director, had tried to take him to London, but Celtic was his club and an offer he could not turn down. There he hired a team of five data analysts. 'John would bring me footage of players through a package his team had put together, or via Wyscout,' Lennon remembered. 'I looked at the clips of Virgil and thought, "Wow, this kid's really special." But you never really know until you see him in the flesh. I was thinking, "There's got to be something wrong with this guy – he can't be that good." '

Lennon flew to Amsterdam to watch him play for Groningen against Ajax. 'Straight away, I was thinking: "Woah, what a player – the next Rio Ferdinand but better." He was broader than Rio, he had a bigger chest. That made him more powerful but it didn't make him any slower. He could really move, he seemed to get faster the further he ran. It seemed as though he was able to glide across the pitch. A physical specimen in every sense. I was looking around wondering where all of the other scouts were. I was hoping and praying I could get a march on them if they were hiding. Apparently, a couple of Russian clubs were offering lots of money. Virgil's representatives never played that card, but we realized we had to get the deal done as quickly as possible. He suited our style of play,' Lennon concluded. 'We'd reached the last sixteen of the Champions League the year before using two really quick centre-halves in [Efe] Ambrose and Wilson. Wilson was a good passer so I wanted someone like that considering he was leaving. I wanted a fast, aggressive defender who could take care of the ball for us.'

Van Dijk's agent played a crucial role in his move to Celtic because he recognized the Scottish league was a good pathway for him: going to a huge club, playing in front of big crowds with enormous expectation – as well as the prospect of regular Champions League football. Victor Wanyama had recently been sold by Celtic to Southampton having played in Belgium for Beerschot previously, and his development provided the sort of example Van Dijk wanted to follow. There were still some gaps in his play but that did not translate into a doubt for Lennon. 'He saw the danger but sometimes he did not react quickly enough, that was the message that initially came back,' Lennon explained. 'Because of his style, to some this may have come across that he was a bit complacent. It was only a slight bugbear – the only flicker of question mark. But when he was fully on it and fully concentrated he was unstoppable.'

Bertie Auld was one of Celtic's Lisbon Lions, a ferocious European Cup winner and later, a manager at Partick Thistle. It is fair to say that he was not Alan Hansen's biggest fan before Liverpool signed him in 1977 – the defender's languid movement giving Auld the impression that he wasn't quite as interested as he should have been. Hansen would emerge as the greatest centre-half in Liverpool's history, and Lennon saw Van Dijk similarly: 'They're different in terms of their physical attributes but in terms of their play, their class – he's probably the best since Hansen, for me.'

Lennon is also a believer in later bloomers – Van Dijk was 22 years old. 'Roy Keane didn't come to England from Cork until he was 19 and he became one of the best players in my generation,' Lennon acknowledged. 'There's always a nugget to be found out there.' After the first training session, Lennon told Van Dijk: 'Enjoy your time at Celtic, you won't be long here; you're that good.'

'Everything you dream of in a centre-half, he had it,' Lennon thought. 'He was quick. He was really comfortable in possession. He could play left and right at centre-half. He could play through the lines with his passing or bring the ball out of defence like a Hansen. Then, in both boxes, he was brilliant in the air. At set-plays he was a massive threat.'

Van Dijk's closest friend in the Celtic squad was the captain, Scott Brown. Like Lennon, the midfielder divides opinions.

Brown is a footballer who appears to revel in conflict. 'Virgil was a good mixer with a strong sense of humour. One of the things that struck me the most about Virgil was, he had more of a British mentality than Dutch,' recalled Lennon. 'He was very aggressive around game time and hugely competitive. He didn't take any nonsense. If things weren't going well in training he was quick to get after people. He didn't suffer fools. He was a winner. Some players might let things go but he'd be the first to step in if something was wrong. He was off the pitch as he was on it: calm and easy-going but very confident without being arrogant. When he wanted to be front foot, he could be. He was very straightforward to work with. For me, he was the perfect player to work with, extremely professional and respectful – desperate to improve. You didn't have to tell him twice. If you gave him an instruction, he got it. But then, you didn't really have to tell him much.'

Celtic lost one league game that season – at Aberdeen, when Van Dijk was sent off for two yellow cards after 20 minutes.

'His impact on the team was ridiculous,' Lennon reflected. 'Virgil is one of those defenders you very rarely see go to ground. He stays on his feet because he reads the game so well. He doesn't have to make many last-ditch tackles because he's already there, ahead of the ball or the opponent. You'd see players that looked to be miles in front of him then Virgil would open up his legs, cut across and take the ball as clean as a whistle.

'I contemplated putting him in midfield for a league fixture ahead of a Champions League game when I wanted to give some of the boys in front of him a rest. When I told him, he said, "No gaffer, that would be a bad idea." I wanted him to be a number 6 but Virgil knew better. "No, I'm a centre-half – that's me." He was so persuasive, I had to listen to him. I said, "OK, Virgil, that's fine." It said to me that he knows what he wants. He was smart, he appreciated which path he was on.'

For Lennon, Van Dijk scored Celtic's goal of the 2013–14 season in a victory at St Johnstone: 'He received the ball on the halfway line, saw the space and charged forward through the midfield with that elegant run of his, before opening his body up and taking it past the last defender. When he reached the edge of the box, he toe-poked it like Ronaldo at the 2002 World Cup.

'He also took a free-kick against Hibs at Easter Road, bending it into the top corner. Charlie Mulgrew was our usual set-piece man and, in fairness to Charlie, he was excellent at free-kicks with his left foot. But Virgil said, "No, I'm taking this one." When it flew in, I thought, "Oh my god – that's our centre-half, he can do everything. The guy's incredible."'

Lennon believes Van Dijk suffered from a stigma that players in Scotland receive – like Andy Robertson. 'For all people denigrate the Scottish game, two players have, inside four years, emerged as key players at one of the best teams in Europe,' Lennon said. 'People question, "Are players really getting tested in Scotland?" But don't forget, Virgil was also playing in the Champions League against Barcelona and AC Milan and coming out on top against some really good players. I was surprised no one came in for him after being so good in his first season.'

Lennon left Celtic for a new challenge at Bolton Wanderers. 'I had chief scouts ringing me, asking about what he was like even while I was there at Celtic. Obviously, I didn't want to lose him. But I accepted the reality that he was going to go and the club would get the best price. I asked some of these scouts, "What are you waiting for? What are you worried about?" They suggested that sometimes he switches off. I told them, the further this kid goes the better he'll get. The challenge will stimulate him more. It wasn't like he wasn't having to concentrate for Celtic. He made the game look easy.'

Van Dijk – to Lennon's surprise – remained in Glasgow for another year under Norwegian Ronny Deila before moving to the Premier League. 'I'm not being disrespectful to Southampton but I thought he'd go straight away to a bigger club. It's crazy that the world's most expensive centre-half was right on the doorstep of these clubs, even at Groningen – bearing in mind Luis Suárez had been there as well. Why it took so long for him to get to a place which matched his talent is one of football's great mysteries. I feel lucky to have been able to have worked with him for a while,' Lennon concluded. 'He's now one of the best defenders in the world, if not the best. Who else is there? Thiago Silva at PSG? Or Raphaël Varane at Real Madrid? Perhaps Varane is a bit quicker but Virgil is better technically.'

Lennon had been a Liverpool supporter growing up in Lurgan, Northern Ireland. On his wall were posters of Kenny Dalglish. He believed that the club's signing of Alisson Becker had also been significant to the team's development. He remembered with anguish watching Liverpool throw away a 3–0 lead in Seville to draw 3–3 in November 2017. 'That doesn't happen now,' Lennon said. 'Alisson and Van Dijk have transformed the defence. And that has transformed the image of the team.'

Virgil van Dijk became the world's most expensive defender when Liverpool signed him from Southampton in January 2018. Immediately, Liverpool looked a calmer team yet also a much taller one. He is 6 foot 4 inches and the theme of height had, in part, explained his journey to that point. At 16 his younger brother by two years was taller than him. Then, over the summer of 2007, Van Dijk grew by five inches. This led to problems with his groin and knee. He needed to be bigger to become a footballer, but this also hindered his progress as he spent more time in the physio's room than on the training field. Soon, he was wearing football boots with specialist insoles to protect his knee. He had been a right-back but, after a six-week break, he returned to Willem II as a centre-back. He had never been a stand-out player until he was 19, when he became the captain of Groningen's reserve team. He would ride a bike to training sessions. His first pay packet went towards driving lessons. Before that, while at Willem II in Tilburg in the south, he had worked as a dishwasher in a nice area of neighbouring Breda at a restaurant called Oncle Jean – Wednesday evenings and Sunday evenings at the sort of place that offers dim lighting, private dining and a decked garden for drinks in the summer.

That money was spent instead on Saturday nights in the Grote Markt area of Breda where he usually finished his socializing in McDonald's. Van Dijk was 20 years old when he lost 2 stone following a stomach infection from an appendix operation which kept him in hospital for thirteen nights. He had been in his first full season in Groningen's first team and was preparing for the derby with Heerenveen when he began to feel sick. By his own admission, he had not eaten healthily up until that point in his life. For ten of those nights, he was unable to walk and, when he was able to walk again, for three days even ten yards would leave him breathing heavily. The period forced him to think more seriously about his own mortality, and this would benefit his career.

For a footballer who in a Liverpool shirt would appear indestructible, Van Dijk came to understand the fragilities of the body sooner than some. He started training more, arriving earlier than the rest of Groningen's squad. Within twelve months the scouts had started visiting Holland, and Celtic were the first club to make him an offer that would take him away.

His mother came from the colony of Surinam and his father was fully Dutch. His grandfather had been the first in the Van Dijk family to play football, though he was a better referee. In Breda Van Dijk would spend his Sundays between church in the morning and football in the afternoon, playing on five-a-side courts financed by the Johan Cruyff Foundation. Each city in Holland had at least one. Games were unorganized: the team that won stayed on and the team that lost faced a wait. While this helped his technical ability, it also increased his endurance. Some of those he competed against would go on to represent NAC Breda and Willem II. Initially, Van Dijk joined Willem II, a club based half an hour away in Tilburg. Sami Hyypiä had played there before joining Liverpool in the summer of 1998. In the summer of 2001 goalkeeper Frank Brugel, having been a professional footballer at Willem II, still had contacts. He was watching his son play one Saturday for a team called WDS'19 when Jordy Brugel, also a goalkeeper, rolled the ball out to the defender in front of him. It was something about the way the defender took care of the ball that made Brugel senior take notice.

Though NAC Breda had a partnership with WDS'19, they had missed him altogether. Aged 10 Van Dijk went on trial, impressing Jan van Loon, Willem's academy director, with his powerful running. Few strikers were able to get past him. But now and then he'd switch off. Coaches at Willem could not decide whether he was too confident in his own abilities and this made him lazy. It was not necessarily an attitude problem. He just made football seem incredibly easy, though he did make some mistakes.

At 18 both Willem II and Van Dijk had a decision to make. Van Loon wanted to keep him, but not every coach was convinced they should, with some technical directors happy to cut him loose. The first-team manager, who was focused on a relegation battle, did not even know Van Dijk's name, and the player himself once admitted that he felt betrayed by the lack of confidence from those who supposedly should have known more, especially in a country with a historic record of producing world-class talent. What those directors must think now . . .

Groningen spotted in Van Dijk what some at Willem had not seen across eight years. Yet those who defend Willem would say every big club in Holland missed Van Dijk completely. Hans Nijland, Groningen's technical director, believed Van Dijk had become rusty at Willem having endured the same relationships with the same coaches, who were giving him the same instructions for such a long time. He needed to hear a change of voices as well as a new environment to freshen his focus. By listening to the player, Nijland established quickly that he'd take things a little bit too easy sometimes, or maybe not act quite as seriously as others in his position might. Initially, there was also a feeling amongst the coaching staff at Groningen that Van Dijk was too laidback. He was intelligent and talented but did he have the drive to push himself all the way to the top? He'd give opponents too much space and, though he was able to recover, he was told that he might not be able to do so at senior level where the top strikers think and act quickly. He also had a tendency to forget to push up and play a high defensive line as per the coach's request. Van Dijk needed to sharpen up.

His first-team debut came against Den Haag in May 2011. Within a month he was making headlines. Having finished joint fifth in the Eredivisie, Groningen faced the same opponent over two legs in a play-off to decide which club qualified for the Europa

League the following season. Groningen lost the first leg 5–1 but then won the second by the same scoreline, with Van Dijk, still a teenager, selected as a centre-forward. He scored twice, one of those from a free-kick. Though Groningen lost the penalty shootout that followed, Van Dijk's performances carried on into the next season, when he was asked about his career aspirations. He was not afraid to be ambitious: to play for Barcelona was the target. Gerard Piqué was his role model. Eight years later he would line up against his idol and knock his team of choice out of the Champions League at the semi-final stages in improbable circumstances, representing the club he now 'loved'. That club was Liverpool.

They met first in Blackpool, the seaside town where Bill Shankly spent his summer holidays with his wife Nessie over at the Norbreck Castle Hotel to the north of the promenade. It was June 2017 and a meeting had been arranged for Jürgen Klopp to meet Virgil van Dijk at another location, an apartment hired by Liverpool. He would fly north from a private airfield in Southampton and land at another private airfield near Cleveleys. Discretion was necessary because Klopp knew Manchester City and Chelsea also wanted to sign Van Dijk – he knew what it would look like if they were photographed together then he went elsewhere. Klopp laid on the charm, telling Van Dijk what he could become and how Klopp – and the environment of Liverpool – could improve him. Klopp acknowledged that it might be easier to win titles at City but at Liverpool, if the possibility was realized, he'd become a legend for ever. City already had Vincent Kompany and he was the statesman-like figure in their defence and dressing room. Van Dijk could do that for Liverpool and be the first in a long time, rather than be someone else's successor.

Van Dijk nodded and thought back, remembering being at the Champions League final between Juventus and Real Madrid in Cardiff a month or so earlier where Liverpool supporters kept telling him to sign if the opportunity was there. 'Like Celtic,' he thought. He was stimulated by the passion, having come to the realization that his sense of calm brought out a better player in febrile environments: a meeting of characters and approach. He flew back to Southampton convinced by Klopp and convinced by Liverpool. The fee they were willing to pay reflected how much they valued him. And then the move broke down.

Southampton were furious that details of the transfer became a matter for public consumption before the deal was signed off. They had agreed that Van Dijk could meet with Klopp but any developments should remain between the clubs and certainly not feature in the papers. Liverpool retreated, offering a public apology to a club they'd signed five players from over the previous four years. When it was suggested to Klopp that he could move on to other targets he rejected the idea. 'Virgil,' he promised over a phone call, 'if you wait for me, I will wait for you.'

He would waft over Liverpool's defence like a cool aftershave, acting as a human roadblock that even the wardrobe that is Watford's Troy Deeney could not intimidate because he was 'too big, too strong and too quick – he also smells lovely, but I hate playing against him'. Indeed, in games against Watford during the 2018–19 season Liverpool would win on aggregate 8–0.

Van Dijk's signing marked Liverpool out as a club that would push boundaries again to put things right. Whereas the defence used to be the team's tender spot, it would become the tightest in the league. Van Dijk's arrival reminded of where Liverpool had been and where they were going. In 1961 when Shankly wanted to make Ian St John a record signing, one dismissive voice in the boardroom insisted the club could not afford it. Eric Sawyer, a big supporter of Shankly, stepped forward and said, 'We cannot afford not to sign him.'

Klopp was absolutely sure about Van Dijk's abilities but he sought reassurances from Mike Gordon, the figure at Fenway Sports Group most invested in Liverpool, that the club was not overstretching itself by paying £75 million for a player that none of the biggest clubs in Holland wanted to sign just four years earlier.

Liverpool's interest in him had begun at Celtic but their scouting of him intensified when Klopp realized that a top defender was a priority. Liverpool looked at more than thirty centre-backs, following their progress in between fifteen and twenty games. This led to two lists being formed: four category-one targets and four category-two – the latter being younger defenders who could rise into the higher bracket if their expected development was realized. Napoli's Kalidou Koulibaly and Athletic Bilbao's Aymeric Laporte were on the same list as Van Dijk but Klopp believed the Dutchman could settle at Anfield straight away considering his four years already in Britain. One of Klopp's earliest games in charge of Liverpool was a 6–1 victory over Southampton in the League Cup. Van Dijk had not made a healthy impression when facing what was mainly a reserve team that night but, a year later, Klopp made his mind up to try to sign him after a 0–0 draw in a game at Southampton where Sadio Mané tried to pull away from Van Dijk only to find his options terminated when the Dutchman somehow caught up with him, blocking a shot. Klopp needed a leader but he also needed pace, given the way Liverpool pressed opponents. Klopp would lean over to his assistant Peter Krawietz and whisper, 'He is the one.'

He would become a £75-million bargain. The last time Liverpool won the title, in 1990, they kept eleven clean sheets. Another on a damp night in Wolverhampton on the Friday before Christmas was already Liverpool's eleventh of a season which had not reached its halfway point. Virgil van Dijk scored that night, sliding in Liverpool's second to secure a comfortable 2–0 victory over a tricky opponent whose record against the top six teams in the Premier League was outstanding. Wolves would qualify for Europe for the first time since 1980, but the distance between the levels of these teams was marked not only by the standard of Mohamed Salah's opener but by Van Dijk's performance at Molineux, where he played like a planet with its own gravitational pull. When Adama Traoré, supposedly the quickest player in the Premier League, tried to speed past him, Van Dijk followed like a tank fitted with a Ferrari engine, pushing the winger to one side like it was the easiest thing to do – as natural an act as breathing or sex.

By the end of the campaign Van Dijk had come up against

Lionel Messi, Cristiano Ronaldo, Eden Hazard, Neymar, Kylian Mbappé, Karim Benzema, Harry Kane and Lorenzo Insigne across the previous eighteen months, and none of them had managed to dribble past him once.

'He is everything I expected him to be,' Klopp reflected, though that could not be said of the directors at Willem II. By the summer of 2019 Van Dijk had not only emerged as the most expensive defender in the world but he had also become only the sixth defender in history to be crowned PFA player of the year, as voted for by his opponents. He had played in more minutes than any other Liverpool outfield player, he had more touches than any other Liverpool outfield player – only Jorginho, Chelsea's midfielder, had attempted more passes over the course of the season – and he had made more than double the amount of clearances than the nearest Liverpool teammate.

Statistics, though, would only support his value rather than define it. In the weeks after he first signed for Liverpool, scoring the winner on his debut against Everton in the FA Cup, Alex Oxlade-Chamberlain was asked about Van Dijk's impact, even after such a short time at Anfield. 'Well,' he said. 'He's a cool character, that's for certain. It's like having your big brother on the same team as you in the playground.'

6. IN MY LIVERPOOL HOME

STEVE ROTHERAM WAS LOOKING OUT OF THE WINDOWS FROM HIS office, which offered panoramic views both of the city he represented and the Mersey river, the waters which brought Liverpool its wealth and then, in part, its decline.

Thanks to the slave trade, Liverpool was once the richest British city outside London and the biggest port in the Empire, but the Second World War had a profound long-term impact on its prospects, with incredible damage inflicted on the city including its port area. Once the Commonwealth disintegrated Britain lost many of its trading partners and, by the 1970s, Liverpool was on the wrong side of the country when the European Community was formed – with containerized ports in the south-east now preferred. Liverpool's economic relevance was then wiped out almost completely by the Margaret Thatcher-led Conservatives. In 1981 her chancellor Geoffrey Howe recommended that the government abandoned Liverpool, setting it on a programme of 'managed decline'. The subsequent period ushered in Liverpool's modern identity, a city which, like Glasgow, was once a bastion of sectarianism as well as a centre of conspiratorialism. Between 1983 and 1985 its Militant council was the only one outside London to fight back against the tide of Thatcher, and this contributed towards its sense of detachment. Thatcher's non-interventionist policy led to the death of many major industries, and in Liverpool that meant the docks. The rates of unemployment in Liverpool were worse than anywhere else. Most firms relied on the port and, without the port, the main source of work,

Liverpool's collapse was swifter and arguably more dramatic considering the mobilization and the sharpness of the resistance.

Looking inland from Rotheram's office three decades later, Liverpool's city centre transformation is clear. Beneath the dark-fronted glass of the fourteenth floor of the Longitude Building, a facility built in 2008 – the year Liverpool became European Capital of Culture – are hundreds if not thousands of tourists making their way between the Liverpool One shopping centre and the Albert Dock, a restored complex of warehouses which first opened in 1846 before it became a symbol of Liverpool's past, decaying like so many other parts of the docklands.

Liverpool managed to re-establish itself as a popular tourist centre because of the Beatles and because of the presence of Liverpool Football Club. Peter Moore, the club's chief executive, who was brought in from the games division of Electronic Arts in the summer of 2017, having spent most of his adult life living in California, estimated that Liverpool FC now drove more revenues for the city than its most famous band. Matches and the associated tourism is worth close to half a billion pounds for the region.

For Rotheram, this displays Liverpool's importance but it also represents a great challenge. He is Merseyside's metro mayor and a season ticket holder at Anfield. The club has to balance its 'local heartbeat and its global pulse', as Moore had branded it. 'Get that wrong and you end up with fans feeling marginalized,' Rotheram acknowledged. 'But if you don't have the visitors, the city suffers.'

Ironically, the local heartbeat, global-pulse mantra was first championed not by Peter Moore but by another Peter, Peter Furmedge – known as 'Furmo' amongst the Liverpool supporter base. A qualified accountant and a socialist, Furmedge learned how to set up football clubs having helped reform Darlington in 2012 after they were expelled from the Football League. In 2015 he was one of the founder members of City of Liverpool Football Club – the city's first socialist club.

Rotheram too describes himself as a socialist. His mother and father had left Anfield before he was born to live in Kirkby, a new town eight miles away. Out of squalor and into the utopia of houses with inside toilets as well as front and back gardens. His father worked as a forklift truck driver but his mother was influential in terms of politics. Dorothy Rotheram was a matriarch. The house in Kirkby was always filled by aunties who were not really aunties, and they'd cook together. 'If my mum had three potatoes and one of my aunties had four carrots, they'd stick it all in a pot and make something for everyone,' Rotheram remembered. 'Everyone mucked in to create something.'

It was important to interview Rotheram because his background and beliefs reflect those of Liverpool widely – and show what Liverpool supporters want from their owners in terms of leadership, and explain why outsiders see the club in a very particular way.

'People here see unfairness and are prepared to personally get involved in fighting against it,' Rotheram said. 'Maybe in other areas people are sympathetic but observe more rather than participate. We stand up for other people but ourselves as well as a city.'

Liverpool, Rotheram thinks, once believed itself to be the epicentre of the whole world. That was in the 1960s when the Beatles emerged, Liverpool FC emerged, and the docks still served thousands of working men who bundled and packaged up cargo before sending it on voyages to all four corners of the globe. Self-confidence and civic pride could, however, sometimes overspill into blind belief. The DNA in Liverpool was harvested by immigration from Ireland during the potato famine, and Ireland had long railed against British rule. In Liverpool this manifested itself in the General Strike of 1911, which led to Winston Churchill sending gun-boats up the Mersey. Because of the docks, Liverpool was a melting pot – not just of Irish but of Scottish, Welsh, West Indian and West Africans, people who have historically felt repressed. Liverpool also has the oldest Chinese community in Europe. 'Scouse,' Rotheram said, 'is a mix of all of those cultures.'

Rotheram was a teenager when Thatcher became prime minister in 1979 and set about changing Britain for ever. In Liverpool, there were few jobs and youth unemployment rates were staggering. Football, which was then cheap to attend, offered solace.

'Football was all you had to look forward to,' Rotheram said. 'There was literally nothing else. You worked to go to the match and hopefully to be able to get out on a Saturday night. Everything revolved around the footy.'

Later, his status as mayor would bring him into contact with his hero, Kenny Dalglish. He would tell him the story about his mother buying a 'Kenny pillowcase' from Kirkby market, which he still slept on when he was in his late teens and old enough to date girls.

As a casual labourer, to fund going to Liverpool matches, he would dig ditches, form manholes and build roads. One of them was just outside his office on Mann Island. When, in 1983, he was offered a full-time job in the Falkland Islands just a few months after the cessation of hostilities between Argentina and Great Britain, he was 21 and full of bravado so he went. By the time he'd returned, Liverpool's reputation as a city had turned. Militant – the left-wing faction of Labour – was an understandable response to Thatcher, considering her plans, but it nevertheless accelerated a feeling of otherness about Liverpool because so few councils followed their lead.

Then there was Heysel, a disaster which led to the deaths of 39 (mainly) Juventus supporters who were crushed after clashes before the 1985 European Cup final. The stadium was unfit for purpose and Liverpool's administrators had raised their concerns about arrangements, with Liverpool's supporters given a reduced allocation of tickets due and placed next to a supposed neutral section which ended up being taken up, as feared, by Juventus fans from Brussels' large Italian community. The courts sentenced the head of the Belgian FA as well as two police chiefs for their role in the disaster while 26 Liverpool fans later stood trial for manslaughter.

Thatcher immediately withdrew English clubs from European competitions before Liverpool, whose supporters had torn down a chicken-wire fence at Heysel before charging into section Z of the stadium, were rightly banned from Europe anyway, along with every other English club due to the level of violence that had seen terraces become battlegrounds for football hooligans.

Everton, Liverpool's closest geographical rivals, arguably received the greatest punishment because they were English champions and never got the chance to see whether they could reign in Europe's elite competition.

Initially, this did not drive a wedge through Liverpool, a city which was so entrenched in fighting back against Thatcher, but many years later – amongst supporters of both clubs too young to really appreciate the social struggle of the era – it became a reference point for bitterness and divide. Further afield, supporters of other clubs missed out because of the five-year ban that followed, and this heightened resentment towards a club which came from a city that was already under attack.

Rotheram, as a leader, studied other leaders. In his maiden speech as an MP he quoted Bill Shankly, whose socialism he believed not only formed the foundations of the club he supported but much of the city's newer political outlook. 'The things Shankly said resonate today just as they did in the 1950s and 1960s,' Rotheram thought. 'He remains a huge political presence.' Shankly died in 1981 but he was never interested in party politics. His socialism was a way of being and a way of doing. 'Even if I was scrubbing the floor,' he said, 'I'd want my floor to be cleaner than yours.'

Rotheram sees similar determination and charisma in Jürgen Klopp, who he described as being 'much more than a football manager'. Like Shankly, Klopp is not party political but he will 'always vote for the left and not the right. He says things that are outside what normal football managers feel comfortable speaking about but uses a softer, more persuasive power which isn't ruled by fear. I've listened to the players and they play for Klopp because they don't want to let him down. Shankly was the same.' Klopp, according to Rotheram, had helped Liverpool's supporters connect with the club again. They could identify with him and they could identify with the backstories of players like Andy Robertson and Virgil van Dijk who, like Liverpool as a place, also felt misunderstood.

At a very localized level the mood around Anfield in 2019 was better than it had been for a long time. For longer than a century, the stadium had been hemmed in on all sides by streets of terraced housing, and this had made it almost impossible to expand without human sacrifice for the working-class families that lived there, as well as the small shops and pubs which came to need the Saturday trade from Liverpool home matches in order to survive. An uneasy relationship developed. While Liverpool became a multinational company known all over the world and filled with millionaire players, the place where they earned their fortunes struggled desperately.

Rotheram had been the councillor for the Anfield area when Liverpool's stadium move to Stanley Park was first discussed. Liverpool had since become 'better neighbours' but the uncertainty around what was going to happen had contributed towards the district's decline, and the club had played a shameful part in the dereliction, buying up houses and leaving them empty for years. 'I don't think Liverpool handled that issue or that period particularly well,' Rotheram stressed. 'The target for the abuse became councillors. The community was concerned that a new Anfield was being imposed upon them without consideration for the families that lived there, and this brought a sense of hopelessness. The full benefits of a regeneration scheme, which would act as a catalyst for the economic improvements for everybody eventually, was drowned out, I have to say, by a fairly limited group of individuals who kicked off very, very loudly.'

There are now housing projects all the way down to the King Harry pub and out towards Goodison Park. There are neatly appointed homes next to Anfield. The completion of Anfield's new main stand in 2016 brought certainty: Liverpool would be staying in the area. This inspired confidence, and since then new ventures have thrived like the Homebaked bakery, a community co-operative which sells the popular Shankly pies. The 'tinned up' terraced houses have also been taken over by a housing association. Things seem to be getting better but Liverpool as a club cannot solve every problem that exists.

Since the return of the Conservatives to government power in 2010, Liverpool – Anfield especially – has suffered. Thatcherism destroyed Conservativism in Liverpool, which now has no Tory councillors, and this means the city is hopelessly underfunded by central government. Under Labour there had been a plan to invest in housing around Anfield but the Tories wiped £600 million from the housing budget. Government policies have since had even more of a detrimental impact on the area of Anfield. 'Those people affected the most are unlikely to ever be able to go to a football match now,' Rotheram rued. 'We're talking about people in work who are low paid or on zero-hour contracts, but if you read the right-wing elements of the media, you'd believe this was a lifestyle choice.'

Ian Byrne lives in Anfield, four roads away from the ground. A Labour councillor in the Everton ward which runs up Walton Breck Road and towards the Kop stand, he's been a community activist since he was a teenager. When the Fans Supporting Foodbanks campaign began in 2016, it started in Liverpool with Byrne and his friend, an Evertonian called Dave Kelly, another social campaigner as well as a trade unionist, who recognized the collective struggle on Merseyside under Tory rule. 'Poverty doesn't wear club colours,' became their slogan and subsequently similarly well-organized initiatives have been set up by supporters at Huddersfield Town and Newcastle United.

It frustrated Byrne deeply that all of this had to happen. He and Kelly would stand behind the Anfield Road stand before every game and take collections. Whenever Everton were at home Byrne would help out at Goodison Park. Peter Moore, Liverpool's chief executive, has supported the movement by purchasing a purple van which provides an opportunity to advertise the campaign on roads across Merseyside as well as a vehicle to transport key materials to different areas of the city. While Liverpool's city centre had benefited from EU funding ahead of 2008, many of the outer boroughs remained impoverished and, to some extent, this explained why Liverpool voted to remain in the EU in 2016 as expected, although the vote was much closer on Merseyside than many expected.

Byrne described foodbanks as a 'dereliction of duty by the government – we're digging them out of a hole'. He's had sleepless nights wondering what will happen to the most affected communities if he and other people like him stop. He's wondered whether it would force the government to do something, but he doubts it. He likens the period 2010 to 2019 to the miners' dispute, 'when our class was under attack' and believes the Conservatives are trying to starve communities out of existence. 'It feels like 1984,' he stressed when I met him before Liverpool played Huddersfield at home. 'The government aren't lifting a finger to help the most vulnerable in our society out.'

Byrne believes a sense of resistance has always existed in Liverpool because socialism was strong in the city. Socialism had risen because the capitalist system had thrived out of the casual labour system that did not yet exist in other English cities or towns where workers did shifts and had regular salaries. This made people think about a different way of living.

'We've always fought against injustice,' Byrne said. 'Maybe it comes from our Celtic heritage.' He considers the fight for justice in the wake of the Hillsborough disaster, where 96 Liverpool supporters died and then had their memories smeared through newspaper lies, as the greatest example of fan activism that has ever been seen – or ever will be seen, 'because we took on the establishment and never stopped'.

'Even with the goodwill and fantastic work of all those community figures like Ian and Dave, you can't absolutely put right what society has got wrong,' Rotheram concluded. 'It's the same with other manifestations of Tory policies such as the increasing number of people living on the streets. What we need to ensure is people don't need foodbanks and don't sleep rough. What we need is a change of government to ensure that happens.'

It was Boxing Night and Liverpool were already leading Newcastle 1–0 when the first chant came from the away end. Bill Corcoran, who was the visiting team's version of Ian Byrne, had asked Newcastle's supporters not to sing 'Feed the Scousers' like they had on Newcastle's last visit to Anfield. 'Our cities are under attack and we need to stick together,' he concluded. 'Those kinds of chants are divisive. Nobody should be singing them.'

Yet they did – or at least, some of them did. 'Younger kids who don't know the harm or significance,' Corcoran said afterwards. 'We'll do our best to educate them,' which made sense considering Newcastle United's foodbank campaign accounted for 30 per cent of collections across the city which, reflecting the level of poverty on Tyneside, had more donations than any other in the country in 2017.

The singing made Steve Rotheram 'deeply depressed'. He could understand why it might happen with supporters who backed clubs from wealthier areas, Chelsea being an example. 'But I'm not having fans from Newcastle or Manchester singing it. They should actually know and see the effects of Tory policies on their cities. They are being hit as much and are hurting by successive Tory governments as Liverpool. All football clubs are guilty of singing hurtful songs but this one does not do any favours to the working classes.'

It was 'just banter', came the reasoning on social media. Yet the singing, which became more widespread as Liverpool made it 4–0, was a suppressant, rooted in anti-Irish sentiment that preserved the view Liverpudlians had too much to say for themselves in the same way women with an opinion are 'feisty' or black people who push back have 'chips on their shoulders'. The song has origins in the 1980s, the decade Liverpool resisted the force of Thatcherism which had sent the city plunging into a social darkness. Liverpool as a city went in the opposite direction when the Prime Minister won her second term in 1983 by a landslide, with the local council now dominated by Labour, and sixteen months later came the release of the Band Aid song that gave football supporters the ammunition they needed – just at the point when jealousy towards Merseyside's football teams heightened, with Liverpool and Everton winning eight out of the ten First Division championships during the 1980s.

There were three games over the Christmas period where 'Feed the Scousers' was bellowed out by different sets of fans who came from cities where employment rates explained deprivation and detailed why match-goers with a social conscience were leading foodbank campaigns (subsequently promoted by football clubs trying to do the right thing). When Manchester United came to Anfield many had travelled from Victoria, a train station where rough sleepers try to get warm – a sight that had prompted Andy Burnham, the region's metro mayor and a close friend of Rotheram's, to donate 15 per cent of his salary to help tackle homelessness. The same feature of life in Manchester that had caused the city's bishop, the Rt Revd David Walker, to accuse ministers of 'taking their eye off the ball' on poverty, warning that the crisis in Manchester is now at an 'unparalleled level', with the poorest families 'torn apart' by welfare cuts that have led to destitution on an unprecedented scale. When Liverpool went to Molineux on the Friday before Christmas and were encouraged – just as Evertonians had been in August – to 'sign on, sign on', it seemed to have been forgotten that not only does Conor Coady, the Wolverhampton Wanderers Championship-winning captain, come from Merseyside, but also that 34 per cent of children in the Black Country now exist below the poverty line; a desperate fact when you consider the majority of those, according to the Joseph Rowntree Foundation, live in households where parents or guardians are actually in paid work.

From his office overlooking the city he loves, Rotheram was excited about his team's possibilities. For the first time in a decade, a challenge in Europe would await in the second half of a season where Liverpool had led their own domestic championship. 'The jealousy towards the football team could lead,' he warned, though, 'towards an increase in the mocking of the city, whether Liverpool end up winning or not.'

7. THE END OF MONEYBALL

BETWEEN THE MUNDAÚ LAGOON AND THE ATLANTIC OCEAN IS A PIECE of Maceió called Trapiche. It is where Roberto Firmino comes from, the scorer of a hat-trick for Liverpool against Arsenal in the final game of 2018 – a 5–1 win which put his team ten points ahead of Manchester City going into the new year. Liverpool would face City next and a victory for Pep Guardiola's side in that match, however, had the potential to reduce the margin very quickly indeed – to just four points.

Firmino's first goal against Arsenal, Liverpool's equalizer, was a tap-in – though he finished the chance by not even looking at the ball or the net. His second, moments later, was the culmination of a slalom run through Arsenal's defence. He celebrated with a somersault. The third was a penalty, after which he pretended to play the drums, baring his floss-fluorescent teeth. His mother, Mariana, described him as, 'Pure energy, I thought he was hyperactive. He lived and breathed football.' Yet he also loved music – 'He'd play football with his headphones on.'

At Christmas time in Trapiche Firmino would dress like his musical hero Wesley Safadão, who also has nice teeth, wore his hair in a ponytail and comes from the north-east of Brazil, traditionally the poorest area of the country, which has led to the mass migration of workers to the south-east, where they've formed their own distinctive subculture. There are twenty-seven regions in Brazil, and in *The Atlas of Human Development* the Alagoas region, the capital of which is Maceió, stands 27th on a list that marks prospects according to education, employment possibilities and health.

An extrovert in appearance, an introvert in personality, Firmino rarely speaks about himself. Though there has been much interest in his story, he has granted only one interview in his four seasons at Liverpool, and that was back when he joined in the summer of 2015. Reluctantly, he spoke about his childhood in Maceió, a city with one of the worst gun problems in Brazil. Through an interpreter, he said only a few words. 'Tough . . . but a lot of places are tough in Brazil.'

His journey would ultimately involve a move to the south-east for work as well. He had grown up dreaming of playing for local club CRB (Club de Regatas Brasil), whose ground was just at the end of his street. 'It was about five minutes' walk from my house, I could hear the noise from the crowd when I was going to sleep at night,' he recalled in 2015. 'All I cared about was football, I'd take the ball to bed with me.'

His father José had been a street-hawker, selling soft drinks, beer and water from his bike at nightclubs and sports events like CRB football matches. 'I'd probably have followed him,' Firmino thought, had it not been for his own ability. Trapiche was the sort of place where kids could play out all day long if they wanted to, and for most of the night. The education system in this corner of Brazil is either non-existent or relaxed. Firmino's mum would try to draw him in from the street but he'd always climb over the back wall when she wasn't looking and start a game of football on a nearby corner.

CRB would sign Firmino on the second day of a trial. He seemed to play everywhere and they could not figure out what his best position was. A central defender initially, he also played right-back. Scouts from the south were always operating in the north-east because they knew of the talent there and the willingness to travel elsewhere to earn professional contracts. Florianópolis was thousands of miles away, a place that got cold in the winter. Figueirense was a second division club offering just a one-year deal but Firmino went and, inside two and a half years, he had emerged as the young player of the year for the league, the season Figueirense were promoted to Série A.

Hemerson Maria was Firmino's youth coach in the early days

and, for a fortnight, he called him 'Alberto'. The player never corrected him and Maria only found out he was called Roberto because of a colleague rather than the player himself. Maria thought this reflected Firmino's shyness as well as his modesty. His mother would not see him for eighteen months because he did not have the means of getting back to Trapiche. When he was 17 years old Maria remembered a week where all of the other youth players at Figueirense went home to be with their families but Firmino stayed alone in Florianópolis. Firmino told him: 'I want to stay here. I need to practise more. I don't want to lose time. I will stop only after I make something good with my life.' Maria was taken aback, telling the *Guardian*: 'He is shy but he has a strong personality and mentality. He knows what he wants in his career and his life.'

Firmino had never played in Brazil's top flight but Hoffenheim were prepared to pay £3.5 million for him when he came on the radar of Lutz Pfannenstiel, Hoffenheim's head of international relations and scouting. Pfannenstiel too had an interesting backstory, having been the only player to represent clubs in each of the six Fifa confederations. In England, one of those had been Bradford Park Avenue in the Northern Premier League. His global experience meant he knew a thing or two about the sort of players who have the character to adjust to new surroundings. He thought of Firmino as an 'unwritten paper' – the sort of player Hoffenheim could shape into becoming very disciplined, once instilled with a German mentality.

Firmino would take time to settle in Germany, but he never complained. One of his former agents called him every couple of days to check up on him. He was again living alone, but this time in a foreign country that was different culturally to any of his prior experience. Hoffenheim was a village of fewer than 4,000 people, but its football team had leapt from the fifth division to the Bundesliga in less than a decade thanks to the financial backing of software mogul Dietmar Hopp. The agent reminded him that he was there to help if anything was wrong, but Firmino told him, 'If I wasn't happy I would have already left the club and country.' The agent concluded that he was shy, a man of few words. But his personal resolve exceeded others who maybe had more to say.

At Liverpool Jürgen Klopp would describe him as 'a footballer from his head to his toes'. Though Firmino remained an interesting yet elusive figure for the media, the spotlight was usually shone on Mohamed Salah instead, and this suited the Brazilian. Salah's performances and his domination of the headlines contributed towards a sense Firmino was undervalued, but those who knew him best, and those in a position to know quite a lot about what he was trying to do, thought of him as an elite-level footballer. 'Undervalued?' Klopp asked. 'This discussion has never happened in the club or the team.' Thierry Henry believed he was 'the most complete striker in the league'.

Without Klopp, though, maybe Firmino would not have received such acclaim. He had joined Liverpool in the summer of 2015 under a different manager with different ideas of the way forward. Except, it felt back then, like Liverpool were going backwards.

Eighteen months earlier, in May 2014, Brendan Rodgers had almost led Liverpool to the club's first league title in twenty-four years. They would fall almost right at the end, literally, with Steven Gerrard's slip against Chelsea allowing Demba Ba to score in front of the Kop. The moment had felt like a car crash in slow motion. Gerrard would soon be 34 and time was running out on the Liverpool career of the club's greatest modern player.

The chance to change history was gone. A Chelsea team made up largely of second-choice picks – one that contained Mohamed Salah, who was the first player to be substituted by José Mourinho – won 2–0. This let Manchester City back in. Though Liverpool would draw 3–3 with Crystal Palace, having led 3–0, the damage had been done by Chelsea at Anfield eight days earlier. By easing to victory over a West Ham United team on the final day – one that had been given the week off by Sam Allardyce – City finished top and Liverpool came second.

The progress made by Rodgers, however, was reflected by an improved long-term contract. He had arrived at Liverpool in

2012 from Swansea City, back when Liverpool's owners wanted a bright, young coach who bought into their philosophy, which was built around the development of bright, young players. Youth promised a brighter future but it also gave Fenway Sports Group the time they needed to understand the new environment they were operating in. Wigan Athletic's Roberto Martínez and Rodgers were the outstanding candidates and John W. Henry met both of them. Though Fenway would have liked Jürgen Klopp, he was out of their reach at the time. Liverpool were only in the Europa League; Borussia Dortmund were German champions and heading towards a Champions League final.

Rodgers would take the place of Kenny Dalglish. Liverpool's players had respected Dalglish's status in the game but not his ability as a coach. He was Liverpool's last title-winning manager and a legend of the game. Fenway believed he spent too much time on the golf course. While the training sessions of the Scottish assistant manager Steve Clarke were good, many of Liverpool's foreign players could not always understand what Dalglish said. He had lived in Birkdale for thirty-five years but his thick Glaswegian accent had never left him. The appointment of Dalglish was the first major decision made by Fenway after their purchase of the club in 2010, and his presence did help unify Liverpool for a short period after the misery of Roy Hodgson's tenure, but many of Liverpool's players felt underprepared for games. And while ahead of 2018–19 Dalglish still remained the last manager to win silverware for Liverpool, in his one full season back in charge he guided the team to their lowest league position since the Graeme Souness era nearly twenty years earlier. By finishing 13 points off the Champions League places, Dalglish's fate was sealed.

Initially, Rodgers had leaned towards staying at Swansea. He did not like the idea of working with a sporting director, another structural change that Fenway implemented early into their reign. Though Damien Comolli had been sacked following the failures of 2011–12 – notably his recruitment of Andy Carroll as a record transfer despite his dubious injury record – in the summer of 2012 the club were still searching for Comolli's replacement three months after his departure. Rodgers agreed to come on the provision he worked with a team of scouts instead. The infamous 'transfer com-mittee' emerged, a term first coined by Fenway and one they came to regret, because it naturally led to suggestions of divisions when it came to decision-making. The word 'holistic' appeared in their language, but football clubs are not day spas or beauty centres. They are brutal worlds where opinions matter and staff don't always get on despite the gleam all clubs like to present.

Rodgers' first season fell neatly under the description of 'transi-tion', but the start of his second was foreboding, with Luis Suárez wanting to leave in search of Champions League football and the Uruguayan – the first big signing under Fenway – training away from the rest of the Liverpool team after he accused the owners and Rodgers of broken promises. Though Rodgers was later able to maximize Suárez's outrageous talent – which propelled him towards 31 league goals and eventually a move to Barcelona – it had been the persuasion of Steven Gerrard that brokered the peace between Suárez and Rodgers, with the Liverpool captain acting as a mediator between the pair at a meeting held at Melwood.

Liverpool were back in the Champions League in 2014–15 for the first time in five seasons and for the first time under Fenway – but without Suárez, and much of the money gained from his sale was wasted in creating a lopsided team that lacked the firepower of before. Rodgers had promised journalists in the pre-season tour of the United States that under no circumstances would Liv-erpool sign a cut-price Mario Balotelli, the Italian forward who eighteen months earlier had been sold by Manchester City after they grew tired of his behavioural problems. A fortnight later Balotelli joined Liverpool, where he would score just one league goal for a team that tumbled out of the Champions League at the group stages and dropped to sixth in the league – losing Gerrard's last game for the club in humiliating fashion. A 6–1 defeat at Stoke brought more pressure on Rodgers, who conducted his final post-match press conference with all of the conviction of a man destined for the guillotine.

In Rodgers' first weeks as Liverpool manager, Jamie Carragher – who was closing in on his final season as a player too – saw an 'outstanding' young coach who delivered training sessions different to anything he'd seen before. Rodgers had new ideas and spoke confidently about his own ability. Yet within a few months, doubts about him were beginning to creep in around Melwood. He had told staff on the opening day that he wanted Liverpool to be a family and he, after all, was a family man. By the summer of 2013, however, he had left his wife for a travel organizer who worked at Melwood. Though the story remained out of the sports pages, it impacted on his credibility both at Melwood and around the city, where supporters were always quick to point out a flaw in any manager's strategy or thinking. Swiftly, a picture of a dys-functional 'Liverpool family' was drawn.

In 2014–15 Liverpool were eliminated from the Champions League at the group stage, and though they reached the semi-final of the FA Cup a defeat to Aston Villa – a team threatened by relegation – was humiliating. Liverpool fell from second in the league table the year before to sixth. Without the results to justify his position, the questions about Rodgers' suitability as Liver-pool's manager began to grow louder. By the summer of 2015 Rodgers was on thin ground and this prompted him to make some drastic decisions. Sacking his long-serving assistant Colin Pascoe while he was on holiday in Florida was one of them; the signing of Christian Benteke being another. The Belgian forward had performed brilliantly on a couple of occasions for Aston Villa against Liverpool, including the FA Cup semi-final, but his arrival reflected Rodgers' desperation to cling onto his role. He had long been accused of not having a plan B, but the purchase of Benteke meant a previously non-existent plan B suddenly became plan A. Rodgers had lost a sense of what had brought him to Liverpool in the first place, and the first six weeks of the 2015–16 season were torturous, Liverpool's plight illustrated by a 1–1 draw with League Two side Carlisle United at Anfield in the League Cup towards the end of September. Rodgers had named pretty much a full-strength side that night and, though they went through on penalties, it felt like his end was near.

To sign Benteke, indeed, he had compromised with Michael Edwards, whose role on the transfer committee had risen. Edwards was now chief negotiator in place of Ian Ayre, the chief executive.

Edwards had wanted to sign Roberto Firmino but Rodgers was insistent on Benteke. An unhealthy-looking compromise was reached, and though Edwards secured both deals Firmino started his first games on the right wing. He did not look capable of being the 'complete' centre-forward he'd become. For that to happen, Liverpool would need to hire Jürgen Klopp.

Inner Circle Sports is a 'boutique investment bank' based in Manhattan which specializes in the takeover of sports franchises. The bank had represented Tom Hicks and George Gillett when they bought Liverpool from David Moores in 2007. Fenway Sports Group, or New England Sports Ventures as they were called then, knew who to ask for assistance when they decided to make a move for the club three years later.

In 2010 Inner Circle invited a host of individuals with an understanding of Liverpool FC and the Premier League to Fenway Park, the home of the Boston Red Sox baseball team. John W. Henry, who would become Liverpool's principal owner, knew 'virtually nothing' about English football, while Tom Werner, Liverpool's chairman to be, also said he had barely heard of the club, but was aware of the 'EPL' – the English Premier League – and its popularity, and 'certainly knew about Manchester United'.

Rick Parry, Liverpool's former chief executive, had helped form the Premier League and he was one of those asked by Inner Circle for guidance. He had been told there was a buyer interested in the club that he and Moores had sold to Hicks and Gillett before their disastrous three-year reign. Parry was informed that the buyer – a group – was still unsure about elements of the challenge in front of them. Parry already had work lined up that week and this may have got in the way but there was a stroke of luck because that work was in Boston, where Fenway were based. Parry dashed out for lunch one day and met David Ginsberg, the vice chairman of the Boston Red Sox. John Henry was late, turning up in jeans and a baseball cap. The conversation was encouraging, though. Henry asked sensible questions. He recognized the sensitivity around the issue of the stadium. Hicks and Gillett had promised a new Anfield and a spade in the ground within a couple of months without delivering.

The Red Sox under Henry had refurbished Fenway Park but Henry initially believed he'd have to sell Anfield and make a new start elsewhere. Henry came to realize through Parry that the appetite amongst supporters for a new ground was not quite as it was after Hicks' and Gillett's broken promises. Parry had once believed in a new stadium too, because he felt the club was getting limited support from the council and residents to expand Anfield. Liverpool could not buy the houses and his solution was to slide the venue into Stanley Park. Parry now believed Henry had the time to think afresh and advised him not to rush a decision.

Most of the discussion had been around the stadium. Fenway were also concerned about being American and whether Liverpool's supporters would trust them after what happened under Hicks and Gillett. Inside six weeks, Henry and Werner stood outside a London court as Liverpool's new owners. The club had been sold to Hicks and Gillett for £200 million and then on to New England Sports for £300 million. Henry and Werner thought they were getting a bargain and saw an opportunity considering the new television rights deal which made being an owner of an English Premier League club very lucrative indeed. Though they came across as thoughtful and methodical to Parry, he thought it was significant they did not try to pretend they were lifelong Liverpool supporters. They wanted to win but expected the club to break even. They were looking for capital growth without taking money out of the club, lining their own pockets.

In those early days, Henry and Werner were the leading figures. Henry was born in 1949 but soon moved with his parents, who were soybean farmers, from Illinois to Arkansas. He liked baseball but he was thin and asthmatic and not cut out to play. He studied the game, discovering he could calculate batting averages and run averages in his head. This would lead him towards the financial markets where he became a hedge-fund billionaire by predicting the future. In 2002 he bought the Boston Red Sox and within two seasons had won the World Series, breaking the fabled Bambino curse which had lasted for eighty-six years.

Rather than buy a championship team, Henry had built one by using mathematics: using data and getting value out of players other clubs had overlooked. He had looked at the success of the Oakland Athletics baseball team under the guidance of Billy Beane, the general manager whose Moneyball theory had helped elevate the status of the club. The A's were one of the poorest clubs in the league and having had most of his best players taken away by wealthier clubs, Beane looked at the market differently. Though Henry could not pull Beane away from Oakland, he used his model to transform the fortunes of the Red Sox.

Henry had been on a flight with Mike Dee, the chief executive of Miami Dolphins, when Dee handed him the sales prospectus for Liverpool in 2008. 'I thought, "Uh-oh, we have enough headaches," ' Henry recalled two years later. 'This seemed like a lot of work and I didn't think about it seriously again until the [NESV] owners' meeting.'

Dee had leaned on Henry's wife, Linda Pizzuti who, at a baseball owners' meeting in Phoenix, Arizona, in January 2010, told her husband to walk up to Tom Hicks and ask him if he was selling Liverpool. 'My wife kept bumping at me [at the meeting], saying, "Why don't you go ask Tom Hicks if he is selling Liverpool?" ' Henry remembered. He was still uncertain he wanted the challenge – ' "Oh, man, it's a long way away," ' he says he told Ms Pizzuti. But she persisted. 'So finally I went over and tried to approach Tom but he was in conversation so I approached Tom Hicks Jnr and I asked him.' Hicks Jnr apparently replied with a flat 'no'.

Sixty-six days before the takeover, one of Henry's commercial executives at New England Sports Ventures, Joe Januszewski, sent him a text message that was followed up by an email detailing Januszewski's thoughts about the club's appeal, which had certainly increased since it became clear that Uefa's Financial Fair Play (FFP) rules would prevent clubs sustaining huge losses under wealthy benefactors' spending on players' wages. 'In my opinion, it would be the deal of the century,' wrote Januszewski, who was also a Liverpool supporter.

NESV was founded in 2001 by Henry, Werner and other

like-minded investors. Werner was born in Manhattan and earned his fortune through television, where he produced famous programmes such as *The Cosby Show*, *Mork & Mindy*, *3rd Rock from the Sun* and *Roseanne*. He became the chairman of the Red Sox before filling the same role at Liverpool. Werner lived in Los Angeles while Henry spent most of his time in Florida. The latter had bought an apartment in Boston's Four Seasons Hotel and stayed there whenever he was in town for a ballgame. When Henry married Linda and they had a baby, a hotel was not an obvious place to raise a child, so they sold their home in Florida and built a new house in Brookline, the district which hosts the famous golf course. Henry had thought about moving to Merseyside and looked at property in Formby. Yet he also had another older daughter who was entering university. In 2014 – four years after buying Liverpool – he bought the *Boston Globe* newspaper, and with that any thoughts about leaving the US disappeared altogether. He liked it in Brookline anyway, where the houses are vast and secluded – not the sort of place where you really get to know your neighbours.

One of them, however, is Mike Gordon, who regularly pops around for a chat over coffee. Now the president of FSG, Gordon was a minority shareholder when the group was formed in 2001 and a partner who operated in the background nine years later when they bought Liverpool. Gordon was, though, very interested in Premier League football and he strongly advocated the club's purchase, seeing an extraordinary opportunity. Though he was not involved in the negotiations and the handling of the public process, he was heavily involved in the due diligence process. Inside twelve months he had become a much larger owner in FSG and his influence in the day-to-day running of the company grew. It was Henry's suggestion in March 2012 that Gordon come around for a meeting with Werner. There had not been a precipitating moment which prompted the discussion but each partner recognized that Liverpool, seventh in the Premier League, were not doing as well as they had hoped and changes were necessary.

It was soon decided that Damien Comolli should leave his role as sporting director while Kenny Dalglish's position as manager would fall under review. From that summer onwards Gordon would take an active hand in running the club. He had been winding down some of his other activities at FSG and it became apparent to the three figureheads that he might be able to do things at Anfield differently. Henry and Werner remained in the loop about every decision. Inside FSG they thought of the decision as evolutionary rather than revolutionary. Gordon was now in charge.

Like the rest of Gordon's career, his ascent happened quietly. There was no public announcement relating to the decision and, for three years at least, it still felt as though Ian Ayre – the chief executive and the last board member standing from the Hicks and Gillett era – was struggling to steer Liverpool in the right direction. Though Gordon's influence grew by stealth, his anonymity did not help perception. Without highlighting who was in charge, it sometimes felt as though Liverpool were drifting.

'When you think about the best organizations, I don't think the very best ones are necessarily vertical,' Werner said in 2011. 'They take advantage of smart wisdom.' FSG had a multibillion dollar portfolio but it lacked a central structure and did not even have an office. Though the key decision-makers within FSG were comfortable with the arrangement, as well as new titles, the lack of visibility and clarity led to understandable speculation – even in Boston, where the owners were now well ingrained with local culture as well as trusted.

By becoming FSG president, Gordon was now above the legendary Red Sox CEO and president Larry Lucchino in the directory on the team's website, even though very few outsiders really knew a lot about Gordon. This led to suggestions in Massachusetts of a power struggle, one which Henry, Werner and Lucchino dismissed, though they did change the masthead, with Lucchino returned to his original status.

Henry once described Gordon as the most private of all his business partners, and his manner was reflected in his rise through FSG and towards Liverpool. His baseball trajectory had taken him from selling popcorn at Milwaukee's County Stadium to owning the second-largest stake at FSG – above Werner. Gordon worked as Jeffrey Vinik's right-hand man in running Fidelity's Magellan Fund between 1992 and 1996, beginning a partnership of more than two decades during which Vinik estimated, half-jokingly, that he'd spent more time with Gordon than his wife. From 2010 to 2013 Vinik would serve on Liverpool's board before re-focusing his interest on the Tampa Bay Lightning ice hockey club. The pair left Fidelity to co-found a hedge fund, Vinik Asset Management. It was Bud Selig, the owner of the Milwaukee Brewers – the man who'd given Gordon his first job which involved selling popcorn – who introduced Gordon to Henry and Werner when they sought partners to form NESV. Selig described Gordon as 'just an outstanding young man'. He was, according to Selig, 'the kind of owner that commissioners want in their sport'.

Mike Gordon and Michael Edwards first met in the spring of 2012. Gordon spent a fortnight on Merseyside introducing himself to everyone he hadn't met before and Edwards, waiting to see what would happen in the aftermath of Damien Comolli's sacking, was one of those. He had played for Norwich City as a school boy and then Peterborough United's reserve team before he was headhunted by Comolli from Tottenham where he worked as a player-performance analyst having been taken there from Portsmouth by Harry Redknapp. He was clearly ambitious but Gordon was struck most by his intelligence and work ethic. Edwards was willing to stick his neck out and say what he really thought. That translated to Gordon that Edwards was a person of integrity. Gordon realized quickly that he wanted to work closely with him. There was no announcement about this either, though over the next four years Edwards would emerge as the kingmaker in Liverpool's transfer activities.

Major criticism would come Edwards' way before praise – some early signings took a while to bed in, or only really took off under Klopp – though Gordon always felt that the criticism was monumentally unfair. Gordon quickly grew to admire Edwards' objectivity, the way he acknowledges bias as detrimental in analytical decisions, particularly in football where it is nearly impossible to filter out emotional attachments. If the data of a player who is well liked at Liverpool drops below expectations, Edwards would ensure it got flagged and a conversation would start about the future. Gordon feels lucky to have met Edwards, who has had approaches from other Premier League and European clubs that could have taken him away from Liverpool had it not been for the bond forged with FSG's president.

And yet, the path towards such an understanding was not without rocks. It had been John Henry's labelling of the scouting system at Liverpool that first invited scepticism. The branding of a 'transfer committee' became a major regret of Fenway's, conjuring up the image of scouts sitting around a darkened room wearing green eye shades. The word 'committee' was debilitating, creating a sense that division was a possibility. Though Fenway were adamant this wasn't a true reflection of the set-up and that Liverpool's scouting department was more aligned to the top European clubs', it was only really when it was finally announced Edwards had become the sporting director in 2016 that the discussion went away.

Gordon felt strongly that any club cannot scale a mountain in one day, that ambition can sometimes work against success in a profound way. It had to be done in stages. Though those stages were not outlined specifically. This led to tensions between Edwards and Brendan Rodgers, who felt Edwards' daily stream of emails to Boston and Gordon undermined his position as manager. When this became a matter for public debate after Rodgers' departure, the focus fell on Edwards.

But Gordon never stopped believing that Edwards was up to the job. The improvement at Liverpool between 2015 and 2019 owed much to the appointment of Jürgen Klopp, who was used to working with middle-managers, having operated in the same structure at Borussia Dortmund. Under Klopp the rules became much clearer – a player would only be signed if the manager wanted him, but the owners still had the right to intervene if they felt the player did not represent value for money.

Gordon had been the first representative from FSG to speak to Klopp on the phone, and in their first meeting Gordon felt one of the most important elements of the discussion related to whether both he and Edwards and Klopp would be comfortable enough in each other's company to express constructive disagreement. Rodgers, of course, had previously disagreed with lots of things privately and then complained later when he should have intercepted issues before they mushroomed. 'Speaking your mind and disagreeing at Liverpool isn't just allowed,' Gordon told Klopp, who offered a pregnant pause and raised an eyebrow. 'It's required.'

Klopp was told by Gordon that he hated the idea of a good idea failing to take root because of a lack of trust between the affected parties to be able to say what was on their mind. Gordon could see Klopp's integrity and extraordinary talent. Inside his first six months as Liverpool manager he had taken a broken team to two cup finals. Though they lost both, Gordon surprised Klopp in the summer of 2016 when he went to him, saying, 'How about we do this for longer?' It became a meeting of minds: the trendy German football manager with his jeans and Converse, along with his trendy agent Marc Kosicke, and then the cerebral owner. There is now belief in Boston that since 2012 Gordon has created a world-class football operations department headed by the best manager in world football. Gordon's contact with Merseyside is hourly. He speaks to Edwards and Klopp the most, along with Peter Moore, the club's chief executive to whom Billy Hogan, the commercial director reports to. Fenway remain distant and fundamentally, they have always been absentee. But in Gordon they have someone who is very hands-on from afar. Amongst his strengths is communication. In order to challenge his own view he will speak to people at different levels of the club, even if an issue isn't covered in their field of work.

Football club owners have historically done whatever they want because, well, they own the football club. Gordon is different because he does not do what he wants. He has a process to get towards a conclusion of what he thinks is right. This has its benefits and its drawbacks, because it has taken Liverpool longer to realize why certain things need to happen.

Gordon, indeed, recognized that one of the major challenges with running a football club is the actual culture of running football clubs in a sport where whatever the owner says or thinks ends up getting implemented because those below are always willing to please him, even if they think a decision is wrong. Henry certainly did not have all – if many – of the answers and neither did Werner or Gordon. They were accepting of this. But they also needed to find the right people to trust when it came to advice. They wanted better advice: to be told of the options. They appointed Klopp even though they knew he was not a yes man. They appointed Moore because he was not Ian Ayre, who went along with many of their calls even though he disagreed with them but was unable to build a competitive argument. They appointed Tony Barrett as head of club and supporter liaison, even though they knew he was outspoken. By having Barrett in place, it has allowed the owners to form a better understanding of base feelings on key issues that may affect supporters particularly. Barrett had formerly been Merseyside's football reporter for the *Liverpool Echo* and *The Times*, and though the club has not got every issue right since his appointment in 2017 they have got a lot more right than previously.

All of this would only make more sense, however, by the delivery of results like Liverpool 5–1 Arsenal, with Roberto Firmino – the player Edwards liked so much – scoring a hat-trick. In the summer of 2017 the Brazilian swapped his number 11 shirt for number 9. This was partly because that was his position now under Klopp, but also because one of Liverpool's new signings wanted the number 11.

For Liverpool, for Edwards, for Gordon – for Firmino, indeed, to be regarded as successful even as they awaited trophies, it needed movement in thought from the owners particularly. Henry believed Mohamed Salah was overpriced at nearly £40 million considering he'd already failed at Chelsea. Yet he sanctioned the deal because he believed in Gordon, and Gordon believed in Edwards, who had tracked the player since his time at Basel.

Henry had compared dealing with agents in football to the Wild West, but for three years running, between 2015 and 2018, Liverpool topped the league in agents' fees because they recognized they were the key-holders in players' careers. Klopp believed that Virgil van Dijk could emerge as the world's greatest defender, and that resulted in Liverpool paying a world-record fee for a defender, rewarding his agent accordingly – the same with Alisson Becker. It was one of the biggest changes in attitude under Fenway, though this was more of a switch in direction than gradual evolution. The penny had dropped: players were only really as good as the money that was paid to the agents. Fenway came to realize slowly that if you want to be the best you have to sometimes pay the highest rates. In football, there could be Moneyball signings, but not every signing could be inspired by Moneyball.

SHADOWS AND PAIN

8. OLIGARCHS AND SHEIKHS

TWO GAMES, THE SAME OPPONENT, FOUR MONTHS APART. ONE MARKED
the last of the season and the other set off a new beginning. Before
the first, Chelsea's manager Claudio Ranieri compared the challenge of beating Liverpool to reach the Champions League as
'David meeting Goliath'. Before the second, Chelsea's new owner
Roman Abramovich was wearing a sky blue shirt and a navy blue
suit. The boardroom at Anfield had a dress code which stipulated
collars and a tie, which Abramovich did not have with him. 'There
was a kerfuffle with stewards on the door,' remembered Rick
Parry, Liverpool's chief executive. David [Moores] went to the
door and told them to let him in but Abramovich was full of apol-
ogies saying something like, "I'm sorry, I didn't realize; I'll find a
tie" which one of his people went and got. In fairness, he was
quite decent about it, he didn't say, "I'm not following your rules."
He tried to adapt. He seemed quite humble, smiled, but he didn't
say very much. He certainly didn't appear arrogant – though after
that game, he didn't come very often.'

Parry had even sharper memories of Liverpool's previous meeting with Chelsea. 'It was so disappointing because they got into the
Champions League by three points and we missed out. Sami
Hyypiä had scored early on to put us into the lead but it somehow
turned into one of those flat end-of-season games. We were still
reeling from them being in the Champions League and us not when
the news broke. I did not know who Roman Abramovich was.'

The focus of the story in May had been about Chelsea rather
than Liverpool. Had the west London club not qualified for the

Champions League, it was reported that they may have entered receivership. 'And then,' Parry thought, 'there'd probably have been no Abramovich – would he have been interested in a non-Champions League team, if indeed they were still in business at all? At first, I had no concept of how important Abramovich would become, or even the immediate significance. Why would an oligarch or billionaire have any interest in football, particularly a football club from a country that wasn't his own? The mega, mega rich buying football clubs was still new. At this stage, someone mega wealthy with an interest in football was Jack Walker. This took it onto a whole new level.'

Walker was an industrialist worth £600 million from Blackburn who bought the town's football team for next to nothing and turned them into Premier League winners inside seven seasons having vowed to make Manchester United 'look cheap'. He had his own box at Ewood Park and rarely entertained owners from other clubs. Abramovich, from the far eastern Russian region of Chukotka, had no connection with Chelsea but in 2003 his £11-billion fortune allowed him to buy the club for £140 million and his presence in football changed the financial landscape of the game overnight.

'Our aspiration was to have a league-winning team,' Parry said. 'In 2002 we had done well in difficult circumstances [considering Gérard Houllier's heart attack, which meant Liverpool's French manager was on sick leave for nearly five months as Liverpool came second]. In that context 2003 was bitterly disappointing [when Liverpool finished fifth]. But you're still thinking your competition is Arsenal and Manchester United. We didn't have the resources of United but at least we knew what the resources were, which basically came from the income they generated. We believed that if we could build a new stadium and get our revenues up, we'd be able to compete with United. It was more of a level playing field, to that extent. Then all of a sudden: wham, here comes Abramovich. It was back to the drawing board because we had to stop and think about the long-term impact of a new rival with unlimited funds. The most immediate impact was Damien Duff, who we wanted to sign from Blackburn. They'd finished just a place and four points behind us in 2003. A year earlier we tried to get him. The maximum price we could afford was around the £12-million mark. But Blackburn didn't want to sell – they didn't need the money. Duff then signed a new contract. We knew he was a Liverpool supporter and hoped he'd come to us a year later. Unfortunately, the new contract had a £17-million buyout clause, which was just about the least helpful thing that could happen. Who was the first and most expensive signing of Abramovich's first summer at Chelsea? Duff, of course. They paid the buyout clause straight away. Immediately we were thinking, "Oh no – is this how it's going to be from now on?" There was going to be one market for Chelsea and another for the rest of us.'

Chelsea were closer to winning the Champions League than they were the Premier League in Abramovich's first season; reaching the semi-finals where they were surprisingly knocked out by Monaco, while finishing second domestically, 11 points behind an unbeatable Arsenal side. For Parry, though, it was significant they still came a whopping 19 points above Liverpool, who just about crept back into the Champions League by coming fourth.

It wasn't enough for either club, which explains why there were changes of management. José Mourinho was on the verge of becoming a European champion with FC Porto when he was offered to Parry the night before Mourinho took his team to Old Trafford where he celebrated a winning goal by running down the touchline. It worried Parry what might happen if a Liverpool manager did the same thing. While also having a deep respect for Houllier, he concluded that it was more sensible to allow him to finish the season off rather than potentially destabilize Liverpool's pursuit of Champions League qualification by seeking his replacement in springtime.

By the start of the next season Mourinho was in place at Chelsea while Parry had hired Rafael Benítez, whose domestic achievements in Spain had certainly been greater than those of the Portuguese, having overhauled Real Madrid and Barcelona to twice win La Liga as well as the Uefa Cup. 'Though Chelsea went big on Duff and signed a lot of players in the summer of 2003, it wasn't until 2004 that we really began to feel their ability to blow everyone else away,' Parry recalled. 'But if we felt it was impossible not to do better than them, we'd have never been able to persuade Rafa to join us.'

Having hired Mourinho, Chelsea spent £91.5 million on seven players, recouping just £2.2 million on fourteen while Liverpool made four signings worth £33.2 million, but this outlay was only possible because they sold one of the all-time great goalscorers in Michael Owen to Real Madrid in a part-exchange deal that brought £8.5 million back to Anfield.

'In the discussions with Rafa, everyone recognized that there was no point going head to head with Chelsea financially,' recalled Parry. 'We just had to be smarter and work harder and defeat them that way. We never felt they were unbeatable, and this was proven by the results we had against them in the cups. Though it was harder over the course of a Premier League season because we didn't have the same depth in our squad – though nobody ever suggested we couldn't win the league even though we knew it was more difficult.

'Though we were able to knock them out of the Champions League over two legs, I remember the league game at Anfield early in the [2005–06] season when they beat us 4–1. Their squad was incredible. Not only did they not have a weakness, they had two players for every position. It was daunting, but it was daunting for every club.'

Parry saw United, Arsenal and Chelsea as Liverpool's competitors for the Champions League places. 'A worst-case scenario would be us finishing fourth,' he thought, acknowledging that the level of competition at the top then was weaker than it is now, since Manchester City's rise and Tottenham Hotspur's gradual progression into a force. In 2004–05, while City came eighth and Spurs one place below, Liverpool instead came fifth.

Inside six months of Abramovich's landing at Chelsea, Liverpool's owner David Moores had started to think differently. His wealth was inherited and family led. His uncle, Sir John Moores, had owned Everton in an era when they were known as 'Merseyside's millionaires'. John had created Littlewoods, which was sold in 2002 for £750 million. Against Abramovich, there was only so much that David Moores could do. He was a sensitive owner rather than a dynamic one, someone who got upset if anyone complained about his leadership in the letters page of the *Liverpool Echo*. Considering Liverpool had not won the league for thirteen years – and winning the title was about to become a lot harder – in January 2004 he made the decision to sell.

'It was a complete bolt from the blue,' Parry remembered. 'The decision was irrevocable. It came through David's financial advisor Keith Clayton, who was a member of the board at Liverpool. He'd looked after David's family affairs for years and David trusted him implicitly – still does. Keith had one of his periodic meetings with David and he phoned me, saying David had decided to find a new buyer. When I came to Liverpool I thought that I'd be working with David for the rest of my working life. I never had the slightest inkling that selling was going to be on the horizon. To be fair, I don't think it was ever in David's mind, but Abramovich changed everything. He knew that he'd find it almost impossible to compete with Chelsea. Clearly, Abramovich had a fundamental and direct impact on the structure and ownership of Liverpool.'

In the summer of 2004 – spanning the period of Benítez's arrival – Steve Morgan, who ran Redrow Homes, had almost bought Liverpool. When Morgan spoke to Benítez about his plans, the new manager was unimpressed by what he heard. Moores, though, was worn down and had had enough. Morgan went past the due diligence stage but then pulled away from the deal. It became an unprecedented period in Liverpool's history where Moores tried to sell while attempting to keep up with their rivals and finding ways of building the new ground at the same time. With all of this going on behind the scenes, Benítez delivered the Champions League in his first season and then the FA Cup in the next.

'The club was living in constant instability,' Parry admitted. 'We were very open with Rafa from the first meeting when we said, "Here's the chairman – but he's trying to sell." I think Rafa liked David, he loved the idea of Liverpool and he wanted to test himself in the Premier League. We said, "This is what we are now. If we get more money and new investment it will be a lot better." '

Between 2005 and 2007 Benítez did a fine job of keeping Liverpool relevant. Though they did not compete for the Premier League title, they were a threat to every opponent in the Champions League, winning the competition once and reaching the final again two years later. Indeed, in the summers of 2005 and 2006 Benítez operated on half of Chelsea's transfer budget, spending a net of £23.2 million compared to Mourinho's £54.3 million. This came after the year ending June 2005 when Chelsea posted a record loss of £140 million with the club reporting it did not expect to record a trading profit for another five years.

Moores and Parry went around the world listening to proposals from supposed buyers. They travelled first to Thailand where they met Thaksin Shinawatra, the country's prime minister, who organized a state dinner to impress them. They met Robert Kraft, the owner of the New England Patriots, who realized on a night's sleep that he knew nothing about 'soccer' and was better off sticking to American football. Parry was excited most by Dubai International Capital, the sovereign wealth fund of the emirate's ruling family, but a key trip to the Middle East with Moores ended in disappointment when they were not introduced to anyone with real significance in the organization. When DIC fell through completely, George Gillett returned to the scene. Gillett had previously been told by Parry that the wealth of a nation or an organization was always going to be greater than one man, and Gillett had listened – this time bringing Tom Hicks with him. Under pressure to pay for the steel that would build a new ground, Moores agreed to sell to the pair and from there Liverpool's modern history unravelled; a civil war at boardroom level spreading through the club into its management and across the supporter base, a story which is explained later in this book.

Parry and Liverpool were looking to find new owners for a second time in less than two years when, in August 2008, it was announced that Manchester City had overnight become 'the richest club on the planet', as their press officer Paul Tyrrell called them when he rang staff on their day off and told them to come in. Tyrrell would soon hold the same position at Anfield where figures like Parry were mystified as to why Sheikh Mansour of Abu Dhabi had chosen City rather than Liverpool considering the deal was brokered by Amanda Staveley, an intermediary who had met with key brokers like Parry at Liverpool as well as supporters and claimed to be a fan of the club as well as the city.

Mansour was estimated to be worth around £30 billion more than Abramovich, and it is believed that his advisors had identified City as mirroring Abu Dhabi in terms of its relationship with its closest geographical rival. While City were dwarfed by Manchester United, Dubai was far more popular than Abu Dhabi, a place that was looking for a city in Europe which had a trans-continental airport that could act as a hub for Etihad, the airline that would soon sponsor City's stadium. City worked for Mansour in a way that Liverpool did not: City already had a new ground, which had been built for the Commonwealth Games in 2002, and there was an enormous amount of space around it where facilities could be improved and developed. It helped too that City had figures on the club's board who also held positions on Manchester's council. In sporting terms, Mansour wanted to buy a smaller club with less history which he could influence without native interruption. While Liverpool had won the Champions League three years before, City's last major trophy had been in 1973.

The coast was clear to do as he pleased but, as Parry reminded, it took longer than it did at Chelsea to properly get their act together – the first winners' medals of the Mansour reign came in 2011. The power of City had become Fenway Sports Group's problem by then, but Chelsea had led the way in terms of foreign ownership, forcing Liverpool to think differently about their own existence.

'I don't look back and think, "If it hadn't been for Abramovich, we'd have won the league every year – or even once." Because we already had United and Arsenal as strong competitors,' Parry stressed. 'Chelsea were an added pressure who distorted the financial picture. They were never a direct rival in the way United or Arsenal were, because our histories were intertwined in a way they were not with Chelsea.

'Our single core value was respect,' he continued. 'We worked on the basis of treating other clubs with respect and, in turn, we hoped they'd respect us. It wasn't to do with history and standing still because what Liverpool were most famous for in the 1960s was innovation. Bill Shankly was the greatest innovator and change agent of them all. One hundred years' heritage did not act as an anchor because the 1950s had been fallow for Liverpool and in one sense in the sixties we were actually the new kids on the block. There was a similar ethos at Arsenal, and even for all the rivalry, United were a proper football club as well.

'Investing and achieving rapid success wasn't completely unknown because it had happened in England before. I think Chelsea was different because it was through Russia and on such a scale that nobody had seen. This was reflected by David Dein at Arsenal warning Chelsea to keep their tanks off his lawn. In one sense, anything that makes the Premier League more competitive – so there's a different name on the trophy – is a good thing.'

Parry had been the Premier League's first chief executive before joining Liverpool: 'In some ways we opened Pandora's box by forming the Premier League in the first place – a competition that was built out of TV money and encouraged the foreign viewer to buy into it. Abramovich coming along was just another manifest-ation of the decisions made a decade before. Even then, I never foresaw a day where more than half of the Premier League clubs would fall under foreign ownership.'

When the Premier League was founded, the chairmen chasing each other around the debating table were names like Ken Bates, Ron Noades, Leslie Silver, Martin Edwards, Peter Swales and Phil Carter. There was still a presence of local businessman made good. 'I remember asking Leslie one day why he wanted to be chairman of Leeds United,' recalled Parry. 'He said, "There's one hundred millionaires in Leeds but there's only one chairman of Leeds United." The position then was still about a status in the local business community. In the first years of the Premier League, we then had a rush of clubs to be listed on the Stock Exchange. Tottenham were the first then United followed, and Newcastle. Clearly that was not a sustainable model. This led to the oligarchs, led by Abramovich. With City, you now have countries. It's no longer enough to be an oligarch, you've got to be a nation. Where do we go next?'

In the summer of 2018 Roman Abramovich did not renew his corporate box at Stamford Bridge – a ground he owned but had not visited in almost two years. Political tensions between Russia and the United Kingdom had resulted in him spending more time in Israel than London, and his interest in what was happening at Chelsea was reflected by the abandonment of plans to relocate the club to a new venue south of the River Thames. There were suggestions that he was willing to sell, Chelsea were on the brink of a transfer embargo for breaking financial fair play rules – and yet, that decision had not taken into consideration the deal for goalkeeper Kepa, which had eclipsed Liverpool's financial commitment in the world-record-breaking signing of Alisson Becker.

Meanwhile, a series of stories in the German magazine *Der Spiegel* had accused Manchester City of financial doping, of distorting the club's accounts and circumnavigating Financial Fair Play rules. Soon the club would be facing four separate investigations that had the potential to get them thrown out of the Champions League, though the Premier League were yet to clarify whether this could result in them having any of their titles stripped.

With this development in particular, had Liverpool – or any other competitor – felt like those athletes looking along the line at Ben Johnson in the 100-metres final at the Seoul Olympics, it would have been understandable. While Liverpool had spent big in the summer of 2018, the economic world at Anfield was an accurate one defined by smart trading and the development of the team into one capable of reaching the Champions League final, which generated more than £60 million in revenues alone, almost paying for Alisson.

At the start of 2019, in the one table that everyone with an interest in football took serious notice of, Liverpool were top and Chelsea were fourth, nine points behind the leaders. City were second and trailing by seven. Liverpool's performance levels had been remarkable considering what City had achieved the season before when they won the league with a record points total and had broken all sorts of other records in the process before strengthening the squad, with nobody really taking any notice of the figures involved. Liverpool's position was largely a reflection of the impacts made by Virgil van Dijk and Alisson and this led to a perception Liverpool had bought their way to the top. Yet those purchases were only possible because of the sale of Philippe Coutinho and the club's progression to the Champions League final. It meant Liverpool were living in a world of high finance, but it was a real one.

In October 2018 Riyad Mahrez had missed a last-minute penalty which would have given City a priceless 1–0 victory at Anfield following an uncharacteristic mistake by Van Dijk, who tumbled into Leroy Sané – a winger Jürgen Klopp had wanted to sign for Liverpool from Schalke before City came in and blew Liverpool away with their offer. It felt like an important moment, if not season defining; though it did not seem to matter that Mahrez had been signed for twice the money Liverpool had taken Mohamed Salah for barely twelve months earlier, and that Mahrez would be used merely as a back-up in the subsequent campaign, with his cause for inclusion not helped by what happened at Anfield. Sheikh Mansour had achieved spectacular things at City – and not just on the pitch. This helped dealing with any critical reception of City's football performance with those who questioned the origin of all the money being ploughed into the club and how officers working for Mansour may have found a way to navigate around the rules, of which City's supporters believed were unfair anyway because they thought without huge investment the status-quo at the top end of football would never be challenged. *Der Spiegel*'s accusations claimed City's financial matters were built on a 'web of lies' that showed the club's sponsorships were mostly paid by the club's owner, Sheikh Mansour bin Zayed al-Nahyan.

City rebuffed all accusations, telling Uefa that the claims were based on 'hacked or stolen' emails – something *Der Spiegel* denies. It was argued by the club's fans that Mansour's commitment to

City was long-term and based around a desire to meet self-sufficiency. But that ignored the impact City's spending had on the rest of football, particularly at the lowest end where the gap from the top was growing faster than ever. It also ignored the growing reality that despite having complained bitterly why the rules existed in the first place, Liverpool had believed in them, had complied with them, and were flourishing.

The area surrounding the Etihad had once been a series of brownfield sites and poorly maintained estates of maisonettes, but City had cleaned up this part of east Manchester, providing new community facilities as well as a spectacular new training ground which was supposedly the biggest and the most modern in football. Yet Manchester City is no longer merely Manchester City, it is City Football Group: a global enterprise which includes ownership and influence of different clubs in each continent across the world. An investigation by *La Gazzetta dello Sport* in 2018 revealed that City had spent more than any other European club on transfer fees across the previous decade, dwarfing the outlay at Liverpool by nearly £600 million. Chelsea's spending had also been greater than Liverpool's by £180 million. Liverpool had sometimes spent big but they had not spent as frequently – or as well – as either of the clubs whose deeper pockets had helped them overtake Liverpool in sporting terms.

While Liverpool had lifted just one trophy since 2008 (the League Cup in 2012), Chelsea had won the Champions League for the first time, three Premier League titles, the Europa League, four FA Cups, as well as a League Cup. City, meanwhile, were still waiting for the Champions League but had also taken three domestic league titles, one FA Cup and four League Cups. Meanwhile, Fernando Torres' transfer from Liverpool to Chelsea in 2011, and Raheem Sterling's move to City four years later, felt symbolic: that Liverpool had, for the first time ever, become plankton in the pond of English football.

Klopp had started to change that through his charisma, vision and leadership. While by the start of the 2018–19 season he had spent £382 million, he had also sold £289 million-worth of players. That meant a net spend of £93 million had turned a club from finishing eighth into one of the front runners against an oil-rich side managed by Guardiola, who'd achieved a net spend of £450 million in half a season less than Klopp.

Virgil van Dijk's decision to reject City for Liverpool in a world-record transfer for a defender had redressed the discussion, giving the impression that Liverpool were now spending their way back to the top. Yet the eye-watering sums involved in both Van Dijk's and Alisson Becker's moves to Anfield ignored some broader facts about Liverpool's spending compared to the teams they were now competing with again. The rest of the mean defence which Liverpool finished the season with had cost just £8.5 million in transfer fees. Trent Alexander-Arnold came from the academy, Joël Matip was a free transfer from Schalke, and the only other club prepared to make an offer for Andy Robertson when he joined from Hull was Burnley.

City, meanwhile, had spent more than £300 million in recruiting not just one defence but two, giving them experienced back-up options – whereas at Liverpool so much depended on the availability of Van Dijk, who may have been wooed by the charms of Jürgen Klopp when they first met, though it would have been fascinating to compare what his agent was promised by each of the clubs competing for his signature.

Liverpool's spending on agents' fees was almost double City's. This was explained by the reluctant admittance at Liverpool between Michael Edwards and Mike Gordon that if you pay the agent, you've got a better chance of getting the player, and though the sums were preposterous to the average match-going supporter, it was a relatively low-cost way of pushing Liverpool forward by making the necessary improvements to their squad.

In cold sporting terms, between January 2018 and January 2019 Liverpool had signed five players compared to two at City, while also agreeing contract renewals for three star players in Mohamed Salah, Roberto Firmino and Sadio Mané – agreements which Klopp described 'as important as any new signing – and not something I've always been able to do'. City had finished the 2017–18 campaign 25 points above Liverpool but, six months later, as winter turned into 2019, Liverpool were the club being chased. Guardiola had recognized the season would be tougher due to Liverpool's steady improvement but also because City had coasted for so long through the previous campaign and there was a danger of complacency.

All or Nothing, the documentary about City's momentous rise under Guardiola had, in an otherwise glossy screening, presented the manager in a fair light, as someone who tried to get the best out of players by showing sympathy and sometimes leniency. He appreciates their talents, relates to their desires and, most of all – having been a player himself – understands what it is like when the pressure and noise is unrelenting in the pursuit of success. His mindset would change in the summer of 2018, though. He appreciated the patterns that had trailed City following titles under previous managers Roberto Mancini and Manuel Pellegrini, when other teams had been able to topple them quite easily at the summit of the Premier League and European campaigns had fallen well short despite signs of promise. Guardiola decided that a stricter approach was necessary to keep his squad alert, but when Kevin De Bruyne became the first victim of a new tighter fine system, having arrived at training just a few minutes late following an opening-day victory at Arsenal, the fallout could not have been predicted. The Belgian midfielder sustained what was described on City's website as a 'freak' knee injury later that morning but, in reality, it was suffered because he approached the training session that followed fired up and in the mood to prove his commitment.

De Bruyne, whose influence at City was comparable to Steven Gerrard's at Liverpool, was only fit enough to be selected as a substitute when Liverpool went to the Etihad and lost their unbeaten run in the league by the narrowest of margins in a pulsating match. That was a day where City's relentlessness as a club was reflected not only by their style on the pitch but the sight of tourists being given a guided tour around the stadium's press room just two and a half hours before kick-off, journalists having already started to work. It was also a little reminder of the scale of the challenge facing Liverpool or anyone else who fancied the challenge of beating the club led by the greatest modern manager (according to Klopp as well), the greatest players, the greatest budget and, perhaps, the greatest accountants.

City's victory was defined by inches. Possession had been shared – 50 per cent for both teams – along with a similar number of shots, corners and fouls. The ebb and flow had been at pace, the tension incredible and the standard of the football on a different level to the rest of the Premier League. Those inches, though. Their winner was scored by Sané, the Schalke winger Klopp wanted so badly but could not reach so signed Sadio Mané instead. The Senegalese would emerge as Liverpool's in-form forward in the second half of the season but here, unlike Sané's shot which hit the post and went in, his shot hit the post and came out, causing an unruly goalmouth scramble. Roberto Firmino's outstanding equalizer had pulled the scores level after Sergio Agüero's equally outstanding opener.

It may have felt like a load of what-aboutery but had Mané's chance gone in, would the outcome have been different? The thought would linger in the background right until the end of the season, when it felt like City's win had prevented Liverpool going the whole campaign unbeaten, as well as preventing them reaching 100 points for the first time in the club's history. Would it ultimately also be the result which stopped them winning the league for the first time in twenty-nine years?

9. JUST FUCKING LAUNCH IT

ROY HODGSON'S EYES WERE DARTING THIS WAY AND THAT LOOKING FOR exit routes, the jowls beneath his chin wobbling. There was a gentle dusting of dandruff on his shoulders. His hands were in his pockets and he possessed the air of an impatient man. Though he was smiling, it was a nervous sort of smile and clearly he was getting more and more irritated as the same journalist pursued an answer he did not want to give. His Crystal Palace team had taken Liverpool almost all of the way but had still lost at Anfield, 4–3. A month earlier, Palace had won at Manchester City. Naturally, an appreciation of the challenge that Palace had faced against the Premier League's leading clubs would have done nicely but Hodgson was having none of that, as the following conversation revealed. It was one which did not appear in the column inches of the national press due to the sensational pattern of the game that had gone before. Deep beneath the terraces of Anfield's new main stand, Crystal Palace's press officer would ask: 'Any questions for Roy?'

Journalist: 'You played against City and got a win there and now you have played Liverpool. What is the difference in those teams?'

Roy: 'No. Oh no. That's not the sort of question I want to answer. I'm not here . . . I'm prepared to answer questions about the game today. I'll talk about Liverpool against Crystal Palace. I'm not prepared to answer questions about Man City–Crystal Palace because that is too far away.'

Journalist: 'No, what I mean is a comparison of the two teams—'

Roy: 'No, no. No. I don't make comparisons. So, I'm not prepared to make any comments. Any other questions?'

Silence . . .

Press officer: 'Anyone else?'

In 1966 England won the World Cup for the first and only time. Roy Hodgson remembered the year for altogether more personal reasons. It was the year Crystal Palace let him go, and from there he would never make it as a professional footballer. He would spend the next decade darting around the non-league clubs of Kent and Surrey, starting in Tonbridge before playing for Gravesend & Northfleet, Maidstone United, Ashford Town and Carshalton Athletic. A spell in South Africa increased his thirst for new experiences and that partly explained why he moved to Sweden in 1976 to pursue a coaching career.

In turning Halmstads from relegation favourites to two-time Swedish champions, Hodgson earned a chance at Bristol City where he was dismissed after four months with the club in financial turmoil. Undeterred, he became an experienced football coach across Europe, holding fourteen managerial positions in the next 28 years, the longest of which was four seasons initially back in Sweden with Malmö. From there, he went to Switzerland, Italy, Denmark, United Arab Emirates, Norway, Finland and then back to England for a third time (an earlier spell at Blackburn Rovers also ended in the sack) where at the age of 62 he finally earned the respect of his domestic peers by transforming Fulham into a team capable of reaching a European final for the first time in its history, though Fulham were beaten by Atlético Madrid in Hamburg. Hodgson's new status was reflected soon after, however, when he became the LMA manager of the year for 2010, an award which took residence on the mantelpiece at his home in Surrey.

Hodgson would later manage his country and though he led England to its worst World Cup campaign in sixty-four years before getting knocked out by minnows Iceland at the European Championships, it is fair to say Hodgson was generally respected by the public in spite of his lack of trophies or long-term attachment to any major club – which may have actually helped his image. By 2019, indeed, his last winners' medal was the Danish Super Cup with FC Copenhagen in 2001.

Hodgson was a certain sort of manager. He tended to do well with clubs or nations with modest aspirations, pushing them to do better. Where there was demand, however, he struggled. At West Bromwich Albion Paul Scharner, a midfielder known for his courage rather than his skill, perhaps summed up Hodgson's abilities best by describing him as a coach who made average players better but very good players seem average.

It was argued when he became Liverpool's manager in 2010 that he'd helped turn around the fortunes of another giant, Inter Milan, fourteen years earlier, but Inter were bottom of Serie A when he took over and the only way was up at a club where significant investment was waiting for him. At Liverpool he succeeded a Champions League-winning coach in Rafael Benítez and the team had finished seventh the season before. Unlike at the San Siro, there was no owner like Massimo Moratti to make Liverpool great again – in fact he had to deal with the opposite in Tom Hicks and George Gillett who had not spoken in nearly two years when Hodgson arrived.

Hodgson was on a shortlist of three candidates which also included Manuel Pellegrini, whose most recent position had been at Real Madrid, and Didier Deschamps, a World Cup winner as a player and someone who would emerge as a World Cup winner as a coach with France. Kenny Dalglish had been on the selection panel and as a legendary Liverpool player and manager himself, he assessed that maybe he was better than any of the options available. Soon, this became a matter of public debate.

Hodgson had links to Merseyside through his wife Sheila, though he had not spent much time in the region as he travelled the world in search of work. But for Phil Taylor, who was born in Bristol and remains the only manager not to have led Liverpool in the top division of English football, the club had always chosen managers from the north of the country, Scotland or Ireland. Hodgson would become the first appointment from the south since Taylor and though the context of his position was unique in Liverpool's history considering the financial problems not of his making, Hodgson did little to endear himself to a supporter base which hangs on its manager's every word.

At his introductory press conference in the old main stand's trophy room, he sat at a table that was positioned just in front of a wall of photographs and oil paintings. Bill Shankly was literally looking over him. The question came: 'Who are your biggest coaching influences, Roy?' It was an easy one for him to answer and Hodgson did not take any time considering his options. 'That will be Don Howe and Dave Sexton,' he responded, reaching into his soul and enthusiastically picking out two managers with links to London rather than Liverpool. Even Ronny Rosenthal would have scored in front of that open goal.

Across two days, I had waited eight hours to interview Hodgson at the point of his arrival. In fairness, it had not necessarily been his fault that we ended up speaking over the phone as he travelled back to London by train to pick up his belongings. With the signal breaking and the conversation cut up into four stages, I was worried by Hodgson's reaction as he became increasingly prickly about the amount of time it was taking. He was, after all, the new manager of Liverpool but the interest in the position seemed to have taken him by surprise.

When, a couple of weeks later, I tried to introduce myself in person at Melwood – even condemning my own approach on day one by saying something like, 'I was the idiot who called you several times,' Hodgson could have replied, 'Oh yes, don't worry about it.' Instead, he fired back, 'Don't remember,' and scuttled up the stairs as quickly as he could.

The pressure on him by then was already beginning to tell in public. Against Macedonians FK Rabotnički, he looked like a man heading for a court summons rather than someone approaching his first competitive game at the biggest job of his career, suggesting it was 'far from certain' Liverpool would emerge unscathed against an opponent that had edged past the mysterious sounding FC Mika from Armenia in the previous round. Hodgson was again in an awkward mood, complaining about the depth of his media commitments. 'All we ever seem to do at Liverpool is have discussions,' he moaned.

It was a World Cup year, which impacted on availability, but Hodgson's first team selection for a competitive Liverpool game had a stench of mediocrity, if not relegation: Cavalieri; Kelly, Škrtel, Kyrgiakos, Agger; Aquilani, Lucas, Spearing; Amoo, N'Gog, Jovanović. Though none of these players had been his signings, he did not have the same excuse with Christian Poulsen and Paul Konchesky – players he had managed before. Poulsen, a defensive midfielder, had a decent track record at top clubs like Schalke, Sevilla and Juventus but he was 30 years old and not suited to the thrust of the Premier League, while Konchesky simply did not have the vision of a Liverpool player and seemed to be unable to spot trouble coming his way until it was on top of him and too late. In another world, Luke Young might have been added to that list. A deal for Joe Cole had already been sanctioned before Hodgson's arrival – as far back as February when Christian Purslow led a meeting in London before a game with Arsenal. Purslow, who was appointed as Liverpool's managing director in 2009, fancied himself as a football scout and this immediately brought him into conflict with Rafael Benítez before the Spaniard was sacked and then replaced by Hodgson. Purslow's background was in private equity and he would make Cole Liverpool's highest paid player even though his injury record had restricted any real impact at Chelsea over the previous two seasons. 'I would never want to dupe the Liverpool public by telling them all is rosy now because Joe Cole has signed,' Hodgson said on his first day of pre-season training. Though he was right, it was the sort of downbeat message that would be a theme of his reign.

As a man of the world, Hodgson should have known about the mood and expectations at Anfield. There are things you say and things you do not. There was no battle for hearts and minds because Hodgson did not attempt to engage in one. He would soon tell Tony Barrett, the locally born journalist working for *The Times* who became the club's supporter liaison officer, that his 'problem' was that he was 'too Scouse'. Maybe it was simply that Liverpool was too Scouse for Hodgson, a Croydon native. 'He just couldn't help being Hodgson,' remembered Mike Nevin, a writer at the *Anfield Wrap*.

Hodgson would later claim that every Liverpool supporter wanted Dalglish to replace Benítez, but that was not true. At the beginning, his appointment was underwhelming even if there was a wish for him to succeed. He would lose the confidence of many not only because of his results but also because of what he said. Hodgson was a fan of American realist literature of the 1960s but he was received on Merseyside as a cross between Alan Whicker and Quentin Crisp. He was interested in literature and unafraid to talk about his passions outside of football. When writing his programme notes for his first league game in charge, a colleague had asked what he thought of the booing aimed at Sotirios Kyrgiakos in Macedonia where Liverpool had beaten Rabotnički 2–0. According to Hodgson, the defender was at the centre of Greco–Macedonian politics, which was interesting and may have been accurate, but he seemed to know more about what was going on in places he couldn't influence rather than the places he could and was expected to.

This was a time of fan activism at Liverpool, where words and messages were great weapons. Hodgson, though, did not give the impression that he appreciated what was going on around him or how to convince anyone through concise articulation of his thoughts. There was an acknowledgement inside the club that he tended to say too much when he needed only to say less, and said too little when he needed to elaborate. He never seemed to say the right thing when it really mattered, and it didn't help that he tended not to listen to advice. He did not seem like he was ever in control.

When a Turkish cameraman decided to start packing away his gear in the middle of a press conference before another European tie with Trabzonspor, Hodgson interjected with humour by saying, 'Don't worry, we can work around you,' and the room laughed with him. By then, however, he'd delivered an assessment of Liverpool's away-leg victory with less measure, labelling the Europa League qualifier as 'another famous European night', which was quite a claim considering Liverpool had beaten Real Madrid 4–0 at Anfield just eighteen months before.

Similar unusual statements would follow. 'They'll be a formidable challenge,' he said before losing at home on penalties to fourth tier Northampton Town in the League Cup, a night match played in driving rain where Hodgson instructed his defenders to 'just fucking launch it' loud enough for everyone sitting in the press area just behind him to hear.

Daniel Agger, one of the coolest ball-playing centre-backs in Liverpool's modern history, quickly became disillusioned with the guidance he was being given. Agger had 'completely lost' his desire to work because training sessions were so repetitive and sometimes ridiculous. There was one which involved an eight-on-two situation – attack versus defence – which was designed simply to help build Fernando Torres' confidence when he was struggling for goals. When being interviewed during this period Agger would puff out his cheeks and give long explanations of what was wrong under Hodgson, who 'did not really want to play football, just stop it happening'.

Hodgson was more popular amongst other senior first-team players than many of his critics might imagine, with Steven Gerrard and Jamie Carragher understanding that many of the problems at Liverpool were not of his making. Even Torres, someone who would soon leave Anfield amidst claims that playing for Hodgson had pushed him closer to the exit, would later credit him for at least being honest with him while others like Purslow and Damien Comolli, the director of football, were supposedly not.

Respect for him on the terraces had drained by the end of September when he alienated the club's hardcore support by saying the continuing protests against the American owners 'do not help' as he grappled with Liverpool's worst start to a season in eighteen years. 'It is something I have had to live with since I came to the club,' he complained.

When Sir Alex Ferguson accused Torres of diving, Hodgson did not attempt to put the Manchester United manager in his place, as is expected of Liverpool managers, and instead sounded like he was in agreement: 'Sir Alex is entitled to any opinion he wants to have but I'm not going to come here and say I agree or disagree,' he said deferentially. 'I thought the referee refereed the game very well and I have a very ambivalent attitude to those type of things.'

Meanwhile, he would describe José Mourinho as 'a great man', like the Portuguese was a circus ringmaster. It sounded like Hodgson was willing to get fired from a cannon by the Great Mourinho because he'd apparently been right about the challenges at Liverpool where there was a possibility that it would get 'worse and worse'.

There are other stories, ranging from well-known ones like the time Hodgson insisted Torres would definitely play against Utrecht only to be overruled by the new-to-the-job Australian club doctor Peter Brukner, to lesser ones like the time he walked past John McMahon soon after his arrival and abruptly asked the reserve-team manager to identify himself. When Liverpool's players and staff went to Alder Hey at Christmas they were late because Hodgson wanted to have his lunch. Once in West Derby, he would tell those suffering in their beds that it was an honour to be at 'the second best' children's hospital in the country.

Hodgson would last until the first week of January. In mid-November, the word that would haunt Hodgson appeared clearly for the first time following a pitiful defeat at Stoke. That word from the away end would be 'Dalglish'. Then, on a murky night at Anfield between Christmas and New Year – and with attendances falling – Liverpool lost to bottom-placed Wolverhampton Wanderers. For the first time, Hodgson would hear his name chanted by the Kop. 'Hodgson for England,' came a cry that would appear again the following Wednesday at Ewood Park in Blackburn where another defeat left Liverpool twelfth. When the home supporters chanted, 'You're getting sacked in the morning,' those that had travelled from Merseyside in a half-empty away end joined in. His departure would finally be announced on the Saturday and it would represent the shortest managerial reign in the club's history.

The behind-the-scenes circumstances of Hodgson's time at Anfield were testing. Yet he never felt, sounded or looked like a Liverpool manager. Liverpool's febrile supporter base wants to feel like their manager is fighting on behalf of them, that he cares about the welfare of the club as well as the city. Hodgson made it seem like he cared only about the job he was hired to do, ensuring that his own reputation was unaffected by issues he could not necessarily control absolutely but, if he had it in him, could at least show some common concern over.

In his third game in charge his team had narrowly beaten West Brom – the club that employed Hodgson after he was sacked by Liverpool. This had been his first league victory as Liverpool manager in three attempts. Hodgson would feel this sense of peaceful satisfaction only once, because by the time the next league win came eight weeks later against Blackburn it was the end of October, Liverpool were still in the relegation zone and by then the calls for him to go were becoming more audible.

That August Bank Holiday Sunday, Hodgson had dinner with his wife at Quarter, a hazily lit restaurant that serves pastas and pizzas beside the cobblestones of Falkner Street in Liverpool's Georgian district. He was dressed officially in his red Liverpool tie, though uncharacteristically the top button of his white shirt was unfastened. He had come straight from work, he was not trying to hide, but nobody other than Sheila was starting a conversation with him. Quarter is a family sort of restaurant. He left through the front entrance, jingling the keys in his pocket like a caretaker as he passed a dozen or so tables. He was not stopped. Either nobody noticed him. Or nobody cared he was there.

When Roy Hodgson was chosen by Liverpool's selection panel, some of Liverpool's players were asked how much they knew about the managers under serious consideration. While Pepe Reina, Liverpool's record-breaking goalkeeper for the number of clean sheets he kept in his debut season, had played for Manuel Pellegrini at Villarreal and gave the Chilean a glowing reference, both Jamie Carragher and Steven Gerrard were close friends with Danny Murphy, who'd acted as Hodgson's captain at Fulham.

On the Liverpool rumour mill – just as it had been suggested that Carragher and Gerrard contributed towards Benítez's sacking – it became commonly accepted that they had wanted Hodgson. Carragher would dismiss that claim. 'I certainly didn't get him the job. I didn't know Roy Hodgson so I could only go off what Danny told me, which was largely positive,' Carragher said. 'I think they went for him because Roy wasn't going to bring with him an entire new staff like Deschamps or Pellegrini might. We'd finished seventh the year before and I don't think anyone felt Hodgson was going to be there for four or five years. Maybe he might be able to get us back in the Champions League . . . but it didn't work, at all . . .'

For Carragher, Hodgson was a decent man but that didn't mean he was a decent manager for Liverpool. 'He didn't get the club in the way the foreign managers before and after him did,' Carragher reflected. 'He'd managed so many clubs, I think Liverpool became just another club for him – albeit a much bigger one. He'd been one of those managers who does two years maximum then moves on. He was obviously a very good manager at a certain level, but the level at Liverpool is a lot higher and the interest in everything that happens at Liverpool is intrusive to the point of obsession.

'Roy Hodgson was the type of manager who goes into every game thinking he might get beat,' Carragher continued. ' "They've got this, that and the other . . ." It was never, "We're Liverpool, we'll do this." It was the sort of thought process a manager in the bottom half of the table would have: you think you're going to lose every game so you make it as hard as possible for the opponent.

'Liverpool supporters feed off every word the manager says. His word means more than anyone else's. If you're getting that wrong, it's not good. I don't think Roy Hodgson recognized the significance and how to use the media to convey his message. Rafa and Gérard [Houllier] were a lot savvier on that front, even though they both had difficult starts, like Roy.'

When Manchester United recovered from 2–0 behind to draw 2–2 with Aston Villa thanks to two goals in the last ten minutes, Hodgson told Liverpool's players ahead of their evening fixture at Stoke that they needed 'to be a bit more like that' – 'that' being United. Though again it might have been true, it made the players realize that he was failing to grasp the mentality of the club – you could, say, compliment United as the manager of Fulham, but never at Liverpool. The final score in Staffordshire was Stoke City 2–0 Liverpool.

Carragher believed some players let Liverpool as a club down during this period. 'When you've got a manager that no one's having, when you play badly – no matter how bad – you blame the manager for it,' he said. He also thought Hodgson gets too much stick considering he did not leave a legacy that needed untangling. 'He was not a manager who was there for long, bought lots of expensive players that Liverpool could not get rid of. Paul Konchesky and Christian Poulsen were poor signings but they didn't cost loads. Konchesky wasn't any worse than [Emiliano] Insúa. Did he make everything change for the worse or was it already on a downward curve when he arrived? It wasn't as if his work alone in those five months stopped us doing things for years. It was a bad dream.'

Hodgson had described the signing of Poulsen from Juventus as a coup. 'You cannot afford to miss out on players of his calibre,' he claimed. Yet Poulsen's best days were behind him, he was too slow for the Premier League and, while he did not have the snap of the midfielder he replaced in Javier Mascherano, he neither had the passing range of Xabi Alonso.

Carragher's lowest point was losing to Blackpool at home, a club that would do the double over Liverpool in their one and only season in the Premier League. Liverpool had an injury crisis and Carragher, at 32, was asked to fill in at left-back – a position he hadn't played in for almost eight years. 'Having played the full ninety in Holland just a few days before, I was knackered but I was terrible,' Carragher admitted. 'We got beat 2–1 by Blackpool and I went home that night and I couldn't sleep. It was the game before an international break and the next morning I went in and knocked on Roy Hodgson's office. He was having a meeting with the rest of the staff. I said, "I'd like to have a talk about what the fuck is going on" – not to have a go at him but to chat about the way forward. At that time Poulsen was getting battered by the fans. He got booed when he came off against Blackpool. I remember Roy said, "I still think we should play him." And I went, "No! No! You can't do that. Even if you think you're right you'll get slaughtered."

'Many of the wins under Roy were shitty wins,' Carragher concluded. 'It felt so big to win. I remember away at Bolton and at home as well – late wins. It was like, "Fuckin' 'ell, we feel like a small team now." '

Bernard Sheridan was 104 years old. An uncle had first taken him to Anfield in 1923, travelling to the ground from his home in Wavertree by tram. Amongst his birthday presents was a Liverpool shirt, a birthday cake, a signed letter from Jürgen Klopp and some match tickets for the game against Crystal Palace. He had seven grandchildren, fourteen great-grandchildren, but he had chosen one of his sons who lived in Canada to attend the match with him.

When all was settled, Bernard waited in the press room – sat in his wheelchair wearing his warm fleece and Liverpool scarf. It had been a chaotic afternoon, with Palace taking the lead before pegging Liverpool back at 2–2 before piling on the pressure in the final seconds when the score was narrowed to 4–3. When Bernard met Kenny Dalglish earlier in the day, Dalglish had joked that Bernard's age was the same as his golf score. Liverpool had made him feel like a 'celebrity' and when Klopp noticed him, the pair embraced before a photograph was taken which would take residence by his bedside in Crosby.

'You've invited me, a 104-year-old, to the game and spent 90 minutes trying to kill me,' Bernard whispered in the ear of Klopp as he leaned down, forcing Liverpool's manager to release an enormous laugh. It was mid-January and Klopp's Liverpool side had already taken more league points than in 2004–05, the season where they last became champions of Europe. They were one win away from eclipsing points' totals in nine other Premier League campaigns. 'I hope you do it this year, Mr Klopp,' Bernard said. 'I really do.'

10. DOWNFALL

MANCHESTER UNITED WERE BACK. OLE GUNNAR SOLSKJÆR HAD TRANS-formed the mood at Old Trafford following the sacking of José Mourinho, winning eight out of nine fixtures since his managerial loan move from Molde. Solskjær, however, possessed a dirty secret. He had been one of the first card carriers at the Liverpool supporters' branch in Norway – the biggest foreign group of its kind anywhere in the world, with more than 50,000 members. After signing for United as a player in 1996 Solskjær stopped paying his annual associate fee and, three seasons later, he would score a famous injury-time winner against Liverpool in the fourth round of the FA Cup, an occasion which proved significant in terms of allegiances on Merseyside too because it was after that game Jamie Carragher went back to the Chaucer pub in Bootle to be greeted by mockery from even those that knew him well. Carragher had remained an Evertonian until that point – checking out the team's results as soon as he left the pitch as a Liverpool player. He realized then his heart was closer to Liverpool than he'd thought.

While Carragher became a symbol of modern Liverpool, Solskjær's switch had been similarly extreme. As a novice manager he greeted an Irish journalist with Liverpool sympathies covering Sligo Rovers' Champions League qualifier with Molde without any sense of playfulness, telling him: 'If I'd known you were a Liverpool fan, I wouldn't have shaken your hand.' With that, he left the conversation behind, just as he did eighteen months later when, then in place as Cardiff's manager, he lost 6–3 at home to

Liverpool before being asked about the title chances of the club he used to support. 'I couldn't care less,' he fired back, departing a post-match TV interview abruptly.

Solskjær was scheduled to be at Old Trafford until the summer when it was speculated United would move for Tottenham Hotspur's Mauricio Pochettino but the players liked Solskjær, who had coached several of them at youth level, not least Paul Pogba who had been left out by Mourinho at Anfield as the rain fell in December and the Portuguese reached a squelching end. It was now Solskjær's job to lose.

Liverpool were further ahead of United than they had been at any point in the course of a league season since their last title in 1990, yet the feeling around both clubs implied opposite fortune. Perhaps this reflected how far Liverpool had travelled, particularly since the 2010–11 season when they were taken over by Fenway – the season they beat United in March thanks to a Dirk Kuyt hat-trick, an outcome which still left them 18 points behind their greatest rivals who were positioned at the top of the league table. Just as Liverpool's belief ahead of their meeting in 2011 radiated from the stands, United's confidence was more palpable in 2018.

In 2011 Fenway Sports Group – as new owners – decided to hire a club legend in Kenny Dalglish as manager, while the decades-old questions about Anfield's suitability as a modern venue remained unanswered. The club's press man Paul Tyrrell would soon depart – replaced by the even more infamous Jen Chang who warned one mischievous supporter that Liverpool fans would post 'dog shit' through his letter box if he continued leaking information through a parody Twitter account.

Now, the Saudi royal family wanted to buy United from the Glazer family apparently; Solskjær was the legend carrying the torch while Old Trafford was not quite the stadium it used to be, its narrow press box a metaphor for how interest in the game had rocketed since United first modernized their home with Sky TV money while everybody else spent those proceeds on players. Having chosen to leave for Uefa, Phil Townsend had been replaced as communications officer by Charlie Brooks, a recruitment from

Nike. Though Brooks had not made any ridiculous threats to sup-porters, United were considering following Liverpool down the sporting director route as well. Damien Comolli was just a few months into the job when United went to Anfield in 2011. Though Kuyt had scored the goals that warm afternoon, it had been a per-formance inspired by Luis Suárez – the Uruguayan signed by Comolli, the director of football who, ultimately, did not suit Liv-erpool, the club where Bill Shankly had taken the power from the boardroom and the cult of the manager really began.

Since Jürgen Klopp's appointment, indeed, the decisions of Michael Edwards – Comolli's successor – had started making more sense. Edwards could install effective scouting systems and trade players successfully but, without Klopp's leadership and guidance, it surely would have been impossible for Liverpool to emerge and pass United in the league.

At boardroom level, though their positions in the hierarchy were entitled differently, Mike Gordon was a steady and under-stated influence at Liverpool. Could the same be said of Ed Woodward at United, or was it even fair to judge him when it felt like football had moved on from the days when the chief execu-tive made all of the decisions? Woodward came across as a cold character, someone who appreciated how to turn out a profit without the need for that to involve success on the pitch.

It was too soon to claim Liverpool had moved beyond United in every possible way. Progress can be marked by staging points and there had been many at Liverpool – most notably the hiring of Klopp and the bulldozing of the old main stand, with a newer one rising over the city's skyline like a machine beast. Liverpool were settled and set up for the future in the way United were not, even if it felt like Solskjær had brought back some of the old United ways like Dalglish had at Anfield eight years earlier, mak-ing everybody feel better about themselves.

For a long time Liverpool had seemed to be a club that looked too often to the past for short-term answers to long-term prob-lems, while United were more forward thinking, seeing into the future. Yet it had been the vision and power of a manager in Sir Alex Ferguson that made everything seem to join up. A reflection of Klopp's influence at Anfield was shown when it was revealed that Liverpool would tour the United States in the summer rather than Asia, even though it was Asia's turn in the cycle. Klopp hated the summer tour of 2017 when it rained all of the time and training sessions at tumbledown facilities were cancelled, as well as the extra time spent travelling. If a United manager wanted to make the same decision, would there be the understanding above him to allow him to have his own way? Mourinho and his predecessor Louis van Gaal had complained about the club's pre-season schedules, which involved America but more games with more travelling and more PR work and less of a focus on preparation.

Klopp would speak about his relationship with Ferguson, comparing Solskjær's impact 'to one of the biggest – if not the biggest [manager's] in world football', insisting that he had returned United to the principles that Ferguson stood for. 'It makes United a threat again and back on track. It is clear he will be the manager next year.' There was gentle laughter in the room when Klopp said that – a Liverpool manager announcing the next in line at the club which it judges itself against.

Ferguson had wanted Klopp to succeed him and Ed Woodward had met him in Munich but Klopp was unimpressed by the 'Hollywood presentation'.

Klopp had first encountered Ferguson in Nyon at a Uefa managers' convention. Initially it had flattered Klopp that Ferguson was so interested in him. Yet it was a sign of Klopp's singlemindedness and judgement that he was able to resist United. He also did not feel he had to ask Kenny Dalglish for help, following the lead of Solskjær, who suggested he might invite Ferguson into the dressing room to give his players a lift.

Klopp had tried a similar trick in Germany ahead of the Ruhr derby between Borussia Dortmund and Schalke, when three Dortmund legends were brought to the team hotel before a keenly contested draw. 'I don't think Martial and Pogba will understand when Sir Alex Ferguson is on fire,' Klopp laughed, confirming that Dalglish would not be called from the hospitality suites to perform a similar role.

A goalless draw was not the result Liverpool wanted two days later on a warm February afternoon where the flow of an unusual game was disrupted by injuries that forced four substitutions before half-time. Like Bayern Munich at Anfield in the Champions League earlier that week, United had already abandoned their buccaneering style under Solskjær before their first enforced change in an attempt to stifle Liverpool's threat. In Old Trafford's mixed zone, Andy Robertson was both angry and defiant. He had been the emboldened star of their previous encounter. Now he was frustrated with his own team's inhibitions. 'We need to start respecting ourselves a bit more,' he thought. Considering the respect shown towards Liverpool in successive fixtures against two of the world's biggest clubs, it was clear by now that others did.

Four miles away in Manchester's glass-fronted city centre, Maurice Watkins' wolfish grin stretched almost from ear to ear. He was sat in a conference room behind an enormous oval desk in the offices of the law firm he worked for. Watkins had served as United's solicitor for more than thirty years. His name was on every contract. When a player joined United, he had to sign it. When the club agreed a new commercial deal, his signature was there. Later, he joined the board and Watkins knew inside out the club which had risen from perennial underachievers to the most profitable in the world as it moved into a new stratosphere of finance that Liverpool were not able to reach. I had suggested to him that United's push towards dominance had been a grand design. 'Well,' he responded, 'not quite . . .'

Watkins was referring to the determination of chairman Martin Edwards to sell the club in 1989 when it nearly went to Michael Knighton, the ball-juggling training-kit-on-the-pitch-wearing businessman who ultimately did not have the money to push the deal through and later bought Carlisle United where he talked of UFO sightings. There was some stroke of fortune that he was intercepted. Two reporters from the *Manchester Evening News* had been in a hotel lift when they overheard bankers discussing their concerns about whether Knighton had the financial backing to take United from Edwards, and within a couple of hours the story was on the front page of the paper and the takeover was dead.

According to Watkins, Edwards was concerned about the amount of money it would take to make Manchester United successful again. In choosing to sell Liverpool two decades later, David Moores had exactly the same concern about Roman Abramovich's takeover of Chelsea and what his investment meant. In the twenty-six-year gap between league titles, United had lifted the European Cup in 1968 as reigning league champions, then four FA Cups, a League Cup and a European Cup Winners' Cup. During this period Liverpool had won eleven league titles, four European Cups, four FA and League Cups as well as the Uefa Cup. This represented a haul of seventeen more trophies for Liverpool. The level of frustration at United could be measured against Liverpool's, who had won eight major trophies in their twenty-nine-year wait for a title in an era where United's record involved twenty-five.

Edwards, Watkins stressed, was not an incredibly wealthy man. Old Trafford needed developing and so did the team, and he was beginning to think it would be better if someone else took the burden away from him – again, like Moores. Ultimately, there was no Premier League, no sizeable television contracts and so, if a club wanted to advance quickly, cash injections had to come from the major shareholder, and that shareholder was Edwards.

Though Watkins denied the suggestion, United had earlier been at the centre of a plan by British Aerospace who wanted to buy the club on behalf of the Saudi Arabian royal family as a sweetener for a trade deal which also involved building stadiums in Riyadh and friendly matches with the England national team. Watkins did not attend the meeting where Edwards and Knighton discussed figures but on hearing that Edwards had agreed a sale for £10 million, Watkins considered it 'a bit of a steal'.

In United's attempt to keep up, it could have sent them in the direction of Liverpool two decades later when they were sold by a local owner to the wrong businessmen and things got a lot worse. Like Edwards, Moores had been corralled into taking charge at Liverpool as it was passed down through his family and, like Edwards, he wasn't a particularly dynamic figure – though he did recognize the need for change.

In 1989 Edwards could have sacked Ferguson as supporter focus and pressure grew on owner and manager. United were in 15th place on Christmas day during a season where Liverpool would race towards their last league title. It was then that Edwards started to think about floating the club on the Stock Exchange. In following the lead of Tottenham Hotspur two years later, this enabled him to raise the funds not only to clear significant debt but also rebuild the Stretford End.

Edwards appreciated then that if this all worked out, United would eventually be bought out, and that is exactly what happened in 2003 when the Glazer family came along two years after United became the world's most successful Stock-Market listed football club, with a pre-tax profit of £22 million, though nobody could have anticipated the boom of the Premier League or United's domination of it in 1991 – the year Tottenham had a much bigger turnover than United. This was thanks to the vision of Edward Freedman, who had led a merchandising revolution in north London, and his achievements were recognized by the United board who appointed him in 1992 when increased revenues from Sky Television's deal to cover English football helped United quicker than any other club as they became champions of the Premier League in its inaugural season.

In the space of a decade, football jurisdiction had changed dramatically. In 1981 Liverpool, as European champions, had been the first team to wear the logo of a sponsor on their shirts, though the two-year £100,000 agreement with Hitachi only allowed them to brandish the brand in games that were not televised – and not in Europe or the FA Cup. By 1993 Watkins was signing off multimillion pound agreements brought by Freedman which would see replica United shirts sold in the Far East for the first time.

Watkins admitted there had been a degree of fortune along the way, with United able to expand Old Trafford in a way Liverpool could never increase Anfield – due to the space around the ground in Manchester and the rows and rows of terraced homes on Merseyside – enabling United to accelerate into a new financial stratosphere piqued by the interest created by their on-field success.

In the space of five years United's average attendance rose from just below Liverpool's to nearly 16,000 more, even though Liverpool's had increased by 5,000 as well. This meant that Old Trafford was welcoming 250,000 more spectators a season than Anfield, enhancing United's return in the most significant of income fields by a quarter.

'Of course,' Watkins reminded, 'we could have ended up with Mr Souness as our manager.' It had been Knighton's plan to remove Ferguson and replace him with Graeme Souness, who was interested in making a controversial move from Rangers despite being a European Cup-winning captain at Liverpool. Sir Matt Busby, after all, had followed a similar path despite his Liverpool links, and Souness being Souness thought he could do anything because during the 1980s everything he touched turned to gold.

Ferguson later boasted that his greatest achievement was 'knocking Liverpool right off their fucking perch'. Though there is no doubt that his management propelled United towards decades of dominance, his first title – seven years after his appointment – came three seasons after Liverpool's last and at the end of intervening campaigns that saw Arsenal and Leeds crowned champions. United's challenge in 1993, indeed, had come from Aston Villa and Norwich City rather than Liverpool, who finished sixth. Twelve months later Liverpool came eighth – 32 points behind United, who were pushed nearly all of the way by Blackburn Rovers instead. Souness had headed to Liverpool instead of United. Back at Anfield his reputation as a manager would prove very different to his reputation as a player and Liverpool would fall from their perch.

The corridors of the Moat House had welcomed the rich and famous from both sides of the Atlantic. Staff had waited on stars such as John Travolta, Oliver Reed and Richard Harris. When

Dame Judi Dench appeared on stage in Liverpool she too stayed at the hotel with Anna Massey. It was late one blustery afternoon in January 1994 when names of Junior Bent, Wayne Allison and Brian Tinnion checked in for the first time. Bristol City were a football team from the English Second Division. They held Liverpool in an FA Cup third-round home tie to secure a replay, travelling north to Merseyside not in hope but with belief. Liverpool were fifth in the Premier League but had lost seven times already in another disappointing season, which allowed United to open a 21-point gap at the top. Liverpool were unbeaten in six weeks but they had drawn seven of their ten games and frustration at Anfield was being directed at manager Graeme Souness who had been a legendary captain winning the European Cup ten years earlier. For Souness the reality of his position was laid bare as he sat eating tea and toast before heading to Anfield. In the next room he could hear Bristol City's manager Russell Osman telling his players that Liverpool's were as 'weak as piss'. On and on he went about Liverpool's shortcomings, but it was the suggestion they did not have the stomach which hit home with Souness. The next morning, following Tinnion's second-half winner, Souness resigned with Liverpool's blessing halfway through a five-year contract.

The length of the deal reflected how confident Liverpool's board were when they appointed him in 1991. Souness did not have to leave Rangers, where he had a job for life having transformed the Glasgow club into one of the most successful in Britain. Before all of the resplendent stadiums in England there had been Ibrox. Rangers had emerged at Celtic's expense and though Souness had outspent every other British club from 1986 onwards, he had also spent well, and this helped Rangers to four successive league titles, setting them up for an unprecedented ten in a row and a period of domination that was not matched until Celtic capitalized on their greatest rival's financial demise two decades later.

Souness had left Liverpool in 1984 for Sampdoria in Italy following a remarkable performance in a penalty shootout victory over AS Roma in a final on their home ground, where Liverpool won a fourth European Cup in seven years. 'A gladiator,' was how one of his teammates, Michael Robinson, described him. Roma had beaten Dundee United in the semi-final and Robinson can remember hoping the Scottish club prevailed. When he told Souness this, his captain's eyes lit up. 'Rubbish, Michael,' Souness had said. 'We can beat anyone.' To Robinson, this represented what Souness was all about: the greater the challenge, the greater his appetite.

In Scotland, however, Souness had grown tired of the spotlight, into which he had often propelled himself. He had been born into a Hearts-supporting family in Edinburgh and when his debut as a player–manager came against city rivals Hibernian, he was sent off for kicking out at George McCluskey, a moment which provoked a brawl at Easter Road and earned Souness a second yellow card after 34 minutes. Three years later he signed Mo Johnston, the first Catholic player in the history of Rangers. Having separated from his first wife, Souness was regularly followed home along the M8 to Edinburgh by tabloid reporters. By 1991 he was in the middle of a long touchline ban, while an incident where he had shouted at a tea lady nearly led to a fight with St Johnstone's chairman.

Though he enjoyed a close relationship with the Rangers chairman and financier David Murray, who offered him a blank contract where he could fill in the details to remain at Ibrox for as long as he wanted, he could not ignore the lure of Anfield: the place he'd made his name as a player. Murray warned him then that it would be a move that he'd end up regretting. When I met Souness years later, he said, 'I have to admit, David was right.'

Bar his second season in Italy when Sampdoria finished 11th in the Serie A table, Souness – since moving to Liverpool from Middlesbrough in 1978 – had experienced almost unbroken success. There had been five First Division titles at Liverpool in six years as well as three European Cups and three League Cups. In Italy he helped inspire Sampdoria to the club's first Coppa Italia in the club's history. Before the point of his return to Liverpool in 1991, indeed, there had been twenty-four winners' medals in thirteen seasons. Understandably, Souness carried with him what he thought was a recipe for success. Italy had opened his mind in terms of the direction professional football was taking, and one of the first decisions he took back at Liverpool was to try to change the players' eating habits. Out went the pre-match meal of steak and chips and the post-match diet of lager, and in came pasta and vegetables then lower-volume alcohol. When he imposed the same measures at Rangers the club had not won a trophy in nine years, so it was easier to convince the players that his method was the right one to follow. Considering Liverpool had been champions of England not long before – considering too that experienced players had their routines and thought they understood their own bodies and minds best – this was a move met by resistance at Anfield. Just as it did not help that Souness was a ringleader in the Liverpool squad's vibrant social scene when he was a player, earning him the nickname Champagne Charlie, it did not help Souness that he inherited an ageing squad stuck in its ways.

Though he had planned to build a team around two 28-year-olds in John Barnes and Jan Molby, who he'd tried to sign for Rangers, Souness believed he was met by a group which had 'lost its passion for Liverpool', something which enraged him. One of his biggest mistakes was to take the responsibility of contract discussions from Peter Robinson, the hugely respected long-serving administrator. This meant he was having the sort of discussions that Liverpool managers of the past avoided. Liverpool were notoriously low payers despite their success, and it had been a deliberate ploy started by Bill Shankly where Robinson would low-ball on offers which then allowed the manager to promise the player a better deal, getting him on side from the start of their relationship. Now, Souness was having to negotiate, and he considered any player who asked for more to be a player who was more interested in making money than playing football.

Souness admitted he was too fiery a character to play the game to his advantage, and whenever a player mentioned the possibility of the offers made by other clubs he decided to call their bluff rather than thinking about the strategy around recruitment and replacements. Suddenly, he was buying under pressure, and for the first time in three decades Liverpool – a club which had long traded so well, often making signings as long as eighteen months before a player entered the first team on a regular basis – were selling without considering what came next. Steve McMahon and Peter Beardsley had been influential figures in the structure of Kenny Dalglish's team for nearly five years but, aged 30, they were the first to leave under Souness. The new boss may have been right in his belief that the squad was in need of urgent reconstruction but here he was moving too fast without thinking about the short-term consequences or realizing their potential to lead to longer-term problems.

Contrary to popular belief, Souness did not order the demolition of the famous boot room, the space under the main stand where Liverpool's coaches would meet to discuss plans or invite opposition staff on match days. That decision was taken by the board, which decided it needed to increase the size of the press room to deal with the increased interest in football as the Premier League era took off.

But another controversial Souness decision also had roots in the rapidly changing football environment. Anfield had become a tourist attraction and due to the number of tours taking place Souness decided that rather than train at Melwood then take the bus back to Anfield to get changed – as had been the pattern of life since Shankly – Liverpool should instead be based at the training ground. It had been recognized those fifteen-minute bus journeys had been a contributing factor towards the great sense of camaraderie between Liverpool's players and so something was lost forever in this decision.

Ultimately, had Souness got his transfer signings right history underneath his management could have been viewed differently. In two and a half seasons, he spent £30 million on players – more than Manchester United. Yet none of his recruits are remembered as Liverpool legends. His retaining of goalkeeper Bruce Grobbelaar proved to be a significant failing because not only did it mean he missed out on Peter Schmeichel, who arguably became United's greatest goalkeeper (having previously written a letter to Souness asking for a trial which he did not get because of the presence of

Grobbelaar), he then passed on the opportunity to sign Eric Cantona. By that point Souness was fighting fires with Grobbelaar and did not want another 'difficult character', as Cantona had been described by Michel Platini when he recommended the French forward. Cantona, of course, followed the same path as Schmeichel.

The team's style would change under Souness, largely because of the failure of Nigel Clough to reproduce the form he delivered at Nottingham Forest. Souness believed he was capable of replacing Beardsley as the link-man between midfield and attack, but when Clough did not stand out Liverpool's natural flow was disrupted. Molby, who would have his own differences with Souness despite the manager's intentions to make him a key player at the beginning, described two Souness signings – Julian Dicks and Neil Ruddock – as 'long-ball merchants' who were unable to deal with the small-sided games in training where standards declined.

Souness would finish his first full season in charge by winning the FA Cup with a 2–0 victory over Sunderland at Wembley. That achievement, however, was overshadowed by his decision to grant the *Sun* an interview about his triple-heart bypass operation, printed on the third anniversary of the Hillsborough tragedy, an event which had been followed by the newspaper reporting vile lies about the role of Liverpool supporters in the disaster. Its circulation had since plummeted across Merseyside, where copies of a newspaper were burned on British soil for the first time since 1933 when the Jewish community reacted to the *Daily Mail*'s backing of the brownshirts by building pyres in east London. A spontaneous campaign against the *Sun* had waged ever since but this seemed to have escaped Souness, who claimed he'd been too embroiled by matters in Scotland at the time of the disaster to notice the boycott in the city. Current and former Liverpool players like Ian Rush and Tommy Smith had, after all, continued their relationship with the paper post-1989 with no public fall-out, but with families still grieving and still no closer to justice the timing of Souness's story was awful – though he did stress it was originally meant to be printed a week earlier and certainly would not have been printed on the anniversary had the person who'd originally written it not been on holiday. The *Sun*'s Merseyside correspondent was Mike Ellis, and he would ghostwrite Souness's first autobiography seven years later.

Souness later reflected that he should have resigned after the FA Cup final on the principle of his mistake. His position by then was untenable. Merseyside's reporters, who had always worked as a pack, were annoyed that they had been left out of an exclusive story, and in their column inches they did not hold back. In promoting younger players like Steve McManaman and Robbie Fowler to the first team, he bought himself some time with sympathetic supporters who remembered him as a player, but not for long.

The position and direction of Liverpool and Manchester United under Souness and Sir Alex Ferguson was confirmed in March 1993 when United went to Anfield and secured the win which sent them top of the table. While United would win their first title in twenty-six years, the result put Liverpool 15th – just three points above the relegation zone with ten games left. A sixth-placed finish did not prove to be a real recovery, and neither did their 3–3 draw with United at Anfield ten months later, even if Liverpool were three goals behind inside the first 23 minutes. Three weeks later Souness was in the Moat House when he heard Russell Osman's stirring claims in the next room. He knew then how far he had fallen. It was time to go.

Bruce Grobbelaar thought things at Liverpool would go back to normal, that the Souness era was simply a blip and the culture of winning would return with the appointment of Roy Evans. Evans had been assistant to Souness but he had also been the junior member of the fabled boot room. He had absorbed the tricks of Bob Paisley, Joe Fagan and Ronnie Moran, learning about what it takes to build a successful football dynasty. Though he was much younger than the other figures and his initial contribution towards this unique environment was to pin a *Playboy* calendar on the wall, his opinion was always asked for and respected even if his ideas were not implemented.

Evans wanted to take this approach into his own senior management. He would trust the players just as he had been trusted, and to trust youth especially, as he had been a reserve-team player as well as manager once and he thought he related to these lads the best. Within twelve months of his appointment as Souness's replacement the average age of Liverpool's team had dropped by three and a half years to 22 and a half.

One of his first acts was to sell Grobbelaar, who found out about a deal with Southampton through the newspapers. Initially Grobbelaar thought this was Evans being ruthless, but later he figured it was him avoiding confrontation. Like Souness, Evans thought some of the senior players weren't as focused as they should have been. European Cup winners Ronnie Whelan and Steve Nicol were the next to go and they were followed by Don Hutchison, whose disciplinary problems under Souness had been made public.

Evans had made the transition from player to coach early. He was 25 when Bob Paisley called him up and mumbled, 'Er, Roy, we'd like you to come in.' That was his playing career over, after just eleven first-team games. Bill Shankly had believed that because of Evans' 'heart and guts', the club had discovered another Gerry Byrne – the left-back who played 80 minutes of the 1965 FA Cup final with a broken collarbone. Instead, his understanding of football would lead him towards a position which John Smith, the Liverpool chairman, had foreseen in 1974 when Evans became reserve coach: 'We have not made an appointment for the present but for the future. One day Roy Evans will be our manager.'

In his early years as a rookie coach Evans had worked closely with Fagan, whose promotion to first-team status had left the gap on the staff which Evans filled. Like Evans, Fagan was from Liverpool. Walton, in fact, is the next district along from Bootle where Evans grew up, and both men would manage the club they loved, but also questioned whether that made the job harder. Evans admitted he hated it whenever Liverpool lost, and had lost count of the number of cancelled meals with his understanding wife, Mary.

Later, Evans learned more from Moran – who Grobbelaar was not alone in calling 'the barking dog'. Evans believed both coaches had the knack of being able to pass on their knowledge without being overbearing. Having watched Fagan lead Liverpool to domestic and European titles between 1983 and 1985, he learned that the key difference between coaching and management was stepping back on the training field and observing, choosing your words carefully. He admitted that he preferred offering encouragement rather than condemnation – 'young footballers,' he said, 'reacted better.'

Jamie Redknapp, one of Liverpool's young midfielders – who happened to be Kenny Dalglish's last signing – saw Evans differently: 'He was a nice guy but that didn't mean he went about giving compliments to players that didn't deserve them.' Redknapp described Evans as a soft leader who would show disappointment rather than throw cups of tea at the dressing-room wall. He was not a disciplinarian and he trusted the players to do their jobs properly, as he had done as reserve-team manager when he led Liverpool's second string in a period of almost unbroken success in the 1970s and 1980s.

A sign of Liverpool's path under Evans became clear in the first month of his first full season in charge, 1994–95, when Crystal Palace were destroyed 6–1 on the opening day before teenager Robbie Fowler scored the quickest hat-trick ever in a 3–0 victory over Arsenal. Evans had made Phil Babb the most expensive defender ever but within two minutes of his introduction for a debut at Old Trafford as Evans tried to seal a draw, Manchester United scored twice to win 2–0.

Liverpool were rarely that far behind United but under Evans Liverpool always finished below them. Socially, there were similarities between the way the young players of Liverpool and United behaved, but it seemed to matter more at Liverpool because they did not reach the level of achievement realized at United. While there was something innocent about the off-field behaviour at United, it felt darker at Liverpool – a reason why they were not quite at the level they should be. Alex Ferguson tried to break up the drinking culture that existed at United but he didn't mind them socializing. The public accepted it because United were invariably top. For Liverpool, who always seemed to trail United, any nightclub stories explained why they were just short.

Liverpool were capable of a more thrilling brand of football but they also had a capacity for dramatic collapse. If they beat Newcastle United 4-3 one week, delivering the sort of unscripted drama Rupert Murdoch must have dreamed of when he steered Sky towards Premier League football, before losing at Coventry the next, there must have been a reason: was it because Jamie Redknapp was dating a popstar from Eternal? Was it because David James modelled for Armani? Was it because Jason McAteer advertised Wash & Go? Or was it because joint interviews with the inseparable Fowler and McManaman appeared in *Loaded* under the headline: 'BIRDS, BOOZE AND BMWS'?

The *Daily Mail* had been the first newspaper to call Liverpool's players the Spice Boys, after Fowler was photographed talking to Emma Bunton, one of the Spice Girls at a Brit Awards ceremony. McManaman's agent was Simon Fuller, who also represented the girls – and this image had an enduring impact on the way these talented young footballers were historically perceived.

Nobody stopped to think about how it might look if Liverpool lost the FA Cup final of 1996 when the opponents were Manchester United and the Liverpool squad turned up at Wembley wearing white suits designed by Armani, a contract delivered through David James' contacts. Evans was not alone in believing James could have been one of the game's greatest goalkeepers but he was prone to concentration lapses – and twice at Wembley they offered an advantage to United. A dire showpiece was drawing to a conclusion when James flapped at a corner, allowing Eric Cantona – the forward who could have been Liverpool's – to volley in a winner. Ten months later, James' mistakes in a 3–1 defeat to the same opposition meant Liverpool missed the opportunity to go past United at the top of the table with just a month of the season to go.

Perhaps Evans could have been helped more by the senior players at Liverpool, who had self-regulated in the past when United were left trailing in their wake with question marks related to why Bryan Robson and other talented players could not mark their careers with titles.

Evans had spent big to try to turn things around at Liverpool: aside from the world-record fee for Babb there was a British-record fee for Stan Collymore who quickly developed an understanding on the pitch with Fowler which was never matched by their relationship off it. Because of the £8.5 million fee spent on Collymore he came to represent Liverpool's failings under Evans' talented and expensively assembled team, though one which was not ruthless enough when it really came to it. Evans compared Collymore to the Brazilian great, Ronaldo, but according to Evans he never came to terms with the size of Liverpool having been a big fish in a small pond elsewhere. He never moved to Merseyside from his Midlands home and his poor time-keeping allowed ill-discipline to fester amongst a squad which he felt apart from because he was rarely at social events.

Collymore saw the situation differently. He was shocked when Neil Ruddock was allowed to walk onto the training field eating a bacon sandwich, and he wondered whether Alex Ferguson would have ever tolerated being placed in a headlock, like Fowler supposedly had done to Evans. He saw Melwood's ancient training boards where players would hone their first touches as a metaphor, monuments to a time when Liverpool ruled Europe – only now they were rotting away.

Like Collymore, John Scales was a big signing who Evans would sell inside two years. In 1996 he had modelled Liverpool's new kit in a photo-shoot with page 3 girl Kathy Lloyd. Though he too was frustrated by Collymore, he did have some sympathy with him: ultimately, Scales thought, Liverpool just was not a club set up for the twenty-first century and not all of the problems were Collymore's or even Evans' fault.

'Liverpool looked to the past for answers but did not apply those principles to the present,' Scales told me over coffee and cigarettes at a café on a high street in Wimbledon, the borough of London whose team Liverpool had signed him from. Scales, in fact, believed Wimbledon's notorious long-ball and rough-'em-up tactics though not pretty involved more planning than the environment he encountered at Liverpool. Scales was a smart man who struggled with the brutalism of a football dressing room, and he was perceptive enough to understand small margins and how they can be defining. He remembered arriving at Old Trafford where a megastore sold thousands of shirts every game, generating the revenues that pushed United forward. At Liverpool, meanwhile, there was resistance when McDonald's arrived at Anfield and a branded 'M' was spot-welded into the Kop.

Scales would leave after the white suits final of '96 following an argument with Evans on the team bus where he questioned whether Liverpool – including himself – were professional enough to become winners. That night, the squad still held a party in a London nightclub with Robbie Williams and Jay Kay from Jamiroquai in attendance.

Despite breathtaking football, Evans had only been able to deliver the League Cup in 1995. Three years later, following a short and ill-fated joint-managerial reign with Gérard Houllier – a classic case of Liverpool trying to find solutions where the past is married with the future (Houllier became the club's first foreign coach) – a Scales goal helped his new club Tottenham seal a 3–1 win at Anfield. Scales remembered the night clearly because it was his last goal as a professional. 'I didn't take any satisfaction it was against Liverpool or Roy because he was a really decent fella,' he insisted, as he took another drag on one of his cigarettes.

Evans knew then his time was up as well, and like Souness before him he told the chairman David Moores that he wanted to resign. Having served Liverpool for thirty-three years, he would leave Anfield with tears trickling down his cheek. At the end of a season where United achieved an unprecedented treble Liverpool were out of all cup competitions by January, finishing seventh in the league. Considering Liverpool were sixth when Souness left five years earlier, it could be argued the club were further away than ever from where they wanted to be.

Paul Ashcroft's parents had bought him the kit which remains the last in which Liverpool won the title. He'd been selected at short notice as mascot for the all-Merseyside FA Cup fourth-round tie replay in February 1991. Liverpool would play Everton four times in the space of sixteen days. Before that, Liverpool had drawn with Manchester United and a fixture with second-placed Arsenal was coming up, a team Liverpool had already lost 3–0 to that season on an afternoon where Kenny Dalglish selected an unfamiliarly conservative starting XI and the players wondered whether he'd lost his mind. Peter Beardsley had been the team's key link-man between midfield and attack and now he wanted to leave, partly because of what had happened at Highbury where Gary Ablett, a defender, was preferred in his number 7 shirt. Were the cracks beginning to show?

None of this context was apparent to Paul, though, who was 7 years old and excited about experiencing his first Liverpool game. His uncle knew people who worked in hospitality at Anfield and this led to the Ashcrofts gathering in Crosby for the big news, which came via a phone call. When Paul found out he'd be leading the team out at Goodison Park his mum recalled him going white – though the significance of the event was recognized more by his dad, who'd followed Liverpool for more than thirty years. As he went to school the next day Paul tried to remember the word 'mascot'. He wanted to impress his friends by being able to discuss what it meant. Nobody could have foreseen what awaited him at Goodison.

It was February, so it was dark and cold. The police horses seemed gigantic. Paul feared being trampled on and his dad kept him close by. He was overawed by the size of the crowd as well as the noise. When he arrived at Goodison, there was a side entrance to the main stand. His dad knocked on the door, it was opened quickly then slammed shut. Outside, there had been a smokiness in the air and burgers were frying beside onions. Inside, it was clinically lit and the silence was sudden. It felt like he was entering a secret world. Paul and his dad sat on a bench wondering what might happen next and when it was going to happen. There was a corridor with a dozen or so doors that led into other spaces. Staff and official-looking people swept between the rooms and he wondered where they led to. Suddenly, someone directed him towards one of the doors and he was in the Liverpool dressing room.

Paul was struck by the business of the place, which looked

more like an old school PE changing area. It was long and narrow and there was a limited amount of personal space. All of the players had arrived wearing different suits and shirts, which now dangled from hooks with their snazzy patterned ties. Paul thought of the players like a group of office workers who had clocked off from their day job in the city centre to go and play an important game of football. He considered the experience much more authentic than the one mascots get today: kids who might get their own kit with the name of their favourite player on the back of the shirt but are one of many experiencing the same thing at the same time. Paul's parents had bought him new boots with screw-in studs and he was worried he might slip on the floor, sending his autograph book as well as himself sprawling.

Dalglish was standing by the door, a reassuring presence and the first person to introduce himself. He was 39 years old – a month short of 40. He was very friendly and he seemed happy. There was no impression that he was under pressure. To a seven-year-old, he seemed relaxed and in control. Dalglish knelt down and put his arm around him. He was wearing a brownish suit. He asked how he was feeling then shared a joke with his dad, before starting to introduce him to some of the players. Paul felt like a fly on the wall, seeing things that few got to see. Beardsley and Ablett were sharing jokes, two players who soon would be wearing the blue of Everton together and trying to find ways of beating Liverpool.

Imagery of John Barnes was vivid because he'd emerged from a shower wearing a towel around his waist. It was unusual for a footballer to wash before playing a game, Paul recognized, but this had always been Barnes' ritual. He still has a photograph of him sitting on Barnes' knee with a big grin on his face.

In the warm-up Paul took shots at Bruce Grobbelaar, the Zimbabwean goalkeeper. When he scored, there was a cheer from the crowd, and to him it sounded deafening: it felt like he'd scored at Goodison Park against Everton.

Liverpool would get four of their own that night. The game was a rush, 'goal, after goal, after goal'. Liverpool's involved pace, skill and craft; Everton's were scrappy. 'It was clear to me even then that the volume of goals was not normal,' Paul deduced from his position on his dad's lap. His mum was there too, who came from a family of Evertonians. A 4–4 scoreline meant extra-time and this was the latest he'd ever stayed up, getting to bed beyond midnight, where he wondered what it might be like in the dressing room he'd left behind. As the inquest went on, with Liverpool's forwards asking Grobbelaar just how many they needed to score to beat their rivals, Dalglish leaned against the wall saying nothing. 'See you all tomorrow, we'll talk about it then,' Jan Molby remembers him saying.

The next day, as Paul arrived at school telling all of his mates about his amazing night, Dalglish was back at Anfield telling Liverpool's board he'd had enough, that he was resigning. He remains the last Liverpool manager to win a league title. Manchester United had waited. Soon, they were moving.

11. TRENT

THREE GOALS FROM THREE PERFECT CROSSES, ONE VIA A FREE-KICK – and a 5–0 win for Liverpool against Watford, just about keeping them top. A hat-trick of assists for Trent Alexander-Arnold, the local player in the team he loves. No longer a teenager, he is Liverpool's attacking right-back. The staff at the club's academy predicted he'd emerge as a marauding midfielder, until they saw him function in a role Jürgen Klopp identified as essential, one which led to more goals being created by Liverpool's full-backs than any other position during the 2018–19 season.

Trent, as Liverpool supporters now called him having taken ownership of his first name in the same way they did with the local superstar that went before him in Steven Gerrard, was born and brought up in a house close to the club's training ground in West Derby – an area of Merseyside where all of the bins are purple. They are dark grey in Sefton – a separate borough to the north of the city that begins in Bootle and ends all the way up in Southport, which is closer to Preston and feels more like Lancashire than Merseyside. It was in southern Sefton where Trent was educated and where he went to what was primarily a rugby-playing, fee-paying school.

'A flying full-back for the rugby team but a centre-forward for the football team,' recalled Derek Williams, his physical education teacher, who reflected the sporting priorities by mentioning rugby first at an institution where football, in fact, fell behind cricket.

Trent had gone to St Mary's because his intelligence meant he could pass the exams to gain entry while his mum, Dianne, had won a bursary for each of her three boys. Trent was the middle child, between Tyler, the eldest, and Marcel. Trent's father Mikey worked away in London to support his family, leaving Dianne to install focus and discipline in her children's lives.

It made the papers when Williams, a short and stocky sports fanatic, had once caught a burglar by making a citizen's arrest having spotted a thief preparing to enter a house from a school window during break-time. After handing him over to the police, hundreds of pupils cheered him as he returned to the school's premises through the playground. He was an all-thinking, all-action sort of character, believing in Trent's talents with the rugby ball because he saw how good he was at football, and he anticipated his athletic skills were transferable. Initially, though, Trent was unsure of his responsibilities. 'I told him full-back in rugby was like being a sweeper in football: "Stay in line with the ball and when you catch it, run with it and put it down behind those posts down there." That's exactly what he did,' said Williams. 'The first time he got the ball, he ran the full 80 metres. I was shouting, "Put it down!" He then took the penalty kick as well . . . he was that sort of lad.'

Jan van Deventer, a South African rugby player working as a coach at Waterloo whose ground is in Blundellsands, the wealthy area in Sefton next to Crosby, was present that day in Rydal, North Wales. He turned to Williams instantly, saying: 'Derek, that boy can run, mate.'

It had, then, been his first experience playing as a full-back on any sort of sporting field; the beginning of a journey that would take him to a Champions League final and a World Cup by the time he was 19. Five years earlier, he had left St Mary's at the insistence of the decision makers at Liverpool's academy who had forged a link with another school in Rainhill, which allowed intake to balance football with education.

Williams described Trent as 'a very determined young sportsman'. He had taught seventeen students who went on to become professionals during his time at St Mary's, including Carl Fearns, the back-row rugby forward who in 2019 was contracted to Lyon in France, and Gavin Griffiths, the pace bowler who moved from Lancashire to Leicestershire in the summer of 2017. Morgan Feeney, the Bootle-born defender who made his debut for Everton in 2017–18, was also on the list – he'd been in the same school year as Trent without making the same sharp level of progress at first-team level.

'Unbelievable focus, all of them,' Williams remarked. 'Trent was a quiet lad. A tremendous athlete, got stuck in – another Steven Gerrard; thick-skinned, really resilient. Every time he's faced a hurdle, he's found a way to overcome it. He's not a big mouth. He still lives at home with his mum, Dianne, and she has her three boys really well balanced. A lovely family. But so, so determined as well.'

Here was a footballer so talented that when Liverpool first saw him play, realizing he was too young and could not sign forms for another twelve months, they hid him away at a Sunday league team with trusted links to the club. This meant they could keep an eye on him while stopping the vultures from swooping in. They were called Country Park, a team that tended to win their games by a decent margin – at which point, Trent would regularly drop in at central defence and ensure the points came home with them. It was 4–0 in one game when Country Park won a corner. Trent was desperate to take it but a warning came his way. 'If we end up conceding from here, it's your fault . . .' The corner was cleared and from there the opposition forward chased after the ball, forcing Trent to sprint back as fast as he could. The forward was free: he was away, it would become 4–1, surely. Any chance of that happening ended when Trent, 'who was six or seven years old', stretched out his leg as far as he could and deliberately tripped the forward up. 'He knew what he had to do to win from an early age,' was the observation from the Liverpool scout on watching duty that day. 'A Scouse trait.'

Scouts from Manchester United and Everton followed Country Park but Trent knew where he wanted to be. He was wiry and fast and more athletic than Jon Flanagan – another Country Park player; more mobile than Andre Wisdom – once the next big thing at Liverpool's academy; more technically gifted than Jordan

Rossiter – who once seemed like Jamie Carragher and Steven Gerrard rolled into one; and smarter than Brad Smith – supposedly the long-term solution in the problem position of left-back.

After five minutes of trials at Ellergreen school, industrial language was used. 'Who the fuck is this?' There was a real sense of excitement amongst those watching from Liverpool. 'This kid is unbelievable; touch and control as well . . . the best I'd seen,' was the view of the scout, who preferred to keep his identity private.

Dianne, his mum, had been an enormous influence. Trent was a quiet kid and incredibly modest considering his talents, though he would react badly to defeat. It became a regular routine of Dianne's to call the staff at Liverpool and announce, 'He's not playing next week. He hasn't eaten his dinner.' The message was loud, clear and deliberate. The next day, another call would follow. 'OK, maybe he can play next weekend. But only if he continues to behave.' Liverpool became accustomed to the ruse and would play along. His love for the game brought him focus.

While Trent spent the 2017–18 season helping Liverpool reach the Champions League final before making it into England's World Cup squad, Everton's Antonee Robinson spent the season on loan at Bolton Wanderers. He was one school year older than Trent but, because of Trent's ability, he always trained at least one year above his natural age group. In 2008 the pair were in the same team but Robinson decided to leave when Everton made his family a lucrative offer. Similar offers from elsewhere were made to Dianne but they were not entertained. 'He was never motivated by money at all,' said one of his coaches at Liverpool. 'All he cares about is football and Liverpool. He's obsessed.'

To those who helped guide him in the early years at Liverpool, Trent was an introvert. He rarely gave too much away in terms of emotion off the field, instead showing more on it – sometimes resulting in him getting booked or sent off. When he trained for the first time with Liverpool's first team, he trained well but he kept himself to himself for weeks. Jürgen Klopp wanted him to engage more, to bring the confidence out of him. The advice from those that had worked with him previously was to offer him lots of feedback. He craved information – though not necessarily to know that he was performing to the expected standard. He wanted to learn. Klopp made a point of sitting down with him regularly, going through his expectations, outlining his beliefs and speaking to him about football. Klopp was a traditionalist in that sense. Academy players were used to coaches explaining everything. In training sessions, Klopp outlines drills then watches and repeats them until they get it right. Yet the aim is for action to become natural. He only intervenes if there is a collective problem rather than one caused by an individual. He believes it is for the individual to figure out the right path to take. Once training sessions are completed, this is when he becomes more paternalistic. On that basis, the relationship between Alexander-Arnold and Klopp bloomed.

His progress was marked in April 2019 when, against Southampton, he became the fifth-youngest player in Liverpool's history to reach 50 Premier League appearances. Already he was keeping legendary company – hitting the milestone just twenty-eight days after Steven Gerrard. Jamie Carragher, second on Liverpool's all-time appearance list, was three months and three days older when he reached that landmark. Carragher never classed himself as a superstar. 'But Trent is going to be a superstar,' he insisted when we met at a bar which coincidentally was just over the road from Trent's old school, St Mary's. 'He's going to be one of the top right-backs in the world,' Carragher continued enthusiastically. 'He's got a great physique. He moves like a top-class footballer. What will determine his legacy and how people in this city will view him is when things go wrong. Would he look to move on or would he look to stay and get Liverpool back to where they should be?'

Carragher never had that option. Arrigo Sacchi was impressed with his performances against Chelsea in the Champions League in 2005 when the legendary Italian manager was involved at Real Madrid – so were AC Milan. But offers never came. In 2019 Trent is one great young player in a system of great players. 'There will come a time when supporters look to Trent because of his ability as the salvation,' Carragher thought, having been through that process himself. He had always lived in the north end of Liverpool whereas Trent moved from Woolton in the south end to Hale in Cheshire at the start of 2019. Most of Liverpool's players live in Formby or the belt south of Manchester which gives rich people privacy. Would this change him?

'I always thought that when Liverpool weren't doing well, it was my job to get them back doing well,' Carragher said. 'When things are going well, you can't play on the fact you're local and then when things turn badly, disappear. A proper supporter wouldn't do that, would they? There's a difference between being a local lad and the crowd thinking you're one of them. My advice to him would be to stay for ever, no matter what happens.'

The views from the raised front and rear platforms at Liverpool's academy in Kirkby have changed since Jürgen Klopp spent part of his first day in charge watching an Under-18s match on the pitch below while sipping black coffee from a machine that he soon insisted on replacing. Three and a half years later, you can not only see Anfield's new main stand shimmering in the distance, reminding young players where they could be if they realize their talent, there is also the new training ground, visible in the opposite direction rising from playing fields next door on Simonswood Lane.

The academy was completed in 1999, and though pictures of Michael Owen, Jamie Carragher and Steven Gerrard were placed on the walls, each of those players' development had been helped most by the coaching delivered at the previous youth-team base just behind the Anfield Road end of the ground. The centre at Vernon Sangster is now a car park. And despite the tens of millions of pounds pumped into Kirkby, by 2015 the highest number of Premier League appearances by any player to have come right through the system was Jon Flanagan's 40-game stretch across five years between 2011 and 2016.

Klopp identified that geography was hindering the experiences and progression of young players. Calling on a youngster to train with the first team at short notice was not really an option because he'd have to wait for at least half an hour while the player made the journey across town. He could then either start the training session without him or allow him to join in later, but that defeated the point to some extent because he was missing out processing time relating to instructions. That player's absence might then have an impact on any of the plans at the academy throughout the rest of the day too.

When Klopp went to Mike Gordon and asked whether Fenway could move Liverpool's training base onto one site, the ownership group realized it did not have a spare £50 million to grant Liverpool's manager his request. But he was doing well, Liverpool had lost cup finals but at least they were in them – they were nearly back in the Champions League as well. The quick agreement of an updated contract in the summer of 2016 proved he was committed to the club until at least 2022 and Fenway reorganized their finances to ensure Klopp got what he wanted.

When Trent Alexander-Arnold celebrated his 17th birthday, he woke up the next morning to find Klopp had been appointed as Liverpool's manager. Inside twelve months, he had made his full Liverpool debut in a League Cup victory over Tottenham Hotspur. 'I like what I see in this player,' Klopp said with some understatement at the time. By the start of the next season, Alexander-Arnold had established himself as Klopp's first-choice right-back. Liverpool's charge to the Champions League final that season started with a qualifying game in Hoffenheim and the 18-year-old had already taken over set-piece responsibilities despite being the youngest player in the team. It was his free-kick which put Liverpool on their way in Germany, setting a tone of improbability in the campaign which followed.

Alex Inglethorpe became Liverpool's academy manager in 2014 after being promoted from his role as Under-21 coach and he watched the Hoffenheim game from Kirkby with a selection of coaches who had been there throughout the teenager's development. The afterglow of the moment involved thoughts about Alexander-Arnold's path, which had first crossed with Inglethorpe's four years earlier. Back then Inglethorpe saw, 'Clearly a good player but not one who everyone was saying was a definite first-team player. He had things which a lot of people liked about his game, but there was a lot that needed to improve as well. The thing he did have was stability around him. His mum was an incredible woman – a huge influence, who above all was honest, particularly about performance and attitude towards training. She was an extension of the coach's voice. She was sensible and realistic and this meant Trent could never really get too carried away with himself even when it came to contracts. He wasn't paid to fail. By the time he broke into the first team he was still on an academy salary. He played the long game. There was never an argument about money. You'd offer him a deal and he'd sign it, leaving him a few quid richer but not by much. He was a throwback in that respect.'

The free-kick against Hoffenheim and the hat-trick of assists against Watford fifteen months later involved the same technique in the player's armoury, but Inglethorpe believed this was mainly learned and practised behaviour. 'He didn't have then the cross that he's got now,' he said. 'He was technically OK and physically good. But he invested in himself. He never believed that his talent was fixed. He wasn't born with all of his ability. He's worked bloody hard at becoming all of the things we now see. And he has been coachable, which is often an undervalued characteristic in a young player. He might not have liked hearing an honest appraisal of where he was but he'd always respond, coming back the next day working harder and putting it right. He would stay behind regularly. He is obsessive about getting better.

'The big question mark with him was around the theme of quitting,' Inglethorpe continued. 'There are definitions of quitting. One is stopping and standing still. Quitting can also be losing concentration and getting sent off, giving up mentally. As a teenager, his definition of quitting was making a rash tackle, letting his head go too easy. We constantly tried to put him in a position where he could quit and see whether he gave up. Gradually, he became stronger. Now, he's as tough as old boots.'

Inglethorpe described himself as Alexander-Arnold's 'nemesis for some time'. He may have had talent but that did not mean he did not have to work hard at becoming better. He saw a teenage footballer who was desperate to prove people wrong – as well as his coaches. Klopp, he thought, was the best person the player could have had waiting to use him at first-team level. Inglethorpe called Klopp 'the best youth-team manager in the world' because he appreciates how to handle young players, offering a mix of trust and guidance: 'Jürgen understands they'll come with mistakes but he might get a fantastic player at the end of it. With a local lad, especially, he recognizes that he potentially gets slightly more in terms of time: the player might not run as fast as a Salah or Firmino but he might run further because the starting point for his Liverpool career is earlier and because of an in-built commitment to the shirt, it finishes it much later.'

In academy football circles there had for a long time been a view that Barcelona's was the best in world football, a club where identity is defined at youth levels in terms of style rather than by the first team. Inglethorpe considered that model impossible to follow in England because Barcelona were able to cherry pick not only the best young Catalonian players but also across Spain, where the contractual laws meant the smallest clubs were only ever a year away from losing their best talent to the biggest clubs like Barcelona. He described this as an 'incredible advantage', also believing the system at first-team level was so sacred in Barcelona that no manager would dare change it any way so, no matter what, the academy teams could play with the same style.

The way at Liverpool had historically been less about tactical systems and more about mentality: the instillation of a winning belief coupled with humility and a care for the club and the city. This, really, was Bill Shankly's way. Shankly passed that ethos across his staff, into his team and around the supporters inside Anfield – spreading it across the city. His ideal lived on through Steve Heighway, who led Liverpool's youth operation for almost twenty years, delivering talent such as Gerrard, Carragher and Owen for the first team as well as Robbie Fowler and Steve McManaman before them. When Gerrard left Liverpool for Los Angeles Galaxy in 2015 there was a feeling that something was lost because the captain had been the last carrying the baton all the way from Shankly's time. This period lasted for less than eighteen months, though, as Inglethorpe created the space for Heighway's return as a mentor for the Under-13s and 14s, while Gerrard eventually became the Under-18s coach. Inglethorpe appreciates which sort of player Klopp now wants and this correlates with the club's deepest traditions, which continue to be transmitted through the fanbase.

'I think supporters like to have role models who don't give up and are tough when the going gets tough: players who arrive in the big moments,' Inglethorpe said. 'Jürgen feeds into this naturally because he wants young players who have personality on the pitch. Does he have the drive but is he also humble? Is he able to adapt and understand quickly what he wants? He wants them to compete and work very hard – is he robust? They've also got to be able to influence the game in and out of possession. Ultimately, they've got to be better than what he's already got. Can he play?'

The pressure of dealing with the trappings of being a first-team player is always hard to predict because fame and money do change footballers. 'You go on supposition,' Inglethorpe admitted. 'Now I'm a bit older I've got a few examples of players who I've coached and later reached high levels, but there isn't a standard formula which accurately predicts how a player will react when he's released into the wider world. It's impossible to recreate the sort of stress and duress young footballers are under when they step onto the stage of Anfield.'

At Tottenham Inglethorpe worked with a 16-year-old Harry Kane. 'Aged 14, Harry was in the middle of the group,' Inglethorpe remembered of the future England captain. 'Anyone who said he was destined for great things would be a liar – no one knew.' Like with Alexander-Arnold, Inglethorpe saw in Kane a good youth-team player who was obsessed with getting better but still had a long way to go. Even when he was at loan at Leyton Orient or Millwall, when he was failing at Leicester and not doing so well at Norwich, 'Nobody really knew until Tim Sherwood put him back in the first team at Tottenham – that is when he showed mental characteristics that he could not only survive but thrive. The one thing I will say is, the club never gave up on him. It would have been really easy for Tottenham to cash in and sell him. But no one did.'

Liverpool is not the only English club which has found it hard creating a pathway from the youth levels into the first team. There is the wider landscape to consider, one initially shaped by the success of Wayne Rooney – the teenager who all others were judged against. Within twelve months of Rooney's debut in 2002 Cesc Fàbregas – another 16-year-old – was introduced to the first team at Arsenal and this made English clubs realize there was talent abroad to pick at – though Rooney and Fàbregas were exceptions to the rule. At the end of that season, Chelsea were bought out by Roman Abramovich and other clubs followed – including Liverpool; many of them spending more money than ever on readymade foreign stars. This fast-shifting environment and the demand for instant success meant a lot of good work at the academies went to waste. It was not really a combination that would allow young players to breathe.

Inglethorpe still thinks any player needs one hundred first-team games before he can really start to thrive: to be able to make mistakes, learn and then flourish. 'But the pressures facing managers means they aren't allowed [to make] mistakes and if they do, they can find themselves out of the door,' he said. 'Would a 20-year-old Mo Salah take the place of a 26-year-old Mo Salah? There's no chance of that. What separates the two is hundreds of games of first-team football (225 in Salah's case before he joined Liverpool aged 24). Someone looking at Mo Salah aged 17 would think, "Nice player – playing left-back at the minute, got a bit of potential . . ." but you're not going to play him ahead of the 26-year-old version.'

Some players are beneficiaries of circumstance. While Inglethorpe sensed Alexander-Arnold was getting closer to the levels required that should earn him a first-team chance, it was only when Nathaniel Clyne was ruled out through injury that a berth at right-back opened up. He has since learned his lessons while performing at the very highest stage, where the exposure means global fame.

Inglethorpe had high hopes for another player who has since become a leader at a Premier League club, only not at Liverpool. When he first arrived at Liverpool in 2012, Inglethorpe saw an academy which he thought lacked one clear vision. After Heighway's departure following rows with Rafael Benítez four years earlier, Kirkby had undergone three phases of management, firstly with a Dutchman Piet Hamberg, then Spanish through Pep Segura and then back to English under Frank McParland. Inglethorpe had considered leaving within weeks of his own arrival at Liverpool – then he was introduced to Conor Coady, a teenage midfielder who later became the captain of Wolverhampton Wanderers. Though he would only play once for Liverpool's first team, Inglethorpe fell in love with Coady's enthusiasm and professionalism – he was the one player he felt he could work with.

Inglethorpe's own career had been spent mainly at Leyton Orient, where he was a centre-forward. He entered management with non-league Leatherhead while also working in a series of warehouses to support his income. The offer to go to Spurs as Under-18s manager came when he was in charge of Exeter City's first team in English football's fourth tier. Considering his successor Paul Tisdale remained in charge of the Devon club for the next sixteen years, he wondered how his career may have mapped out had he stayed. Inglethorpe left because he considered himself first and foremost a coach. There was talk about him joining the staff with Liverpool's first team before it was suggested he should lead the academy after the club's first-choice option turned them down.

Inglethorpe considered the challenge enormous. He'd inherited a recruitment model from McParland, who bought players like Raheem Sterling from Queens Park Rangers for an initial fee of £500,000 which eventually rose to £5 million. Though Liverpool made a profit of £44 million on the winger, Inglethorpe recognized that Sterling may have stayed much longer had he been attached to Liverpool from the beginning rather than brought in from elsewhere.

He also judged there were huge gaps in Liverpool's programme from Under-8 level to Under-15. Where Liverpool had become very effective at buying in talent at 15 and above, he did not think the club was as effective as it should have been in developing its own talent in the younger age groups. He made it a priority to invest in talent on Merseyside and get more local kids signing for Liverpool instead of their regional rivals. 'We have to go back to basics and pay a little bit more attention to what is in our own back garden before we start looking over the fence into other people's gardens,' he admitted. 'Recruitment is getting harder. It used to be boys joining us at 12 or 13. They had lots of time to develop in the grassroots and that made it easier to identify them. Now we're asking scouts to identify players at six years of age when many have only been playing for a year or so. Equally, there are some six-year-olds who haven't played football yet but might go on to become very good footballers – it means there is a chance someone could fly under the radar. The recruitment has to be very open-minded.'

Inglethorpe's priority was to win the battle on Merseyside first, admitting Liverpool had fallen behind Everton, who had a stranglehold in the area due to Liverpool's decision to widen their recruitment net. This was illustrated by the presence of Tom Davies and Jonjoe Kenny in Everton's first team. While Davies' grandfather Alan Whittle had played for Everton in the 1970s, he grew up – like Kenny – a Liverpudlian.

Inglethorpe worked hard on defining what long-term potential looks like. 'The ones who win you Under-10s games aren't always the ones that reach the first team,' he stressed. Liverpool took more time on background checks, analysing the correlation between birthdates and the chances of success. There was a re-education of coaching. He received full support off Liverpool's owners as well as successive managers: 'Not once have I been asked about a result. I'm in contact with the owners but not once have I been congratulated for reaching a final. The question is always the same: "Who's the next one?" That makes things quite easy. If we can get to cup finals then brilliant. I don't enjoy seeing a Liverpool team lose but I'd rather sacrifice a victory if it meant the development of one player who could make a difference.'

Liverpool won their first FA Youth Cup final in a decade in 2018–19, beating Manchester City. They had beaten City last time and from that team only Jay Spearing and Martin Kelly made any impression on the first team. 'The challenge for any youth-team player isn't just to play for Liverpool it's to win trophies for Liverpool,' Inglethorpe reminded. Spearing and Kelly were only on the bench when Liverpool's first team won its last trophy eight years earlier by beating Cardiff on penalties in the League Cup final. The highest hopes at the academy are for Rhys Williams, a tall defender from Preston, and Jake Cain and Leighton Clarkson, midfielders from Wigan. Paul Glatzel's parents are German but he has been brought up in Liverpool. Insiders at Liverpool's academy describe the teenagers as 'slow burners'. Inglethorpe, meanwhile, is excited by 'lots of players in each age group – I think we have depth now.'

Each of these, of course, is hewn from places out of town. There had never really been a desire amongst Liverpool's Mersey-side supporter base to have a team filled with local players, but it does help the mood when there are more, especially in difficult periods because it removes one discussion about soul. When Liverpool beat Southampton 7–1 in 1999 each of the scorers had been local academy graduates, but none of these players would all win something together.

John Coleman, who was born in Kirkby, recognized the dangers of having too many Liverpudlians in the team. He had taken Accrington Stanley through the non league via four promotions and into League One, initially using players sourced from Merseyside before he realized the pitfalls of this selection policy when players stopped 'digging each other out' and instead turned on those born outside of the area, even if it was unfair.

Inglethorpe thought the challenges came when young local players were pulled away from their family, friends and city. 'Everyone says their city is unique but having come from the outside and having been here for a reasonable period of time I can say that Liverpool is a unique city which produces unique people. In London, you can walk into a room full of supporters and they'll all follow different clubs – including clubs outside London. In Liverpool, there are only two answers you can give. That brings an incredible passion. When you couple that with the history of the city, the hardships it's had, there's no doubt the people are fighters. There's a toughness about the young players – a run-through-brick-wall mentality. They're very authentic, they wear their hearts on their sleeves. You'd go to war with them.'

A recent Liverpool recruit is Bobby Duncan, a forward who in

2016 became the first England player to score a hat-trick against Brazil. The story of his youth-team career underpins the wider challenge at Liverpool. He is Steven Gerrard's cousin and a Liverpool supporter but he still signed for Manchester City, who offered more money. When Duncan began to think he might have a better chance of progressing at Liverpool, he was left out of City's youth teams for a year before his contract ran out and he returned home – joining Liverpool for a quarter of what he was on at City. Inglethorpe thinks Duncan's case is a rare example of a young player making a tough decision based on what might be better for him in the long term. 'Many want paying up front for what they're hoping to do rather than what they've done,' Inglethorpe rued. 'That's not how it really should work. It's instant gratification against deferred gratification, only elsewhere in life you are taught that you put the hard work in and the rewards come much later. Children don't always struggle with that, it's more the people who surround them – the messages that are put into them by agents, parents or sometimes even coaches.'

Phil Thompson became a European Cup-winning captain for Liverpool, but he only joined the club at 14 when he became an apprentice. This meant the novelty of Melwood, the novelty of being around other footballers, never wore off. 'Each morning, I'd thank my lucky stars that I was being welcomed to the club I loved,' he told me. 'I never could have become blasé about my surroundings.'

It worried Inglethorpe that Liverpool – and football clubs generally – might lose the love of players because they have been there for so long. There was a danger that those who have been there since the age of six become institutionalized. 'By the age of 13 or 14, will they be bored of football?' he wondered. 'They're giving up a lot of their childhood. Our challenge is to make it serious with the right age groups, and to recognize when those milestones are. It's important that we create well-rounded good people who, if football is taken away from them, are still good additions to society.'

Clubs are not just on a journey with the boy but with their parents as well. 'If the parents are a bit wonky, you do question whether you want to spend the next ten years with them. He'd have to be Lionel Messi to go through that process. It's so important that parents understand the journey – even more so than the kids – otherwise development is impossible.'

This leads back to thoughts about Trent Alexander-Arnold. A few days earlier, Liverpool had beaten Fulham 2–1 thanks to a late penalty by James Milner. Now aged 20, Alexander-Arnold had said afterwards that Liverpool's endurance was a sign they could win the league. It was a bold statement to make for the youngest player in the team. 'His measurement of success was always higher than a lot of the other kids,' Inglethorpe said. 'That means winning things. And maybe becoming captain.'

The academy manager's fierce blue eyes lit up when he thought of the future: what the first team and the youth system being on one site really means for players. 'Their daily working dream will be visible, which sometimes is important,' he concluded. 'Ultimately, though, the set-up is only going to work if the relationships are right. I've worked at clubs before where the manager has been in the office next door and he might as well be 500 miles away because there hasn't been the desire to integrate the players from the academy into the first team. That isn't the case here. Jürgen's treatment of Trent, and Trent's desire to reward the manager's faith, gives each one of us belief.'

12. DISASTER CAPITALISM

'DO YOU THINK WE DIDN'T TAKE ENOUGH RISKS TODAY? IS THAT WHAT you want to ask? That's a really disappointing question. I tell the boys to take more risks: "Come on, boys, we go for it!" Is there any draw we didn't try to win? What is that? An extra attacker, just to go wild nine matchdays? You think it's PlayStation, bring an extra attacker and football changes? We are offensive enough, football doesn't work like that! Come on . . .'

It was the last question of a post-match press conference inside Goodison Park's main stand when Jürgen Klopp's mood sharpened. It had come from a reporter who not long before had been a part of the club's in-house media team, and it related to Liverpool's intent against Everton: had they showed enough will to win? Klopp's eyes narrowed, as they tend to do when he prepares to unload. In a world where any managerial emotion is received as a form of public breakdown, this was Klopp cracking up.

Though it had been an uncomfortable afternoon beneath dank skies, Liverpool should really have beaten Everton. Storm Freya was rumbling above Merseyside and Goodison's ancient buttresses were juddering. At the suggestion of Tony Bellew, the former world champion boxer, air-raid sirens preceded 'Z-Cars' as the players walked out onto the pitch, giving a sense that Liverpool would need to sustain aerial bombardment. Evertonians were desperate to take something from Liverpool, even a point. In front of the press box, Bellew clasped his hands together and prayed. Two results would represent victory for Everton. Anything but a win would feel like a defeat for Liverpool, especially after the disappointment at Old Trafford.

Liverpool had four clear goalscoring opportunities to Everton's one but Liverpool's finishing was poor. When Mohamed Salah zoomed away from Everton's defence in the first half, it should have been 1–0. When Salah zoomed away from Everton's defence in the second half, it should have been 2–0. Then Fabinho and Joël Matip failed to score despite chances falling to them inside the six-yard box. At the other end, Virgil van Dijk gave one of the most authoritative defensive performances in any Merseyside derby. This, however, was largely ignored due to another frustrating result for Liverpool – another 0–0 draw.

Everton's record against Liverpool this century is worse than Espanyol's against Barcelona or even Getafe's against Real Madrid. Just inconveniencing Liverpool and stunting their title quest was enough to prompt celebrations. At the final whistle a fourth Oasis song was played across the public address system – Everton had done a job for Manchester City who moved ahead of Liverpool at the summit for the first time since the middle of December. Goodison was euphoric. Klopp was damp and irritated. When a ball boy sarcastically clapped as he left the pitch, Klopp confronted him. Once inside, he would unload his thoughts.

It was the result that had most damaged Liverpool in a derby since Everton's last victory nearly nine years earlier when Goodison Park's press room witnessed another sort of unforgettable managerial collapse. Back in 2010 the Merseyside derby had been the first game after New England Sports Ventures bought Liverpool, though the immediate result that followed belonged to the Tom Hicks and George Gillett era because of what Liverpool had been reduced to. When Liverpool had lost to Everton in the past it was usually because they were out-fought, but this time they were out-skilled as well. A car crash of thoughts and messages ensued in the wake of a 2–0 defeat. Hodgson asked for the pressroom window to be shut in order to muffle out the sound of Evertonians gleefully singing 'going down, going down' from the

Winslow pub down below. Hodgson would sneer at a Norwegian journalist for asking him a question about his future – telling him Norway was a country he never wished to manage in again, having been there five years earlier with Viking. Between those moments, there was time for this bewildering reflection: 'That was as good we've played all season,' Hodgson suggested. 'I have no qualms about the performance whatsoever. To get a result here would have been utopia. But I can only analyse the performance. There is no point in trying to analyse dreams.'

With that John Keith, the highly respected broadcaster – someone who had covered Liverpool since the days of Bill Shankly – was heard at the back of the room offering his own instinctive reaction. 'Dear god!' he recoiled. As Hodgson shuffled out of the room Henry Winter, then the *Daily Telegraph*'s chief reporter, was coming in. 'We weren't that bad, were we, Henry?' Hodgson asked, knowing his team were in the relegation zone.

Liverpool's fall had been dramatic. Eighteen months earlier they had finished second in the Premier League, and that achievement had earned Rafael Benítez a new five-year contract. Rick Parry, who started that season as the chief executive and ended it out of work after his relationship with Hicks deteriorated, described Liverpool's league performance as a 'miracle' considering what was happening behind the scenes. Those close to Benítez would describe a 'civil war' at Anfield after Hicks and Gillett fell out, leaving Benítez not knowing really what the game was any more: what to believe and who to follow. If a scene summed up the mood at Melwood it is one from the 2009–10 season when Liverpool finished seventh. Most of the staff had left the training ground late one afternoon but Benítez was still in his office and sat behind his desk. When someone delivered letters, Benítez was surprised by the sudden company. 'Whose side are you on?' the manager asked.

The erosion of a common cause seemed manifest in one moment at Goodison Park under Hodgson when Jamie Carragher sent a pass down the touchline for Fernando Torres to chase. Torres had wanted the ball to feet – though by then he sometimes gave the impression he did not really want the ball at all. The Spaniard stood still. Carragher, quite understandably, roared at him. On the touchline Hodgson grimaced as Everton went 2–0 up. 'John, John!' shouted one Evertonian at John W. Henry, Liverpool's new principal owner. 'You've bought the wrong club.'

'I ask myself, "What makes us special?" Are we one of the biggest cities in the country, or in Europe? Why are we one of the best teams? Why is the team not in Birmingham or London?

'I think it's because the people – the supporters – have a certain nature about them. That's not to say we are better than anyone else. But we're proud and we're never going to let anyone walk all over us. We expect the best and demand the best. We're not intimidated by anyone. And that shows in the defiance.'

Jamie Carragher was thinking about Liverpool the place and Liverpool the football club, which he represented 737 times across seventeen seasons, a record that puts him second on the club's all-time appearance list. 'The connection between the fans and the team,' he said, 'is probably more important here than it is any-where else.'

By 2010 Carragher recognized that connection was shattered. The fans did not identify with what they were seeing on the pitch. The fans did not identify with the way the club was being run off the pitch. There was a genuine fear Liverpool would enter administration and the club would get relegated, though not every-one was willing to recognize that possibility, and this caused a split in the fanbase between those who believed in protest and those who did not. Benítez, meanwhile, was gone. The Spaniard's work divided opinion between those who believed in him and those who considered him too cautious – or even a great divider. In his place Hodgson was acting like a Tory foreign minister on a fact-finding expedition to some war-torn country – unable to come up with any results or even find the right words to bring about any sense of togetherness. This had been an environment created by Tom Hicks and George Gillett, the American businessmen whose supposed investment three years earlier had initially excited Car-ragher for sporting reasons, though he was not alone.

'A big transfer fee was £20 million and we couldn't get there,'

Carragher reasoned. 'We were still operating in the £10-to-£15-million maximum bracket and David Moores recognized he couldn't go any higher. Rio Ferdinand had gone to Man United six years before for nearly £30 million. Our record stood at £14.5 million for Djibril Cissé, a player Rafa inherited because the deal had been sanctioned by Gérard Houllier before he left in 2004. It wasn't until the Americans came in that it felt like we were operating in the same market. Suddenly, there was Fernando Torres, Ryan Babel, Martin Škrtel and Javier Mascherano. These players were coming in for bigger money and it felt like we'd made a jump – that now we were able to get a better level of player that could really push us on and allow us to compete.'

A day after the Americans bought Liverpool they went to a Manchester hotel to meet Carragher and Steven Gerrard who were preparing for an England international friendly with Spain. This was where Carragher encountered Fernando Torres for the first time, who soon became the first big signing of the Hicks and Gillett era.

'George Gillett seemed to know more about Liverpool than Tom Hicks, who came from nowhere to get involved,' Carragher said. Gillett had spent eighteen months trying to buy Liverpool but Rick Parry and David Moores did not believe he had the necessary level of funds to take the club that much further than they were already.

'I remember a new stadium model being brought into Melwood,' Carragher recalled. 'There was a lot of steel and glass. It looked amazing. Maybe I'm wrong but I sometimes wonder how much the global financial crisis impacted upon their plans. We went from a position where it seemed like we had a lot of money to one quite quickly where it felt like we were cutting costs. Clearly, they wanted to build a stadium. That had been their intention. If they build a stadium, the club is worth more and that's what they're in it for. They weren't here because they loved Liverpool, they were using Liverpool to make money.'

Despite his optimism at the beginning, Torres initially did not impress Carragher.

'He wasn't a great trainer, to be honest. If you reduce training at Premier League level to its most basic form, it is a game of foot-ball in small spaces: making the defence organized and tight, keeping possession quick and short, making sure your forward line develops the sort of relationship where one can play off the other. Torres wasn't great at this. But as soon as you had eleven v eleven on a Saturday he became a superstar.

'In pre-season, I was thinking, "*Hmmmmn.*" I wasn't sure about him. I remember him missing a penalty in a friendly during the tour of Asia. He didn't look like he wanted to take it. When I played against him at international level, he looked like a right handful: pace and strength. Rafa obviously knew Torres' game better than any of us but he asked for patience. I don't think he expected anything like what he produced. He [Torres] was very quiet around the training ground – didn't come on many of the team nights out. At Christmas, he came in his own clothes rather than fancy dress. It felt like his missus was his best mate, which is fine, of course. He wasn't one of the boys – a big character in the dressing room. But I always say, if someone is a good player and he's playing well you'll put up with anything. If Torres keeps himself to himself and he's playing well, he's a lovely, quiet lad. If he's not playing well, he becomes a miserable bastard.'

That was what Torres was in 2010, following a summer where he'd become a World Cup winner with Spain and been told a pack of lies by those in suits representing Liverpool about the dir-ection of the club, who convinced him to stay. By then Torres' relationship with the midfielder he'd dovetailed so well with for eighteen months at the beginning had also frayed. In a victory over Sunderland Steven Gerrard avoided Torres when celebrating a goal. Before, they had helped complete each other's game and, in Carragher's opinion, were 'the best number 9 and number 10 in Europe'.

Liverpool finished fourth in 2007–08, the first full season with Hicks and Gillett running the club. Considering the team would push on in the next campaign, the recruitment in the summer of 2008 was sub-standard. Robbie Keane was the big one, a £20-million recruit from Tottenham Hotspur. He was nearly 28 years old, in the prime of his career, and had already experienced big moves to Inter Milan as a teenager and then Leeds United when they were competing for trophies – though they were ones that never arrived.

'Rafa pulled me to one side and told me he was thinking of signing Robbie. "What do you think?" To be honest, I didn't understand it. Not because of Robbie's ability. Mainly because from around February onwards Rafa had started playing Stevie as a number 10 and he developed a brilliant relationship with Torres. Stevie won PFA player of the year. He scored more than twenty goals and set up twenty. There wasn't a better front two in Europe. So, when Rafa bought Keane, I couldn't figure out where he was going to play. Robbie wasn't better than Stevie in the number 10 role. He wasn't better than Torres. Maybe he could drop Stevie back but we had Alonso and Mascherano there already.

'Robbie got games at the start but after a Champions League game in Marseille someone asked Rafa about Keane's chances of getting back in the team. Rafa sort of said, "Well, what can you do when you've got Torres and Gerrard?" I understood that, but why did he buy him in the first place, because it was so obvious? I know people say you need a squad and top players, but when you spend really big – and Robbie Keane was a big transfer for us at the time – he's surely got to be first choice in a system that suits him, when our system didn't, really.

'I think it's easy to forget how good that Liverpool team was. To make a difference, you had to be some player. It probably surprised Robbie Keane just how good we were. You are talking about a really good player in the Premier League. But we were one of the best sides in Europe. In training early on you could see – this wasn't taking us onto the next level.

'We lost only two games that season but still didn't win the league. I always look back at the summer before. None of the signings worked in a big way. Imagine if one or even two had. Could that have pushed us a little bit further? There was Keane, two full-backs (Philipp Degen and Andrea Dossena) – who were really poor, a goalkeeper (Diego Cavalieri) and a winger in [Albert] Riera, who did well for that season but he was only ever good enough to do all right. He was never going to be a game changer. None of them were.'

The summer of 2008 had also been the period that sowed the seeds of Xabi Alonso's departure. Carragher was Alonso's friend but he could understand why Benítez was willing to let him go. The Basque midfielder's performances for eighteen months had been inconsistent and he wasn't always chosen for the biggest matches. Benítez's plan had been to sell Alonso for £30 million and replace him with Gareth Barry for half of that fee, and this would have reduced the need to sign another left-back in Dossena for £8 million, giving him extra cash to spend on other areas of the side.

Carragher, though, had spoken to Barry, who told him that he did not consider himself a left-back, 'or a left midfielder – where Rafa had spoken to him about playing as well, so this idea was never going to work out as Rafa had planned.' Because it became a public matter the Aston Villa manager Martin O'Neill was furious and raised his asking price for Barry to £30 million. Arsenal's subsequent bid for Alonso was just £15 million. Liverpool would end up losing money and Benítez was told that the moves would not receive the sign-off that he wanted. While Carragher could understand why this might frustrate Benítez, this had not been the reality painted by the manager originally when the idea was first suggested and so he could also understand the position of the club as well. The situation had one way or another been poorly managed.

It proved to be the one time where Benítez publically lost a political fight with a figure inside Liverpool. Alonso was enormously popular and the supporters sided with the midfielder. In a pre-season friendly against Lazio at Anfield the chorus of 'you can shove your Gareth Barry up your arse' made collective opinions very audible indeed.

'I don't think Rafa ever forgot that,' Carragher believed. 'He was always going to sell Xabi the next year, no matter what happened. He wanted him out of the club but the only way to save face was to play him, get him back into form and earn a big fee.'

Alonso had been brought to Liverpool by Benítez and their

relationship had been strong. When he found out that Benítez wanted to sell him, however, the feeling changed. When Alonso refused to play in a game against Standard Liège in Belgium – which would have cup tied him in the Champions League and potentially reduced the number of clubs interested in him – Benítez reacted by dropping him for the league season opener at Sunderland three days later, choosing Damien Plessis instead. Plessis was a gangly French midfielder with just two Premier League games behind him. Benítez recognized his decision had been a mistake and introduced Alonso at half-time. Liverpool played much better after that though they had to wait until the 83rd minute to secure their narrow victory through a Torres goal.

In an odd sort of way Benítez won the battle because in 2008–09 Alonso delivered his best performances in a Liverpool shirt. Carragher was thinking, 'Give him a new contract – just do it. No matter what you think of a player, if he's as good as Xabi you find a way of keeping him.'

Manchester United would win the title, finishing four points ahead of Liverpool. 'What cost us were the seven draws at home,' Carragher felt. 'Could we have taken more of a chance from the bench? Rafa was very much a manager who thought, "If you can't win, don't get beat," rather than going berserk and throwing extra attacking players on.'

There were times, though, when it seemed like Liverpool might win the title. A 4–1 victory at Old Trafford ranks as one of the club's greatest results in the Premier League era. Yet Carragher recalled more vividly the game where Aston Villa went 2–1 up at United a few weeks later, only to lose 3–2. Tottenham had also led by two goals at Old Trafford just as the Liverpool team boarded a flight back to Merseyside after a comfortable victory of their own at Hull. By the time they landed, United had won 5–2.

'Every season under Rafa, the spine of the team was getting better and better,' Carragher thought. 'In 2004 we bought Alonso, in 2005 we bought Reina, in 2007 we bought Torres and Mascherano – we'd also bought Agger and Škrtel in this period. Every year, the team was growing. Then one player leaves [in

Alonso] and it falls apart. I look back and I think, *"Argh* . . . we were so good – we were one of the top five teams in Europe, we were so close . . ." '

In 2009–10 Liverpool lost two out of their first three league games. Liverpool had lost two in the whole of the previous campaign. 'Psychologically, that's massive – we're still only a few points off the top but you feel miles behind already,' Carragher reflected. After losing to Aston Villa at Anfield, Benítez mentioned in his post-match interview that the senior players needed to do more. Carragher was unhappy. Steven Gerrard was unhappy as well. Benítez reasoned that the comment had been taken out of context but Liverpool's senior players saw it as a questioning of their commitment. Considering Carragher and Gerrard had missed so few games and made themselves available even when they were injured over the previous five seasons under Benítez, the moment sat awkwardly. In the dressing room after the Villa defeat, Carragher spoke up – Liverpool had conceded from a set-piece again and he believed the organization was not as it should have been. Liverpool rarely conceded from corners and Carragher thought Benítez's argument was overlooking the absence of Sami Hyypiä, a towering figure in defence who had left the club following a disagreement with the manager after he was left out of the Champions League squad the season before. Philipp Degen, a hopeless Swiss full-back, was preferred without the decision ever being explained to Hyypiä, despite his seniority.

'I shouldn't have lost my rag but it was just emotion at the end of the Villa game,' Carragher reasoned. Benítez then appeared in the next team meeting with a statistic-filled chart which he thought proved Carragher's complaint incorrect. When Benítez moved on to direct criticism of Gerrard, Mascherano became involved, which was a surprise considering the Argentine had been viewed as one of the manager's favourite players, especially after he had lost the trust of Alonso. Mascherano had wanted to sign for Barcelona that summer and maybe this explained his reaction.

Details of the tense meeting did not emerge in the press, though Benítez's argument about Liverpool's supposed strength at set-pieces made a column written by the Spanish journalist Guillem

Balague – which led to some of the Liverpool squad becoming suspicious and disappointed. After all, the players had been able to keep the details of the post-match Villa meeting a private matter. Had the manager?

Whereas Roy Evans and Gérard Houllier stayed a year too long because of the strength of the relationships built with the owners and directors, Benítez had one season where it did not go well and wasn't given the chance to rectify his mistakes. Benítez, unlike Evans and Houllier, had, in fairness, for nearly three years tried to plough through fallow fields created by Hicks and Gillett, who were a different breed of operator compared to David Moores and Rick Parry.

'Me and Stevie always get, "You two got Rafa the sack." But we didn't,' Carragher said. 'Rafa got himself the sack, not only by the results at the end but also the fact he called Martin Broughton out soon after he came in as the new chairman.'

Broughton, despite being a lifelong Chelsea fan, had been appointed to the board as chairman having led the British Horseracing Board as well as British Airways. He was brought in with one primary responsibility: to sell the club on behalf of Hicks and Gillett. His arrival reflected just how far Liverpool had fallen – David Moores had feared Chelsea's financial power under Roman Abramovich and now, three years after he ceased being Liverpool's chairman, the club he had sold were looking towards a businessman with no prior links who supported the club he was trying to keep up with in the first place but had even less money than Moores to try to help it stay afloat, rather than flourish.

A fortnight after Broughton's appointment Benítez told the media of his frustration that he'd not met the new person in charge, even though, it later transpired, Broughton had twice tried to arrange meetings only for Benítez to cancel them, though his reasoning had been understandable because those meetings had been scheduled on days after games, and in each of those games Liverpool had suffered disappointing results. Benítez claimed he was instead needed on the training pitch. When they did eventually see each other Benítez spent two hours telling

Broughton about all of the problems that existed at Liverpool and all of the things which needed to happen to improve its state. He had arrived with a shopping list which included another new left-back. When Benítez was reminded that he'd signed six players in that position over the previous six seasons, with none of them working, and was then asked to explain why this one was different, Broughton believed Benítez did not give him a proper answer.

Broughton spoke of a 'polarized' Liverpool, damaged by the paranoia that existed in every person who held significant office. He claimed that he wanted Benítez to stay, but Carragher saw the dynamic of the situation differently. 'I think Rafa had run out of leeway,' he said. While this mess unravelled, neither Carragher nor Steven Gerrard spoke publically about the war at Liverpool. This surprised Pepe Reina, who wondered why this was the case in his autobiography, claiming the reaction of senior players in Spain would be different.

'At Liverpool you weren't raised to question the club, values were never an issue,' Carragher explained. 'You'd never see the United players coming out and criticizing the Glazers. Where do you draw the line when it comes to authority? Would it be OK if I came out and said, "I can't believe Rafa Benítez has sold Xabi Alonso and replaced him with Alberto Aquilani"? Everyone would call it a disgrace. I think a lot of the focus was lost because of what was happening off the pitch. Of course, the owners were not good owners, we all knew that. But as a player you cannot afford to make excuses even if they are there. You have to get results on the pitch. I don't look back at that season and think, "We were shit because of the owners." I think we were shit because of us.'

In 2016, five years after George Gillett lost control of Liverpool, he was still paying £125,000 a month in debt repayments. He never had the money in the first place to buy the club and that is why he introduced Tom Hicks, a Texan businessman he'd worked with before through a series of mergers to form the second largest pork and meat processor in the world. Within a year their relationship had soured. The pair's mix of failed gambles, poor decisions and outrageous social and PR blunders left Liverpool supporters at war, fearing for the club's existence. At the centre of that story was Rafael Benítez. For some critics Benítez exacerbated the problems at Liverpool. For many others he had been the solution.

By October 2010, when Liverpool took to the field at Goodison Park placed just above the relegation zone, Benítez was gone. Gillett and Hicks were also gone. Xabi Alonso and Javier Mascherano were gone. Fernando Torres was about to go. Though Liverpool had been bought out, the club's decline had been swift and dramatic. How had it come to this?

Gillett had already been bankrupt once. He had purchased Storer Communications in 1987 but by 1992, when Liverpool finished their league season lower than in any of the previous twenty-seven years, the investment towards Storer's six TV stations had gone badly wrong, racking up debts of £1 billion. His purchase of the company had only been possible in the first place because of high-risk borrowing. In an interview with *Time* magazine five years later he admitted that he often moved too fast and bought too much without considering what came next. 'I've lived my dreams,' he said. 'But then I blow them up.'

Gillett had been born into the level of wealth that can lead to the sort of self-recognition which says enormous risks are fine when they don't seriously trouble a fortune that is always going to be there anyway. His father had been a Wisconsin car dealer and surgeon but his mother's family were much richer having built their fortune in Milwaukee in a variety of local industries. Privately educated, Gillett started buying into sport when he was still in his twenties, firstly with Miami Dolphins in the 1960s then the Harlem Globetrotters, where he maximized his profit by turning the team into a cartoon series which first aired on CBS in 1970. Gillett would buy radio stations across the country and then invest in the beef industry where he focused on leaner meats just as Americans started to become more health conscious. His ownership of one TV company in Nashville allowed him to buy a ski resort in Colorado, which was just about the only thing he bought with his own money.

His vision, laid-back charm and determination had often won other businesspeople over but it was his success with junk bonds which propelled him into a new stratosphere of finance during the 1980s when Reaganite deregulation meant there were more opportunities and even bigger prizes for those connected to money and those who understood the system most.

Though his experience with Storer was a setback, he found a way to rebuild his empire by floating his ski resort on the US stock market. By 2000 he'd salvaged more than half of the billion-dollar fortune he'd lost, and that is when he bought the Montreal Canadiens ice hockey team. North America's population was becoming more Hispanic, and this led to his interest in Premier League football. Like nearly all of his other businesses, Gillett started, in his own words, 'looking for clubs that had a very strong fan base that perhaps weren't as developed as they might have been'. At first he went to Aston Villa, whose owner and chairman 'Deadly' Doug Ellis was willing to sell to Gillett until he found out through Rothschild's that he was borrowing money to seal the deal. Villa were low cost – more than £330 million cheaper than Liverpool, who were also on the market. Gillett needed help and this led to a conversation with Hicks at an ice hockey convention.

While the diminutive Gillett spoke with a folksy drawl, the powerful-looking Hicks came from a different part of the country – an unblinking Texan. They did not seem like natural partners but were both driven by the pursuit of deal-breaking, making enormous profits and then disappearing over the sunset.

By the end of their involvement with Liverpool Hicks had emerged as the dominant character, but at the beginning it had been Gillett's persuasion that brought him into view. After realizing Liverpool's potential through a Google search that revealed the sums of money all Premier League clubs were entitled to through the latest astronomical TV deal, Hicks quickly became convinced 'it was an opportunity to buy a crown jewel in sports at a modest price'.

Hicks, like Gillett, was a disaster capitalist: a repeat asset stripper whose objective wherever he went was to make vast takings, leveraging the price of a fading institution using someone else's money to do it. His background was different to Gillett's in that he wasn't born into wealth. He was more interested in gridiron and dj-ing as a teenager before enrolling at the University of Texas where he completed a finance degree. There were spells in a venture capital firm in Chicago as well as Wall Street before he returned to his natural habitat in Texas where he began specializing in leveraged buyouts which involved low investments with borrowed money then selling high at enormous profit. He became a billionaire in the 1980s, buying Dr Pepper and 7Up with his partner Bobby Haas for $646 million before selling both companies on for $2.5 billion. Like Gillett, Hicks invested in ice hockey and though the Dallas Stars initially thrived under his guidance, winning the fabled Stanley Cup, by 2010 – with Hicks' fortune diminishing – the team finished last in the Pacific Division.

Wealth brought estate and estate brought Hicks into contact with George W. Bush, whose mansion backed onto his land. Hicks had supported the Democrats before but he would soon become Bush's fourth biggest donor and the pair were behind the purchase of the Texas Rangers baseball team in 1988. When Hicks bought Liverpool, he denied the relationship ever existed. Even he, it seemed, appreciated modern Liverpool was not a right-wing city.

Hicks tried to transform Rangers by signing Major League star Alex Rodriguez, for whom he vastly overpaid in a statement of intent that left him without the money to rebuild the rest of a team. The Rangers finished near the bottom of the league in each of the seasons Rodriguez was there, before he was sold at a loss of hundreds of millions of dollars.

Hicks had experience in football before his purchase of Liverpool, having been involved in a group which pledged to invest more than £40 million in Brazilian side Corinthians. His plan in 1998 had been to make them successful and broadcast their games on his own TV station. Like at Liverpool, Hicks and his partners talked big, promising a new stadium and new players, but when the returns on those promises did not meet expectations Hicks pulled away, leaving the club in a financial mess which would take nearly a decade to untangle.

Liverpool should have recognized that partnerships at management level rarely work. In 1998 the joint-managerial reign of Roy Evans and Gérard Houllier lasted just six months, though both had realized within six weeks that two people could not do one job. Rick Parry had not been a part of that decision. Though he dismissed the suggestion that neither he nor David Moores had completed their due diligence on Liverpool's buyers – they too had consulted Rothschild's apparently – Parry felt that Liverpool had been backed into a corner due to the delays caused by the interest in Liverpool from Dubai International Capital, whose promises had led to the purchase of the steel that would build a new Anfield, which still needed paying for. Meanwhile, Benítez needed funds to raise a team capable of challenging Manchester United, Chelsea and Arsenal.

The scream for change meant any fears about the intentions of Hicks and Gillett were largely ignored in February 2007 when the pair sat in front of a cabinet filled with trophies at Anfield and announced, according to Gillett, that their purchase was 'about our passion and our understanding of the fans of this club'. By the end of that year, their connection – which had been a marriage of convenience consummated through the search for profit – had broken down, with the pair pursuing individual agendas in the running of the club. This was confirmed just thirteen months after their purchase when Gillett told a Canadian radio station that his relationship had been 'unworkable for some time' and that he was already willing to sell his stake to Hicks. Though neither businessman has ever spoken publically regarding what started the problems between them, those observing them closely from the first day noticed an uncomfortable relationship. Buying a football club was not, as Hicks had thought, the same as buying a meat-packing business together, when they got on fine. The pressure was totally different and this brought out the worst in them in terms of emotion and ego. It was believed that a straight 50/50 deal with no deadlock provisions was a huge mistake, causing conflict over the biggest decisions.

Both insisted they would 'not do a Glazer' by loading Liverpool with debt but their summer transfer splurge, which included the record signing of Fernando Torres, was made possible by a £350-million loan agreement with the Royal Bank of Scotland and Wachovia, another North American bank. A Hicks spokesman admitted that the loan would see Liverpool paying interest of around £30 million a year on their borrowings, which for context was nearly a third more than it cost to bring just one player, in Torres, to Anfield.

Ultimately, Hicks and Gillett did not spend a single cent of their own fortune on Liverpool. Gillett had claimed as he sat in charge in his first hours as a new owner that a 'shovel needs to be in the ground in the next 60 days'. Though plans were indeed rolled out via a Dallas-based architect firm, and Liverpool City Council granted permission to build a futuristic new Anfield, work would never begin. In Liverpool's annual accounts three years after their departure, it emerged that the club had footed £35 million on design fees as well as legal and administrative costs on the unbuilt arena.

Whenever Hicks spoke in public he made everything seem worse. He admitted to targeting Jürgen Klinsmann as Benítez's replacement, the German manager having got to know Gillett through sharing the same surgeon in Colorado. This led to a period of discord between owners and manager which culminated in Benítez's famous press conference where he answered every question with 'I am focused on training and coaching my team' after being told by Hicks what he thought his responsibilities were following a row over potential transfer targets. As the chasm between Hicks and Gillett deepened Hicks would eventually side with Benítez by rewarding him for Liverpool's second-place finish in 2008–09 with a new five-year contract of which he would only see one season.

When, in January 2010, the *Liverpool Echo* ran with the headline 'For God's Sake, Get Out . . . Before You Kill Liverpool FC' and the newspaper's Liverpool reporter Dominic King wrote an article entitled 'Rafa Benítez should not have to manage Liverpool's debt' it led to Liverpool fan Stephen Horner forwarding a copy to Tom Hicks Jnr, who had been implanted onto Liverpool's board and dispatched to Merseyside in his father's absence.

Because of that move, George Gillett appointed his son, Foster, to the board as well – a board which now had no clout or understanding of football whatsoever. Initially Horner received a one-word response – 'Idiot' – before further exchanges led to Hicks Jnr's infamous 'Blow me, fuckface. Go to hell, I'm sick of you' reply. Hicks Jnr was removed from his position, but getting rid of his father and estranged business partner was proving altogether more challenging.

It would require the mobilization of Liverpool's supporters to push them over the edge, though the cost of politicization was great, splitting the fanbase for a long time between those who believed that action was necessary and those who did not believe it was the responsibility of supporters to wash their dirty laundry in public.

Jay McKenna was in his early twenties when he became the chair of the Spirit of Shankly pressure group, which formed early in 2008 in the months after it became known that Hicks and Gillett had lined up Klinsmann to replace Benítez. McKenna remembered seeing Hicks on his first day in charge at Anfield, emerging from the swinging doors of a city centre hotel wearing a pair of cowboy boots with the Liverpool badge stitched onto the side.

'At the beginning they were welcomed with open arms,' McKenna admitted from the trade union offices in Liverpool's city centre where he worked twelve years later. 'We'd seen Chelsea running into the distance with a lot of foreign investment. Benítez had forced us back towards being a serious trophy-winning club again, on a limited budget, but we still needed more money to get that trophy everyone wanted (the league). Like a lot of fans, I wasn't politicized and I didn't have an understanding of football finance. A financial meltdown doesn't happen at a club the size of Liverpool, does it? There were a few warning signs in the corner of our eyes, but we were doing so well on the pitch, and another Champions League final felt more important than worrying about the new owners.'

Initially, the split on the Kop involved those railing against the owners and the 'support-the-team brigade'. The 2007–08 season was marked by marches and stay-behinds but the campaign to bring focus on Hicks' and Gillett's commitment to Liverpool, as well as their relationship, intensified after it became public knowledge they had discussed Benítez's successor in Klinsmann. While Rick Parry reasoned this was purely the reaction of two hard-nosed American businessmen after Benítez did not dismiss the possibility of him returning to Real Madrid, Spirit of Shankly – which formed two months later – considered the revelation an undermining of the office of Liverpool manager, regardless of who happened to sit in the position.

Opinion about Benítez, despite delivering two Champions League finals (one of which was won) and an FA Cup in his first three seasons, was divided by that point, with those willing to back him all the way because of his achievements on a budget, set against others who were dismissive, believing the fear of losing often stopped him from developing the courage to go and win what Liverpool supporters really craved – the Premier League title.

Benítez was now at the centre of the war and Spirit of Shankly considered it important that he was well-briefed about supporter activities. Then came a level of antipathy towards SoS. Already some supporters thought the protests were not the right thing to do, claiming the owners were surely not as bad as they were being made out. Some concluded that Benítez might use the environment as an excuse. Then there was, as McKenna put it, 'that Scouse thing of "who are you to tell me what to do?" The, "I should be meeting Benítez, what makes you so special?"' It was concluded by many that Benítez was playing a game within a game. Because nobody was running the club on fair means, perhaps he could use the inertia to gain more power over recruitment and the academy. Benítez thought Parry acted too slowly when it came to signings, and he wanted Steve Heighway out, the legendary winger who had helped bring through Steven Gerrard and Jamie Carragher at junior levels. Though Liverpool had reached two FA Youth Cup finals in three years, Benítez believed none of the players were good enough for the first team, and this eroded his relationship with Heighway, who had the sympathy and support of Gerrard and Carragher. Whether Benítez was right about the quality of those players is hard to gauge. There were some suggestions that he didn't really believe the players were not good enough, rather he just wanted more control. That none of them enjoyed long Premier League careers at other clubs might suggest he was right if he did feel that way, though.

SoS would eventually attract more than 50,000 members but interest in the demonstrations against Hicks and Gillett only accelerated when the team's fortunes slipped and fans realized they were merely turnstile fodder, that their hard-earned cash was being used to pay off the loans taken by the owners rather than improve the standing of the team.

Though it wasn't viewed this way at the time, perhaps Benítez's relationship with Xabi Alonso deteriorated because he was forced into selling him to raise the funds to ensure Liverpool remained competitive. McKenna saw it that way, 'a consequence of what was happening off the pitch: if the manager had the money he would not have had to wheel and deal, thinking about how to maximize what he had. I think this was the first time what was happening at boardroom level affected the team and the harmony at the club.'

McKenna looked back at the Hicks and Gillett era in two phases: 'The first, between 2007 and 2008, everything was muddled, not very professional – they were actively at war with their own staff. Parry goes, press officer under suspicion: it was very chaotic. They're making mistakes, giving interviews and saying mad things. This makes them easy to be got at.

'Then there was a professionalization of the operation. Christian Purslow comes in. Paul Tyrrell follows . . . dossiers are made on fans.'

Purslow had been hired as a managing director to renegotiate the outstanding £350-million loan but could not resist involving himself in football business, of which he had no experience. This led to clashes with Benítez. Tyrrell, meanwhile, became the club's new head of communications and he was more combative than his predecessor, Ian Cotton. In 2013 it was revealed that Tyrrell had compared Liverpool supporters fighting for change to the

Khmer Rouge. In a document he stated that some fan groups were like 'the sporting version' of Cambodia's 1970s revolutionaries, wanting to 'get to Year Zero to start all over again and see the opportunity of furthering their general political beliefs through LFC'. Spirit of Shankly said it was disgusted to be compared to a 'murderous genocidal regime just for taking a different stand to the club's management'.

McKenna: 'No longer were we just fighting for the club, no longer were we fighting Hicks and Gillett, who were like two punch-drunk boxers where you just had to keep hitting to grind them down; it felt like there were people who were actively coming after us. They were willing to fight back, and elements of the club were at war with their own fans.'

When McKenna heard Gillett was staying at the Crowne Plaza he led a march to the hotel and it became clear to him then that, at the very best, the owners were way out of their depth. 'Gillett was sat in the foyer and we surrounded him before security and police turned up. He pretended to be on his phone and agreed to meet one of us providing everyone else left. He denied he'd said half of the stuff that everyone was understandably so wound up about, and then he tried to blame Hicks. He had no proper understanding of what was happening and he was an owner who was trying to spin his way out of it. They didn't know what they'd bought or who they were taking on. They just saw Liverpool as an investment opportunity.'

There are owners in Premier League history who will be remembered as worse because of how far a club tumbled, but Hicks and Gillett had the potential to be the very worst because of Liverpool's size. Had it not been for the sharpness and intervention of people like McKenna – and many others, some of whom were not SoS members – Liverpool may have been docked points and possibly suffered relegation in 2010–11 as a consequence. It was their meetings and marches which led to an email campaign that forced the banks to reconsider their support of Hicks and Gillett.

'It would have been even worse had they been like the Glazers, who were bad but clever with it,' McKenna reflected. 'Hicks and

Gillett were bad but not that good at being bad. They made themselves an easy target – said too many things, never delivered success – but had Liverpool won the league in 08–09, we never would have got rid of them inside eighteen months.'

There were many initiatives led by SoS but the most significant was the most modern: an email campaign which placed pressure on the banks supporting Hicks and Gillett. This lead to a 2010 court battle and a series of failed legal challenges by the owners which resulted in them being labelled 'untrustworthy' by a High Court judge. Hicks had fought ferociously to prevent the sale of the club to New England Sports Ventures, a group led by John W. Henry, and he made a final attempt to negotiate an agreement with Mill Finance that would have seen the US hedge fund repay Hicks' and Gillett's huge loan. The move, which would have enabled Hicks to sell his shares and leave Liverpool with a profit, failed when the High Court approved NESV's £300-million takeover, which Hicks called an 'epic swindle', announcing he would seek $1.6 billion in damages. When those proceedings were concluded between the club and its former owners in 2013, both Hicks and Gillett walked away empty-handed.

McKenna held pride at the resistance that contributed towards the owners' removal and the rise of an organized movement that has since given supporters a collective voice able to challenge the club over all sorts of issues. Yet there was a sadness that supporters could no longer only be simply supporters – that paranoia had infested a place fans like McKenna used to escape life's problems rather than extend them.

'Everyone was jaded and the new owners met a very different fanbase to the one that greeted Hicks and Gillett three years earlier,' McKenna said. 'So much about the club was broken.'

REALITY

13. IF I HADN'T SEEN SUCH RICHES, I COULD LIVE WITH BEING POOR . . .

THERE WAS STILL EXCITEMENT ABOUT THE NEW TAKEOVER. TOM HICKS and George Gillett were making all sorts of promises and, in early May 2007, Liverpool had their second Champions League final in three seasons to look forward to.

On a Wednesday night they had knocked Chelsea out in a semi-final via a penalty shootout. On a Sunday afternoon they went to Fulham in a Premier League game where the outcome did not seem to matter because elite European football had already been secured for the following campaign.

It was by chance that just at the point the Chelsea squad were preparing to travel the short distance to Arsenal, whom they were playing the next night, boisterous Liverpool supporters made their way to Craven Cottage passing down King's Road and beside Stamford Bridge, Chelsea's home.

Impossibly, there was no security and one supporter – egged on by his mates – saw his opportunity, boarding the Chelsea team bus with a red Athens banner draped over his shoulders. Chelsea, of course, would have gone to Athens instead of Liverpool had the outcome been different at Anfield a few days earlier. A Benny Hill moment ensued: no sooner than he'd got on, he was being chased off by two members of Chelsea's coaching staff, as well as John Terry, the captain who symbolized the club he'd always represented. Those present recall the steam shooting from Terry's ears and a volley of abuse going both ways.

It proved to be the incident which led to the formation of *Boss* magazine. Dan Nicolson had not been in London for the Fulham game which Liverpool, fielding an under-strength team ended up losing, but lots of his mates had. Upon hearing the story, he realized lots of unusual things happened on away days but nobody was documenting them, certainly not in a memorable way. Occasionally, one of the tales would appear on a fans' forum, reach page four within a couple of hours, and then get forgotten. 'A lot of the lads were around the same age, in their early twenties, and we came to realize that we wanted something down in print so thirty years later we could look back and smile,' Nicolson explained.

Liverpool's casual culture had been chronicled before in *The End*, whose contributors included Peter Hooton, the singer from The Farm, as well as author Kevin Sampson and the *Daily Mirror*'s Brian Reade. Hooton had described *The End* as a dig at anything that was in fashion and, with Britain in the grip of Margaret Thatcher's rule, that made the editorial line strongly anti-Conservative, though politics was always discussed in an indirect manner. In many ways *The End* became a social commentary on Liverpool itself: not only the trends but the city's history, nightlife, music, pubs, football and those that went to the football. It moved away from the traditional music fanzine and, in the words of James Brown who later edited *Loaded*, 'created the new template for ground-level football writers'. Fundamentally, *The End* represented scally culture, which was about as far away from the hipper cliques of art student types and London-oriented trendies as you could be. Paul du Noyer, the music writer, summed these lads up as 'potentially the least lovable rogues you would never wish to meet', but Nicolson believes he and his mates a quarter of a century later fall into another category which du Noyer described: 'ordinary boys, inclined to naughtiness but hardly vicious'.

The End ran between 1981 and 1989. In the gap of eighteen years before *Boss* the fanzine void was filled with football-led publications that catered more for the anorak: the recording of on-the-pitch moments came first, taking priority over anything that happened off it. Nicolson thought the casual culture had remained throughout that period, only there was nobody willing to record it.

While Liverpool might have millions of followers all over the world, the base of their hardcore home and away support probably amounts to no more than 200 people, or 200 'divvies' as they are known between themselves. 'That means only a small number will play music or write a fanzine,' Nicolson reflected. 'In 2007 that became me and my mates.'

The following year, Liverpool would become the European Capital of Culture. After decades of underinvestment from central government and a subsequent social slide, the city was beginning to feel valued again. Visitor numbers were on the up and new venues, bars and restaurants lent a more cosmopolitan sheen. Liverpool's signing of Fernando Torres helped push this feeling along and, for a while, it seemed as though the city felt more of a connection with Spain than the rest of England.

Nicolson had always read the fanzines of rival teams and admired the observational witticisms in Everton's *When Skies are Grey* as well as *United We Stand*: 'It made me realize that although we supported different clubs, we tended to get up to the same sort of mischief.' He wanted *Boss* to cover both of Merseyside's football clubs. He wanted it to be a black and white anonymously written magazine, appealing to no particular market of people other than those who were interested in football fan culture. There would be no by-lines or fame attached to the stories: 'We weren't pretending to be writers.'

There would be no commercial angle either. He knew a group of Evertonians who were going to Kharkiv in Ukraine for a Europa League game. 'They were taking the overnight train from Kiev,' he said reverently. 'On the way home from a Half Man Half Biscuit concert in Manchester I plucked up the courage to ask them whether they'd like to be involved in *Boss*. But they laughed it off as Kopite behaviour.'

The first issue was designed using desktop publishing software. Nicolson printed it out and photocopied it at Hope University where his brother was studying. Then we went home and stapled it all together. Between 2007 and 2015 there would be sixteen issues of *Boss*: 'We didn't think we needed to commit to one every quarter, but only when it felt right. There was no big fanfare behind it, no sales pitch or strategy. We'd print 1,000 copies at a pound a go and it would sell out every single time.'

Boss magazine morphed into *Boss Nights*. Nicolson and his mates knew lots of lads who were in bands. As young Liverpool supporters from Liverpool, they wanted somewhere to go after the match that served cheap lager and played good music – for the afternoon to be extended into the evening. The first gig was at the Static Gallery in Liverpool's city centre. The popularity of the magazine meant that 300 tickets for the night sold out straight away.

'This was just a hobby – alongside our other hobby of going to the match,' Nicolson stressed. 'We couldn't have turned it into a business in the early days because Scousers just don't buy into that. You're meant to give something back rather than shout about what you're up to.'

Boss Nights became non-ticketed and free entry. After a goalless draw at a Merseyside derby in May 2013 there were hundreds inside the venue and what seemed like as many waiting outside. When a firecracker was thrown underneath the wheels of a police car which had turned up to check on the gathering crowd, the vehicle reversed out quickly like it was Northern Ireland at the height of the Troubles. A convoy of police cars did not shut the venue down that night but it did show just how popular these events were becoming amongst Liverpool's younger local fanbase.

When riot police tried to break up another event held at Sound on Duke Street after a victory over Manchester City in 2014 seemed to put Liverpool in touching distance of another title, Nicolson appreciated *Boss* needed more space. Jayne Casey had been respected on Liverpool's music scene ever since the heyday of Eric's on Mathew Street. She ran Cream for years and now she was involved at District – located in the city's largely underdeveloped Baltic Quarter where the warehouses around Jamaica Street were slowly being turned into party venues and work spaces. The Baltic Quarter felt disconnected to the rest of the city in 2014 but it became *the* new area to go to – thanks, in part, to the popularity of the nights at District, as well as the emergence of other venues like Camp and Furnace.

The early *Boss Nights* at District, however, did not run smoothly and on one occasion someone set off a Marine-grade warning flare. From behind the fire and the smoke, Nicolson assessed there was nothing malicious about the intent because the events were never violent or even particularly aggressive. 'It's just what happens when young boisterous lads are having a good time,' Nicolson thought. 'Those early events were 100 per cent a hardcore Scouse thing. If someone turned up wearing a replica shirt they'd feel really out of place, maybe even intimidated.'

Jamie Webster was wearing an Under Armour tracksuit and a pair of black Adidas equipment trainers. He had rented out some space in a recording studio in the Vauxhall district of Liverpool, just to the south of the city centre. In the reception area of the studio there was a snack machine with no snacks next to two battered pieces of a three-piece suite. His room was newer and slightly brighter: bare walls but carpeted floors, two couches, a table with coffee, tea, juice and an ashtray. There were five guitars and he planned to install recording equipment. Webster worked for the rest of the week with his father as an electrician. *Boss Nights* had sent him on a trajectory that he could never have predicted, yet it did not make him much money.

'People make the assumption I'm loaded,' he said. 'My car's outside and it's an 05 Ford Focus with the petrol cap missing. I'm losing a day's pay to rehearse. The music industry is dead and the only way you make money is by doing gigs. Footballers are the new popstars, really. In the past you could be a mediocre band and have a cult following but still make a load of money because everyone was buying records. They don't now. Paul Weller's most recent album sold 25,000, whereas years ago he'd have done millions. Apparently, he couldn't get his head around it.'

Webster was 24 years old and he'd been at the top of the *Boss* bill since the 2013–14 season when he was still a teenager. He'd listened to Oasis, The Jam and Stone Roses in his early teens and this made him pick up the guitar while most of his mates preferred dance music and nights out at places like the Pleasure Rooms. At 17 he'd been in a band, knocking around the gigging circuit in Liverpool, but football always came first. His dad had followed Liverpool all over Europe and Jamie wanted to do the same thing. Having left school and entered employment, he now had just about enough money to travel to away games. 'The gigs here and there,' he reflected, 'only paid for the football – that was all I was arsed about.'

It takes time to develop relationships on the coaches because so many friendships are already formed and long-lasting. Webster had been quiet during those first few months amongst older boys and young men: 'When you're a newcomer you want to fit in so you don't reveal too much about yourself, you try to keep up drinking with them, try to be as angry about the same things as them. I didn't want anyone to know I played acoustic guitar because I didn't know how well it would go down. A lot of the lads were into dance and I got the impression they saw anything else as being shite.'

But the coach, he would come to realize, invited friendships between lads from different parts of the city who would not normally meet: 'I've now got mates who are surgeons, mates who are on the bins, mates who are painters and decorators, mates who are gravediggers and mates who are heads of departments at secondary schools – as well as mates who work illegitimately. But when we all go to the match that gets left behind. Whatever shit you've had to deal with through the week, when you step onto the coach or into the pub before the game it feels like everything goes away. That's why following the footy is the best days. Sometimes the ninety minutes gets in the way because so much else happens at other points in the day. Supporters from different clubs might not understand this because for a lot of them it's all about the result.'

Dan Nicolson echoed this impression: 'Liverpool fans more than any other set of supporters, I think, are about the party,' he said. 'We can get beat and it's disappointing but we'll still be able to put it to the back of our minds, get on with it and have a good time. I think the fellas who go straight home after the game or travel back to wherever they're from, it has more of a tendency to spoil their week. For our lads, once they've got their first pint down them, it's all about the party.'

For Nicolson, supporters were spending so much money following their team, the experience had to be more than just about the result – though that remained crucial.

'Fans of other clubs take themselves far too seriously,' he stressed. 'For the hardcore at Liverpool, it's party time win or lose. If you end up at a bar or venue where there's decent music, you're five or six pints in and you're hugging your mates, the result doesn't matter. To paraphrase Jürgen Klopp: football is about enjoying the journey. As much as you want that trophy at the end and that has to be the aim for the club always, as supporters it's about waking up the next morning and thinking, "Had a laugh there . . ."'

It was because of music that Webster came to be accepted on the coach. One of his more vocal friends had joined him in travelling to away matches and played a video clip of one of his performances. At his next gig in the Head of Steam, next door to Liverpool's Lime Street Station, more than twenty lads from the coach watched him, and that was when one of them suggested he should get involved with *Boss*.

There were no football songs at these early gigs, until Webster played 'Mrs Robinson' by Simon and Garfunkel, using Jordan Henderson's name instead. The reaction from the crowd suggested they wanted more. He remembered the scene vividly from the night Liverpool beat City in 2014, when the possibilities for Brendan Rodgers' team seemed endless, and the floors shook as he suggested, 'We're gonna win the football league again.'

Boss and Webster, however, remained niche or even underground until the 2017–18 season.

'It became much more popular because it became much easier to upload a video to Twitter or Facebook,' Nicolson explained. 'In 2014 the idea of filming something on your phone that might be really pixelated, and trying to upload it to a social media platform, it didn't really happen. All of a sudden technology caught up and you had amazing-quality video and there were all sorts of likes, retweets and shares. This made the interest explode.'

The first song that went viral was one about Mohamed Salah. Webster had performed in the Halfway House pub down the hill from Anfield when he heard someone at the front of the crowd yelling Salah's name to 'Sit Down' by James: 'So I joined in. I thought it was a perfect song to use by Liverpool fans because of the line "If I hadn't seen such riches, I could live with being poor" which relates to all of our frustrations over the last thirty-odd years.'

In Porto, where Liverpool won a Champions League game 5–0, Webster heard 'Allez, Allez, Allez' being belted out for the first time by the away end, a song adapted originally from a 1980s disco hit by the Italian duo Righeira, 'L'Estate Sta Finendo' ('Summer is Ending'), which was taken across Europe by different sets of supporters before being embraced by Liverpudlians Phil Howard and Liam Malone who had recognized it could become the new 'Ring of Fire', the Johnny Cash soundtrack to Liverpool's improbable 2005 Champions League win.

The key moment, both Nicolson and Webster recognized, was after a defeat to Manchester United at Old Trafford in March 2018. Webster recalled Liverpool supporters singing the song incessantly, even though Liverpool were losing: 'Our end was bouncing to it, swinging scarves,' remembered Webster. 'We got beat 2–1 and the whole game, it didn't stop. United were trying to give us shit at the final whistle but we carried on singing at them. They looked confused: "What, we've just beaten you – what are you so happy about?" I did wonder whether everyone would come back to District because they'd be pissed off. Wrong. Everyone was waiting for it. As soon as I started singing, the smoke bombs went off. I had a chest infection that day as well.'

Nicolson had commissioned a music photographer who recorded the gig. The next morning, within an hour of Webster's rendition of 'Allez, Allez, Allez' being uploaded to YouTube, Facebook and Twitter, there had been more than a million hits.

Nicolson: 'The question was now being asked: "Hang on, what's going on there?" We went from being an underground thing to people asking, "Who are they? Why are they so happy? Why are they singing a football song?"'

Liverpool's run to the Champions League final in 2018 was underpinned by the sound coming from the terraces. After Nicolson suggested to the club that it should promote an event hosted by *Boss* with Webster front and centre, the scenes at Shevchenko Park in Kiev resembled a religious pilgrimage. For Nicolson, it was a reminder that supporter culture works best when it comes from the bottom up rather than the top down. 'I don't think there's been a single example at any football club where the club has tried to impose something on the fans and it's looked good,' he said. It helps enormously when the team does well but Nicolson was not the only one to sense something changed around Kiev: 'Local supporters started to feel really good about the club again. When we'd fallen out with Liverpool as fans in the past it was because we felt we weren't appreciated, listened to or noticed. There were times when Scousers felt like the tourists, and out of towners were getting more attention and were worth more to the club than us.'

Nicolson recognized the Scouse and out of town debate was more about where a person is at rather than where they are from: 'I don't think the Scouse hardcore has a problem with a fella from Norway who's really dedicated towards Liverpool, or the fella from London who comes up on the train every other week and looks like us. What they've got a problem with is someone who turns up with a St George's cross flag which says "DEVON REDS" singing, "*Who are ye?*" That's a different problem to one with out of towners as a whole. It relates to a fear about our culture being eroded. "Allez, Allez, Allez" meant all of a sudden the out of towners wanted to become a part of what we were helping create.'

Liverpool lost the Champions League final in Kiev but for those present at Shevchenko Park outstanding memories were formed. The success of the pre-match event led to *Boss* being invited on the club's pre-season tour to America. Nicolson believed it was possible to bottle up Liverpool fan culture and take it elsewhere without losing something. He thinks that providing no concessions are made, these events – supported by the club – can strengthen the sense of Scouse resistance and help others understand better the history of the city: 'If you're a United fan in America, you're buying into the fact the club is the biggest in the world. If you're a City fan in America, you're buying into the probability of success. I think if you're a Liverpool fan in America you're buying into those factors but just as much buying into the off-the-pitch stuff: "You'll Never Walk Alone", the flags, the scarves, the history, "Allez, Allez, Allez". Other clubs will cringe at that but I think our club realized our newer fans want this as much as they want to see a former player at a community event with Mighty Red or a $90 ticket to a friendly game. They want to see Jamie Webster getting up and singing some Liverpool songs because that's what they've seen on YouTube and that's what they think the hardcore are into.'

For Webster *Boss* has provided a platform which helped him form an unlikely reputation for himself considering where he'd come from. He'd grown up in Croxteth, the area of Liverpool where Wayne Rooney was born, and is more synonymous with gang problems. He did not know any other musicians and he wondered what path he may have followed had it not been for football as well as music. He wanted to become a musician in his own right, known for his songs which did not relate to the team he supported, but it has been difficult to escape. 'I'd like people to hear me and not have "Allez, Allez, Allez" in their heads,' he admitted.

His experience ahead of Bayern Munich's trip to Anfield in March 2019 reminded him of how far his voice now travels. In a pre-match gig he opened his set by simply saying hello to a crowd where he struggled to pick anyone out – and the crowd roared back. 'I was like, "Shit – is that for me?" This sort of reaction could only happen in Liverpool to someone who hasn't even released any music yet. It's fucking mad but great.'

Backstage, Munich. That was the name of the venue for the latest *Boss* gig, ahead of the second-leg tie in the Champions League where the aggregate score was locked at 0–0. Jamie Webster was due at 3.30 p.m. but it was 4 p.m. by the time he appeared. The demand for him, amongst an audience of more than 1,000, was absolute. Again, his performance was filmed and within half an hour more than 100,000 people had watched it online. The crowd was different this time, though: more replica-shirt wearers – even more out of towners; proof, it was argued by some critics, that the *Boss* audience was changing.

Nicolson, though, had a plan for the end of the season where he'd booked out the Olympia, a big venue in Liverpool which could hold all of the originals with space for more. Invitation would be by word of mouth amongst those really in the know before a late public announcement, possibly even after the result of the final match against Wolverhampton Wanderers had been settled. 'If we win the league,' Webster said, 'the city won't go to sleep for weeks.'

What happened in Munich helped stimulate belief. It had been an awkward few weeks for Liverpool but a 4–2 win against Burnley got them back on track in the league. Bayern's conservative approach in the first leg had been surprising but Jürgen Klopp recognized that this was an opponent which specialized in results rather than performances. The outcome at Anfield heaped more pressure onto Klopp and Liverpool, but Klopp saw it differently: 'Disappointing 0–0 draw against Bayern when you've had enough chances to win, eh? Maybe it shows you how far we've travelled together already. It's not the first time it has happened to us but it's a very good sign in general for us as a club that we have that respect again within the game. We are a proper contender in a difficult competition with only fantastic teams left. They thought 0–0 was the perfect result. Now we have to show it is not like this.'

From the railway tracks that connected Munich's Hauptbahnhof with Augsburg, the lurid lights of the Allianz Arena had been a reminder of where Liverpool wished to be. That was three Februarys before, when Klopp was less than four months into the job and the Champions League seemed like a dazzling speck in the distance. The opponent, indeed, was a Bavarian club but not the one whose company is a barometer of status.

It said much about Liverpool's progression under Klopp that the competition which the club was desperate to get back into after just one appearance in eight years felt in 2019 like it was no longer a priority, that an exit at the first knock-out stage would not be considered season-defining.

Klopp could have been appointed as Bayern's manager twice but the first time they decided to go for 'the other Jürgen', as Uli Hoeness told Klopp, in choosing Jürgen Klinsmann. The second time, Klopp decided against negotiating their approach because he was so attached to Borussia Dortmund by then he did not think it was right to leave one rival directly for another, especially as he'd compared Bayern to the Chinese because they simply hoovered up all of the talent – and then a James Bond villain because they seemed to take pleasure in the process.

It was argued later that Liverpool had met Bayern at precisely the right moment and this helped ease their progression to the next round, but either side of the tie Bayern had won both league games 6–0. Perhaps that reflected just how far German football had slipped, that their best team could be so dominant domestically but slump out of Europe when they could have even left at the group stage.

It was Sadio Mané's night, his two goals securing a 3–1 victory which was as impressive as any Liverpool had achieved in Europe across three decades. Klopp would claim Liverpool were 'back amongst the top level of European football', but this was already undeniable considering where he'd taken them the season before. It would mean that Liverpool became the only British club in history to win in Madrid, in Milan, in Barcelona and, indeed, in Munich.

Somewhere in the concourses or in the stands, Jamie Webster was there with his mates, amongst them the lads from *Boss*. '*We've conquered all of Europe, we're never gonna stop*,' came the chorus, only now he'd reverted to being a supporter in the crowd rather than a musician playing to an audience. '*Allez, Allez, Allez . . . !*'

14. THE QUIET BOY FROM THE VILLAGE

THE JOURNEY FROM DAKAR TO BAMBALI IS LONG, A NEAR SEVEN-HOUR drive across 450 kilometres of almost entirely dust roads that cut through the Gambia and then back into Senegal, a country where the deep south from a map looks like a finger hanging from the rest of its hand by the scales of skin.

The completion of the Trans-Gambian Highway in 2019 included the building of a bridge at the River Gambia's narrowest point, but back around the time Sadio Mané was discovered, a football scout from Mbour had used a more challenging route, crossing the river by boat at its mouth via Banjul before continuing on towards the remote agricultural and forestry region by bus.

Mané was found in the *navetanes* of Sédhiou – the neighbourhood football leagues where he'd begged his parents to let him play because he was smart and recognized that nobody would go as far as Bambali, a small village 15 kilometres further into the countryside. They had told him that he would be better off trying to become a teacher.

'They thought football was a waste of time and I'd never succeed at it,' Mané recalled when he signed for Liverpool. 'I always said, "This is the only job that will enable me to help you. And I think I have a chance to become a footballer."'

The scout returned north from Sédhiou but rather than stopping at Mbour he went straight to Dakar – another 80 kilometres up the road. He knew Abdou Diatta, a veteran recruitment agent at Génération Foot, an academy set up in 2000 by Mady Touré with the support of his childhood friend, Youssou N'Dour, whose dreams of a professional career in Europe were wrecked by injury before he became a singer and released a song with Neneh Cherry. While '7 Seconds' reached the top three in the United Kingdom in 1994, it remained number 1 in the French charts for sixteen weeks.

Mané's trial took place on the recreation pitches of Dakar's police academy. On initial inspection, Diatta had doubts. 'Sadio came very shy,' he recalled. 'I did not think he would do anything because it seemed like he did not want to go and play.' The impression, however, was quickly dispelled. 'When I saw his touch of ball, I thought, "He a really good player." After two days of testing, I went to the coach and said, "This one, we take it directly."'

That coach was Jules Boucher, a former Senegalese international midfielder. He would meet Mané on Diatta's recommendation and spend fifteen minutes trying to find out more about him. Boucher described him as 'friendly' and 'observant' but understood that he 'did not come to Dakar with great means'. As a footballer Boucher soon witnessed what he thought was a 'high-level player – qualities of speed, dribbling sequences. He was a boy who was always hungry.'

Diatta was concerned about Mané's reluctance to socialize with the other boys his age, whose backgrounds were urban while his was rural, even though that did not show during games where his skill melted into the collective. 'One day I went to him and said, "Sadio, you're a footballer. When you're here, put yourself in the group, with the group, together, all the team." I warned him, "If you continue to be shy like this you risk ending up going back home, because football's like that. You have to be part of this team not outside it."'

The conversation had an impact. Soon Mané was mingling more and Boucher could remember him at times, 'making as much mischief as any of the other players'. Though Mané was loved in Senegal for his football ability, Boucher was just as proud of his development as a person. From Liverpool, Mané would call him regularly asking about news of his family. 'He's a very grateful boy,' Boucher said. 'He has not forgotten his roots.' This was illustrated, Boucher believed, by the player's gesture before the

Champions League final in 2018 when he sent 300 Liverpool jerseys home to wear as they gathered in front of a television in the village square of Bambali. Mané's photograph would hang above the door in every classroom in Bambali, where the school was made out of mud, but he also provided the funds to build a new education facility, one out of bricks and mortar. 'He did not want the publicity,' Boucher insisted. 'But in Senegal, everything Sadio does gets picked up.'

Though Diatta and Boucher provided guidance in the early days at Génération Foot, Mady Touré was the greatest long-term influence on Sané, a powerful-looking man who always wore a *boubou* – the long, colourful loose-fitting dress worn by both sexes in West Africa. Touré was capable of big statements and he compared the ability of Mané to Lionel Messi and Neymar. 'Of course, I am very proud of Sadio,' he said. 'But he is not my player. He's my son.'

In 2003 Touré agreed a partnership with Metz which meant Génération Foot were obliged to produce at least one player a season for the French club. Papiss Cissé and Diafra Sakho would later appear on the radar of Premier League clubs but they left Senegal before Mané, who Touré described as better, being 'much, much faster – a player able to repeat skill without ever stopping or even slowing down'. Touré believed Mané's naturally introverted personality helped him in the long run. 'He has always led a quiet life. He trains, plays, rests. Even if he makes a lot of money, he has a head on his shoulders. Sadio was an attentive and very wise boy. I never had any problem of discipline with him. He knew there was only football to help him,' Touré thought. 'He might be a shy boy, but he's always believed in himself. He does not doubt. This is his strength. He often said to me, "Do not worry, President, I will succeed."'

Mané's father had been the Imam at the mosque in Bambali. He had grown up in a country where almost 90 per cent of the population was Muslim, yet his best friend in Bambali – Luke – was a Christian. It showed, according to Touré – also a man of faith – that Mané was indeed a person who mixed well with different cultures even before he went to Europe.

Then, he did not tell his family that he was going – only his uncle. His mum Satou thought he was still in Dakar when the call came from France – a call that was only possible because Mané persuaded some friends who were already at Metz, having followed the same path from Génération Foot, to lend him the money to buy enough telephone calls to reach Senegal.

Those early months were difficult for him, mainly because he could not play many games due to a hernia problem which his mentor back in Dakar thought had been sustained at the end of the Senegalese championship. 'He hid his wound from me because he wanted success so much,' Touré reflected. 'When he went to France he carried on playing with pain and this affected his early performances.'

Mané was dropped into the reserves, where his coach was José Pinot, who had played more than 500 games in a fifteen-year career outside the French top flight with just one club, Beauvais. Pinot was well established at Metz by the time Mané fell under his wing and, having recovered from his injury, he was quickly able to show a more accurate reflection of his talent. Though Mané struggled to complete 90 minutes, Pinot remembered him as being 'calm, with a little temperament, but attentive and always ready to improve'.

When midfielder David Fleurival was suspended for a first-team game, he went to play in the reserves. 'I immediately realized this kid had something extra,' he said of Mané. 'He made the game look easy because of his speed, as well as his ability to hit shots with power. I found it really wicked. I spoke directly with the coach to tell him that this player had to come and train with us, though I think the staff had already noticed. It was only a matter of time.'

Mané's professional debut came in January 2012 against Bastia in Corsica. Bernard Serin was the president of Metz and, from his position in the stands, he recalled the 'meteorite' of Mané, who should have won a penalty inside the first two minutes only for the referee to judge that the ball had gone out of play when it had not. Metz would lose 5–2 and it proved to be a significant result. Bastia had been mid-table with Metz and while one club

would climb towards promotion, the other hurtled towards relegation and the Championnat National. These were troubled times
for Metz. Joël Müller had started his relationship with the club as
a player in 1971 – four decades later he was the technical director. He described 2011–12 as 'the worst season in the existence
of Metz' because of where it took them, for the first time to the
National. Metz had struggled for the previous three seasons and
were dangerously close to relegation the year before. Remarkably,
Kalidou Koulibaly was beside Mané on the team's roster, a
defender who was born nearby in Saint-Dié-des-Vosges but ended
up representing Senegal before emerging as one of the world's finest players in his position at Napoli – a team Mané and Liverpool
would knock out of the Champions League seven seasons later.

Back then, Mané and Koulibaly were still teenagers and the
balance of the Metz squad was not right, according to the coach
Dominique Bijotat, a former Monaco midfielder capped eight
times by France, who said, 'It lacked a core of experienced players
who could have helped bring unity.'

Like Mané, Koulibaly had problems settling in a new city when
he was younger and this led to him returning to Vosges for a
period when he felt the club did not believe in him. Koulibaly was
an awkward mixer too, but was prepared to raise his voice if he
felt other players his age were not pulling their weight. This
resulted in promotion to a group three years his senior. The senior
Metz coaching staff were unable to ignore him. For Bijotat, Koulibaly became a conduit in the dressing room, someone he could
trust to spread positive messages. When Mané arrived in the
summer of 2011 Bijotat asked Koulibaly to take care of him.
While Mané remained shy but aware of his talents, Koulibaly
was forward and hard-working. Unlike Koulibaly Mané was not
the type to give his opinion if nobody asked for it.

Bouby saw a 'talented kid' in Mané with above-average physical and technical skills. 'He was fast, he could run forever, would
try to dribble past anyone and had a huge spirit. He was not there
to laugh, but had the intention to progress to the next level. He
had ambitions and he was someone who listened, but he was also
sure of his qualities. I knew very quickly that he knew he was

coming to work,' Bouby emphasized. 'I never saw him arrive late for training or even brag about anything he'd done.'

Metz's general manager Philippe Gaillot was pushing Bijotat to use Mané because of his ability to 'quickly bring the ball from one foot to the other'. 'He had an exceptional relationship with the ball,' Bijotat recognized. 'He had some gaps to fill, such as his positioning and his relationship on the pitch with teammates, knowing when to pass. But at the time he was already able to string together technical acts of a very high level. He was already phenomenal.'

Bijotat's deputy Patrick Hesse had never seen a player who could influence what was happening so quickly: 'He was driving his opponents crazy with his explosiveness on that first touch of the ball. We were always amazed. It was hard to catch him without making a mistake. His first touch was extraordinary.'

While Mané's first professional goal came in a 5–2 defeat to Guingamp, Koulibaly became the team's first-choice centre-half and the reference point in defence after the sale of Fallou Diagne to Freiburg during the winter transfer window. A broken foot, however, meant Koulibaly could not play the final ten league games as Metz dropped into the third tier for the first time. 'Had Koulibaly been fit, then maybe we'd have stayed up,' said Bijotat, who would ultimately select Mané and Koulibaly in the same side at Metz on only twelve occasions.

Bijotat wondered how defining this period had been for both players – suggesting that, actually, the sinking feeling of relegation could have been beneficial for them in the long term. 'I think that it remains a favourable experience, in an unfavourable context,' he said. 'They have developed personally psychological qualities that they might not have had if they had never suffered disappointments like this.'

Koulibaly's £1.2 million move to the Belgian side Genk preceded his career in Italy and, similarly, Mané did not go straight to one of Europe's elite leagues after leaving Metz, where he'd played just 19 games. The 2012 Olympics in London gave Mané the opportunity to showcase his talents, but right until the end of that summer's transfer window his future was uncertain. While

Marseille, Lille and Bordeaux made enquiries, he was forty-eight hours away from staying at Metz for at least another six months after an offer from Nice was deemed too low.

His lack of international experience had put Premier League clubs off because of work-permit issues. When Red Bull Salzburg met Metz's financial expectations in a deal which, at £3.5 million, would be the third-most expensive sale in the club's history, Mané's former agent Thierno Seydi recommended that he should go to Austria, build his reputation and then bounce into the Bundesliga or the Premier League. Back in Senegal the press were indignant at the choice. 'I was called a pariah but now I am seen as a genius,' Seydi later reflected.

The sum nevertheless was huge for a player with just a few Ligue 2 matches in his legs. For Metz, £3.5 million allowed the club to regroup in the National, where they earned promotion at the first time of asking. Mané's former teammates agreed that he made the right decision to try Austria first because the move allowed time for development and steady progress rather than a dramatic rise in standard which he might not have been ready for. 'This is what happened when Marouane Chamakh went from Bordeaux to Arsenal where he never reached his potential despite all of the promise,' Patrick Hesse suggested.

Mané came to the attention of Salzburg because of Gérard Houllier, who in 2019 remained the most successful Liverpool manager since their last league title in terms of trophies. At Anfield he had used the French market poorly and it had been his purchase of another Senegalese striker in El Hadji Diouf that undermined the last years of his reign. When he saw Mané at the Olympics, though, he was straight on the phone to Salzburg where he worked as a consultant for Red Bull. He had seen him before on French television but having watched him in the flesh Houllier did not hesitate in recommending that his employers do everything to ensure he did not go elsewhere. 'What I liked straight away was his speed and ability on the ball,' Houllier said, comparing him to Kylian Mbappé, the French World Cup winner. 'The potential was there and we just had to make sure he was well looked after.'

Houllier had introduced a player-liaison scheme during his time at Liverpool, where new foreign signings would get help from the club as they settled into their new environment. He made sure Salzburg adopted the same system when Mané went there. Though he had cost so much money, for the first few months in Austria he lived with a French-speaking family. Across two seasons under Roger Schmidt, a German coach who would later take Bayer Leverkusen back into the Champions League, Mané scored 45 goals in 87 games. Interest in him gathered quickly. Houllier recalled fielding phone calls from Bayern Munich after Salzburg beat the Bavarian giants 3–0 in a mid-season friendly where Mané scored one and set another up. 'Bayern wanted to sign him after that,' Houllier revealed, though he did not know this was also the game where Liverpool's scouts started to produce dossiers.

From afar, Mané's former teammate Pierre Bouby watched his development and he saw a new maturity that he thought could place him on the same level as Franck Ribéry or Douglas Costa – Bayern players who at their peak retained the ability to not only accelerate but have the 'gas' turned on for 90 minutes.

Though he would ultimately join Southampton for a fee which gave Salzburg a profit of more than £12 million, Mané could have joined Borussia Dortmund instead had it not been for the hesitancy of Jürgen Klopp, who – like other coaches in Mané's story – questioned whether he had the sort of outward personality the German tends to work better with.

'I have made a few mistakes in my life and one of the biggest mistakes ever was not taking Sadio when I was at Dortmund,' Klopp confessed. 'We were together in my office but I wasn't sure about signing him. It was completely my fault.'

When Mohamed Salah was named African player of the year in 2017 and 2018, Sadio Mané was the runner-up. The voting patterns took into consideration not only club form but impact at international level. Considering Salah's goal sent Egypt to Russia for Egypt's first World Cup in twenty-eight years – a moment which sent Egyptians pouring onto Tahrir Square in central Cairo, the scene of popular protests against Hosni Mubarak seven years earlier – it was recognized that the euphoric scenes were reminiscent of the intoxicating days and nights of the revolution.

Mané was facing a different emotional challenge in Senegal, a country which last qualified in 2002, sensationally beating France in the opening game. Ever since, aspiring Senegalese players were told they did not have the collective sense of a squad led, ironically, by El Hadji Diouf – who became a Liverpool flop.

Alain Giresse, a classy European Championship-winning midfielder with France, had made Mané the focal point of his attack after becoming Senegal manager in 2013. 'He is able to tip a match,' Giresse said, who at the time had more experienced players to choose from ahead of Mané. Because of Demba Ba, Papiss Cissé and Moussa Sow, Mané 'had to fight for his place' – though Giresse was soon fielding questions about why the player was unable to reproduce his form for his club at international level. 'We asked a lot from him,' Giresse admitted.

Mané received support from Diouf, who recognized the challenge of switching between styles – there was a sense that Mané had become Europeanized in his approach to the game. 'He should not take refuge behind that excuse,' Diouf said. 'He is a footballer who is able to make the difference thanks to his qualities in acceleration, dribbling and technical background. But it is easier for a player when he trains with the same system every day rather than, maybe, just four sessions every couple of months.'

Unlike Diouf, Mané was able to express himself best in a Liverpool shirt. He was not the sort of personality to add his voice into a national debate even if he was at the centre of it. According to Mané's headmaster in the village of Bambali, football had always been the release from any problems not the extension of them. It was only on the pitch where he was able to communicate fully, otherwise, 'You could easily miss him . . . he's a young man who can pass unnoticed and shy.'

When Mané signed for Liverpool in the summer of 2016, James Milner remembered him not saying anything to anyone for weeks. 'Or if he did raise his voice, he spoke very quietly.' This impression would be supported by journalists who interviewed Mané, observing him taking his time to consider his answers before delivering them quietly and with a minimal amount of words.

It was after his debut that Milner noticed a difference in his presence and a sign that he was beginning to seem more comfortable in a new environment. There had been a mazy darting run and a superb left-foot finish at Arsenal on the opening day of the season – an outstanding goal which eclipsed even Philippe Coutinho's sublime 30-yard free-kick earlier on in the game. Mané reacted to that by sprinting over to Jürgen Klopp before climbing on his back like a jockey. 'I was like, "Oh, there he is . . ."' Milner recalled. Mané absolutely loved the moment. 'The biggest goal for the biggest club in my career,' he called it.

The season before, Mané had been sent off at Anfield having scored Southampton's equalizer late on in a 1–1 draw to dull Liverpool's spirits. It was Klopp's first home league game in charge of Liverpool and the challenge in front of him was laid bare because Southampton – inspired by the pace and raids of Mané – could quite easily have won. When Liverpool went to Southampton deeper into that campaign Mané scored again – this time twice to seal a narrow victory after Liverpool had led 2–0 at half-time. His performance and telling contribution made a defining impression on Klopp who acknowledged then that Mané had the skills and spike to inject his team with what it was missing.

Thirteen weeks later Mané became Klopp's first signing of the summer at £30 million; his first big signing for the club. 'He had everything we needed,' Klopp said. 'A player who is always on the front foot. He is a nice boy but he can be very aggressive when he wants to be.'

It had been the late Bill Green, Southampton's former chief scout, who first recommended Mané for the same reasons. Red Bull Salzburg played the same high-tempo style under Roger Schmidt as Mauricio Pochettino when he was Southampton's manager. Schmidt has similarities to Klopp in that he is a thoughtful coach with a track record of getting the best out of thoughtful and sensitive players. Pochettino would later try to sign Mané as Tottenham's manager only for Klopp to beat him to the signature even after Mané had toured Spurs' spectacular new training ground.

At Southampton, Mané flourished under the guidance of Ronald Koeman who, before arriving in England, had seen him score twice for Salzburg in a 6–1 aggregate victory over Ajax in the Europa League. Koeman is a colder sort of manager than either Schmidt or Klopp, but he did help improve Mané's confidence by telling him straight that he had the power, pace and endurance to become one of the best forwards in the world.

It seemed an unusual lapse of character when Mané arrived late for a game at Norwich and Koeman reacted by dropping him. Koeman noticed how determined he was in training the following week to prove his commitment, that his mistake was merely a one-off slip – a mistake that did not happen again.

Mané scored ten and 15 goals in his two seasons at Southampton then 13 in his first at Anfield, though that campaign was interrupted by the Africa Cup of Nations – when he was really missed by Liverpool. In 2017–18 he would score 20, though that achievement was eclipsed by Mohamed Salah's sensational haul of 44 as well as Roberto Firmino's efforts, who weighed in with 27. There had been so much talk about the contributions of Liverpool's two other forwards that Mané's importance went under the radar – though Klopp appreciated what he was doing.

'He does not realize how good he is,' Klopp said during 2017–18 – a view which he revised when his goals in the absence of Salah's drought a year later decided the outcome of many games. 'We all know that he's a world-class player, and he has started realizing that for himself,' Klopp concluded after a 4–2 victory over Burnley where Mané scored Liverpool's second and last of the afternoon.

The trip to Munich followed. His goals at the Allianz Arena blew Bayern away and they were two of his very best for Liverpool – 'Maybe in my life,' Mané said, with untypical grandeur. The first came from Virgil van Dijk's long pass, which swerved through the air with the sort of grace a Masters' champion delivers on the 18th hole. From there Mané had the strength to swat away Rafinha and then the creativity to embarrass Manuel Neuer, a goalkeeper as large as a villain's Alpine retreat. The former World Cup winner was stranded when Mané then sent a twisting chipped shot into the empty net with the sense of ease that had been missing from Salah's game for weeks. His header – which later made it 3–1 and could have been scored by Pelé, the way he hung in the air like a viper before striking downwards – meant that since the start of 2017–18 Mané had now scored more goals in the Champions League than any other player aside from Cristiano Ronaldo.

Since the start of 2019 Mané emerged as Liverpool's go-to man. While Salah endured the worst goalscoring spell of his Liverpool career – albeit a period which would stretch across just eight games – the Senegalese stepped up, scoring in six successive home games, a feat once achieved by Michael Owen. Klopp thought the focus on Salah had helped Mané, making more space for him to be so deadly. 'Two or three players mark Mo,' Klopp said. 'But two or three players cannot mark Bobby as well as Sadio – otherwise the other team runs out of players.'

Klopp recognized Mané's talent first but it was his 'attitude and work-rate' which had the potential to push him further than even the player's own expectations. During 2018–19 he won more tackles than any of Liverpool's attacking players while also making more attempts to tackle, which translated into the type of pressing football that Klopp believes in to a semi-religious level.

Mané is a man of faith. He helped out at the Al Rahma mosque in south Liverpool by cleaning the toilets only hours after featuring in Liverpool's win at Leicester City at the start of the 2018–19 season. Like Salah, he celebrated goals by performing the *sujud* – touching his head on the grass and worshipping. It felt significant that when he scored again for Liverpool at Fulham four days after his exploits in Munich, he instinctively raced away and embraced with his teammates rather than thanking god. That ritual would wait until later when James Milner belted home Liverpool's winner from the penalty spot after Mané had been hauled down by Fulham's goalkeeper, Sergio Rico. Behind Milner, Mané fell to his knees. While the terrace in front of him erupted, he quietly thanked his blessings.

15. THERE CAN BE ONLY ONE

WHEN JORDAN HENDERSON WAS A YOUTH-TEAM PLAYER AT SUNDER-
land he would intervene if he thought the set-piece routines
needed freshening up. Kevin Ball, his coach, remembered him
stopping the session and coming up with his own ideas.

Years later, a boiling Easter Sunday in Cardiff – the hottest of
2019 so far. Though Liverpool were creating chances against an
opponent fighting to escape relegation, the score was 0–0 at half-
time. Henderson entered the dressing room with an idea. He had
seen how Cardiff's defenders left space on the edge of the box
when marking corners. 'Put it there,' he told Trent Alexander-
Arnold. He promised a Liverpool player would be waiting and a
Liverpool player was waiting when the full-back slung in a low
corner. Georginio Wijnaldum nearly broke the back of the net
with the shot that followed and the relief was incredible, with the
Dutch midfielder celebrating by running around the back of the
goal and jumping for joy in front of the travelling Liverpool
supporters.

One of the conversations that had followed Mohamed Salah
around since joining Liverpool would soon return. He was grabbed
by Sean Morrison, the defender who'd spent the rest of his career
in the Championship. He was pulled and dragged back but Salah
remained on his feet. With referee Martin Atkinson not awarding
a penalty, when Morrison used his arms again in an attempt to
regulate his movement, Salah fell and Atkinson finally pointed to
the spot. Neil Warnock, Cardiff's anvil-headed 70-year-old manager described Salah's tumble as an Olympic dive, but he had been

fouled and it was a penalty, and from there James Milner confidently secured a 2–0 Liverpool victory.

Milner is not really a routine sort of footballer when it comes to celebrations. He had once described himself as a Yorkshireman wearing his mining boots. Here, he pretended to use a walking stick. Virgil van Dijk was constantly telling him he's getting too old for football but Milner, at 33, gave the impression he could go on for ever. He was the man to rely on in pressure situations. When Liverpool needed him to score a penalty against Fulham, he scored. When Jürgen Klopp needed him to fill in at full-back as Liverpool searched for a winner at Southampton, he plugged the hole and Liverpool won. At Cardiff, he was again introduced as a substitute and his impact was telling.

Milner had grown up a Leeds fan. He'd played for Leeds as a 16-year-old, and he'd played for Newcastle and Manchester City. All of those clubs have reasons to hate Manchester United. 'It'll be the first time in my life!' he admitted enthusiastically as he stopped to talk in the narrow corridor at Cardiff which led from the changing rooms towards the exit and the Liverpool team coach, where hundreds of supporters were screaming for signatures as the furnace of the afternoon cooled into the evening.

Milner was referring to the Manchester derby at Old Trafford. City had four games left and Liverpool needed them to draw at least one game to have a chance of winning the title. Milner thought watching the game would be a waste of energy considering he could do nothing about it. He was planning to leave his phone at home and go to a restaurant to distract himself. He did not believe that Liverpool's destiny rested in Manchester anyway. He thought back to his own experiences as a City player in 2012 when the club won its first title in forty-four years by narrowly beating relegation-threatened Queens Park Rangers on the final day in Manchester. Joey Barton's red card meant Rangers had to play nearly half an hour with ten men but they still managed to take the lead in that period as the pressure told on City. Somehow, they recovered and Sergio Agüero's stoppage-time winner sealed the championship. 'To beat anyone is tough when it's all on the line,' Milner thought. 'Trust me, I know.'

Jürgen Klopp watched the Manchester derby sitting on the couch with his wife Ulla at their home in Formby. In the background his dog Emma sat placidly on the mat near the fireplace. It was a rare moment in Liverpool's history, where the club's supporters were desperate for their greatest historical rivals to do them a favour by winning. Fourteen miles away, Liverpool's local supporters gathered in the pubs near Anfield. The Arkles was almost full. The Flat Iron or 'the Flatty' was packed to the rafters. The Sandon – where Liverpool FC was formed – was busier than a normal Wednesday.

'It was the result I expected,' Klopp said cheerfully the next morning at Melwood when he was immediately asked about City's comfortable 2–0 victory. Though United had caused a few problems in the first half, after the break City moved up through the gears. The introduction of Leroy Sané, the winger Klopp wanted so much eighteen months earlier, changed the pace and flow of the game and, after Bernardo Silva gave City the lead, the German sealed the victory by racing clear of United's defence, staggering by then like drunken sailors on land leave. 'They were a bit unlucky in one or two moments, but over 95 minutes it was clear they can't stand up to City at the moment,' Klopp reflected. 'I was not surprised by the result.'

The fine weather from the Easter weekend had disappeared and the cloud above Merseyside was grey and continuous. City's win at Old Trafford had made the gloom stick to Liverpool's supporters like a thick sheet. Yet Klopp appeared unshaken. These are the moments where he comes into his own. He was confident but he was also convincing. He was able to make people happier through laughter. Liverpool were facing the very real possibility that they would take 97 points from the season and still not win the league. Pep Guardiola suggested that both teams deserved to finish as champions. Klopp agreed with that, but he had his own way of putting it. 'It's like *Highlander*, only one of us will be there at the end,' he joked, though he was not asked whether he saw himself in the role of MacLeod, who prevailed instead of his great enemy Kurgan in the 1986 movie, which Klopp, who likes cinema, watched when he was 22 years old. He stressed, as he had done for months, that this was only Liverpool's first time competing for the title, 'not the last time'. It had been revealed that morning Liverpool had four players in the PFA team of the year but Klopp believed they could have had all eleven. City, he reminded, had finished 25 points above Liverpool the year before and that was more than the total number of points Liverpool's next opponents Huddersfield had gained in the whole of the 2018–19 campaign. Yet he certainly had not given up. Away from the cameras in a side-room, Klopp sat perched on a table as he always did even though everyone else in the room was standing up. He was given an opportunity to deliver a rousing message to Liverpool's supporters, who saw the league slipping away. Give us hope, Jürgen, come on – give us some hope . . .

'It was not the last chance before the game; why should it be the last chance after the game?' he asked. 'If anybody really thought that United, in the moment, are capable of hurting City . . . City are just too good for that. There is always hope until the last whistle of the last game,' he insisted. 'That never changed. In your mind, the best-case scenario is City lose last night and so we are two points up. Then we play Huddersfield and we win or not, we will see, but then Newcastle. Massive pressure, everyone talking about that. You wouldn't feel a little bit better. You wouldn't. If we win that, which is difficult enough, and City win their game and then we play the last game against Wolves who can go with a win into the Europa League – and they want that, not like the others – then that is unbelievable pressure too. That is exactly the situation we have now only with the little difference that they are one point up. That's the only difference. It's not allowed for us to lose concentration or focus now. It is not a lie, I watched the game in front of the television and I was not a little bit nervous. I was not like, "Oh my God, why did he do this? Lingard!" I don't like watching these games because we have nothing to do with them. I like to have the information, but that's all. Everything is still fine and if somebody doesn't believe any more then I can't change that now. If you still believe then welcome to my club.'

Huddersfield had been relegated from the Premier League in April 2019 following two seasons in the top flight. Their manager David Wagner – Klopp's great friend and best man – had resigned in the January. Their last victory over Liverpool had been fifty years ago and this emphasized the scale of their task at Anfield. Yet there was an intertwining of histories at Liverpool and Huddersfield, a cross-over of paths and a suggestion of if-only. The Liverpool Way involves faith, even when it seems all hope has been lost. This outlook comes from Bill Shankly, who'd abandoned Huddersfield for Anfield in 1959 after delivering another defeat on the club he would come to shape in his own image. Ironically, his first Liverpool game in charge would be against Cardiff at Anfield, where Liverpool lost 4–0.

Back then Huddersfield were beating Liverpool routinely. In 1958, following a 5–0 defeat at Huddersfield's old Leeds Road ground, Shankly was in such a triumphant mood that he reminded the press that his team had delivered 'the result of the bloody year' despite playing with an injured player for most of the game. It was the day where Shankly later recalled a scene involving Liverpool's directors 'leaving in single file with their shoulders slumped, like a funeral procession'.

That sight did not put him off when Liverpool approached him. At Anfield he would turn a second-tier club into English champions in less than five years, winning the title two more times in a glorious period where he'd also deliver the first FA Cup in Liverpool's history, despite claims of a curse. Shankly transformed the culture of Liverpool, how supporters felt about themselves – defining the way outsiders think about Liverpool as a city today. Without Shankly there is no modern Liverpool. On the wall at the entrance of Melwood, beside a bronze bust, are the words:

Above all, I would like to be remembered as a man who was selfless, who strove and worried so others could share the glory and who built up a family of people who would hold their heads up high and say, 'We are Liverpool.'

While Shankly and Liverpool conquered the country, then Europe under Shankly's successor Bob Paisley, Huddersfield fell into the bottom division. Across four decades Huddersfield finally worked their way back to the top flight, but many of the Terriers' supporters who'd witnessed Shankly's team in action all those years before wondered whether Liverpool's story could have been theirs.

Shankly had been Andy Beattie's assistant originally, having arrived in West Yorkshire from Workington. He had managed Grimsby Town and before that Carlisle United, the club where he'd started his playing career. It was at Preston North End where he met Beattie as a teammate and realized his own potential as a tough right-half, but his best years were taken by the Second World War and this frustrated him immensely. There are entire books which explain Shankly's personality but, fundamentally, he was a quick-thinking socialist who found the right words to inspire footballers. It annoyed him to the point of distraction when others – mainly board members – did not meet his ambition, and that is why he resigned from Carlisle, Grimsby, Workington and, ultimately, Huddersfield.

Ken Taylor had been the defender whose injury in 1958 did not prevent him from scoring in a 5–0 rout. Taylor was also a cricketer who represented Yorkshire and England, playing in the same county side as Fred Trueman and Geoffrey Boycott which, under the inspirational captaincy of Brian Close, won seven championships between 1959 and 1968. While Taylor's brother Jeff balanced a First Division football career at Huddersfield with a university degree in geography (he later became an opera singer under the name Neilson Taylor), Ken studied too – winning a place at the Slade School of Fine Art in London. It is hard to imagine today two working-class brothers doing all of these things almost at once, not that the achievements mattered much to Shankly, whose commitment to football was absolute, calling cricket a 'lassie's game'. Taylor, who irked Shankly by taking to the football field with a handkerchief tucked inside his shorts so he could wipe his nose, combined his love of art and football by releasing an illustrated biography in conjunction with author Stephen Chalke entitled *Drawn to Sport*. Despite their differences Shankly picked Taylor because he was a very good footballer. Taylor once recalled a conversation with Shankly about motor cars and how flashy some of them were. 'It's what's underneath the body that counts,' Shankly remarked.

Shankly had initially been put in charge of Huddersfield's reserves by Beattie. Amongst the squad was Ray Wilson – England's 1966 World Cup-winning left-back. 'Roy Goodall was the first-team trainer and his sessions were so boring,' Wilson told Chalke. 'All you did was lap and lap and lap. And when you did have a game, first team against second, there were to be no serious challenges. Then Bill came along, and he was full of enthusiasm.' Training was mornings only – but not with Shankly. 'We'd come back in the dressing room,' Wilson remembered, 'and he'd point to some of us. "You ... you [and] you: come back this afternoon." He used to have us playing outside on the car park. The pitch would be marked out. There'd always be five Englishmen, four Scotsmen and him. "And here we are," he'd say, "going out at Hampden Park now." And we'd walk out onto the car park. We [English] could never score a goal. If there was ever any doubt he'd say, "Not in." We used to play till it was nearly dark. So, we'd nod to each other and we'd say, "Let him score the winner." And as soon as he did, he'd blow for time.'

The first-team players saw this natural enthusiasm and realized they wanted to be trained by Shankly. When Beattie was sacked following relegation from the First Division in 1956, they got their wish. Beattie had spent a great deal of time trying to work out what the opposition was planning. 'But Bill wasn't worried about the opposition,' Taylor recalled. 'His idea was to collect good players and to let them play. We never had a proper pre-match talk. He would just go around building up our confidence, telling us how good we were, how the other side "weren't fit to be on the same park". He'd walk around the table. "The police are going to be upset," he'd say. "There'll be eleven murders out there this afternoon."'

Where Klopp has interests outside of football, Shankly possessed no hinterland. He would ignore players that were injured for months because they were no use to him, and he banned marriages between players and their girlfriends between the months of August and May. Yet Shankly was emotional like Klopp, and Huddersfield's players would always remember his reaction to a 7–6 defeat at Charlton Athletic in 1957 having led 5–1. That day, even the reserves did not escape Shankly's wrath, 'For not being good enough to get into the team in the first place.' While Taylor said Shankly sat alone in silence during the train journey home – 'he didn't speak to anybody for days' – Wilson's account offered a different view. 'Shankly was pacing up and down. He was muttering to himself: "It's just one of those things . . . it's history." He was trying to sort it out in his mind, how it had happened.'

Huddersfield would not lose any of their next ten matches, so amidst his agonizing Shankly had figured out some of his team's problems. Two years later, Liverpool's problems became his own. And there were many of those.

The cult of the manager began at Liverpool when Bill Shankly took on the directors and won. Before his arrival at Anfield there had been a team-selection panel at every club across the country. That soon changed. Before his arrival, Anfield looked and smelt like a toilet. That soon changed. Before his arrival, training sessions involved long runs and a little amount of ball work. That soon changed as well. There were so many battles for Shankly to win, he penned his resignation letter several times, but he never walked the same path as he had at Carlisle, Grimsby, Workington or Huddersfield. He sensed he was onto something with Liverpool, where he believed he was 'made for Liverpool' just as 'Liverpool was made for him'.

His staff were Brylcreemed pensioners. He kept everyone on and learned about the club from their experiences, so retaining Liverpool's identity while also developing it – he sent the club in a new direction according to his vision. Ian Callaghan became Liverpool's record appearance holder, playing 857 games. His debut came in Shankly's first full season in charge. 'He fell in love with the Liverpool people and they instantly fell in love with him because,' Callaghan pondered, 'he made promises and then he kept them.'

Before the war, Shankly had travelled to Liverpool for a nose operation. He'd returned since to watch the fights of his favourite boxers, Peter Kane, Jimmy Warnock, Ernie Roderick and Henry Armstrong. He realized he liked Liverpool because the bustle reminded him of Glasgow and Edinburgh. Liverpool people, he thought, were like Scottish people.

The belief and consciousness of Liverpool's people, however, was not reflected on the terraces of Anfield's Kop. Liverpool were in the Second Division and way below Everton. 'For a city the size of Liverpool and considering the potential support, the situation was appalling,' Shankly wrote in his autobiography. 'The dyed-in-the-wool supporters were just hoping a miracle would happen and they would have something to cheer about. People on the Kop were shouting and bawling, but not with the same unity or humour or arrogance that made them famous later. Everton were in the First Division, of course, and I went to Anfield to see a Liverpool Senior Cup game. Bobby Collins turned Liverpool inside out, Everton dusted them up, and the atmosphere was awful. The mockery was embarrassing. It was pathetic. But, deep down, there was something.'

Shankly had replaced Phil Taylor, a decent, honest coach who was hard-working but a typical gentleman of the time. If the board of directors told him how something needed to be done, he'd agree with them. Shankly decided it was time for a shake-up in attitudes and, with the help of one director in Eric Sawyer, he set about redressing the balance of power. Shankly knew that if the fans loved him, they'd support his decisions and love the team; support Liverpool through thick and thin.

Though he was a staunch socialist, Shankly was not party-political or driven by dogma. His socialism was instinctive and this was reflected by the bond he quickly developed with the fans, many of whom had developed socialist beliefs having worked as casual labourers on the city's docks for generations. Whenever he received letters, Shankly would respond by addressing the person he was writing to as 'You'. When he said, '*You* are so important' what he meant and how he made fans feel was: 'You are important to me.' His upbringing beside the mines of Glenbuck had helped define how he treated everyone. Shankly's simple, clear messages were hypnotic, and his power was reflected not in victory but in defeat.

Liverpool had lost the FA Cup final in 1971 to Arsenal when he stood in front of an enormous crowd outside the St George's Hall in the city centre. 'Since I've come here, to Liverpool and to Anfield,' he said slowly, 'I have drummed it into our players time and again that they are privileged to play for you.' Tommy Smith, the team's captain whose ferocious reputation went before him, stood beside Shankly, looking at the floor, coughing nervously as his manager carried on. The mass of people stretched as far as the eye could see, up towards London Road where Shankly and his wife Nessie used to do all of their shopping. Shankly's right hand was in one pocket and his left hand was used to emphasize the points he was making. After a long pause, he returned to the 'privilege' of his players: 'And if they didn't believe me, they believe me now.'

At Cardiff Neil Warnock went up to Jürgen Klopp and told him, 'The work-rate of your team is incredible.' Klopp was delighted by that. For a long time he had felt that he had to make an excuse for not playing like Manchester City. He knew there was only one Manchester City – but he believed he could make one Liverpool as well, clearly identifiable from the rest; their own team, not copying anyone. Warnock had told him that City were very good but Liverpool were more willing to fight to win possession back. There were moments when Cardiff's fast wingers attempted to counter-attack but were pursued by three, sometimes four Liverpool players. In Klopp's eyes that made his players winners before they'd even lifted a trophy. They were not giving up. They were desperate.

Klopp does not believe in destiny or miracles. It sits uneasily with his religious conscience. He prefers to think of remarkable victories as 'big performances'. Protestantism had told him that working hard gets you places. There is no divine right to anything. He realized from an early age that faith was not about going to church and repenting for sins. It was more important to listen to other people and try to help them rather than appearing to do good by sitting amongst a congregation and saying sorry for everything. 'Praying in church did not make me a good Christian,' Klopp said. 'I thought life was more about common sense.' Bill Shankly was a Protestant too, and he did not practise at the altar either. 'I am always interested in people. I am not nosy, I am interested in people. I am a good listener and I really like to hear people tell me their story.' That might sound like Shankly, but really this was Klopp speaking.

In his own words, Klopp will 'never vote for the right', and this appealed to Liverpudlians, for whom socialism is passed between generations. Klopp does not have private health insurance and waits in a queue on the NHS like anyone else. Yet those who know him best describe him as more of a liberal with an acute sense of social conscience. Like Shankly, who was shaped by the mines and the suffering of Glenbuck, Klopp's early life centred around east meeting west and new freedoms. He was born in 1967 and this meant he was 22 when the Berlin Wall came crashing down, uniting Germany under one banner. The period that followed was not without its problems but there were attempts to be more inclusive, and this goes some way to explaining Klopp the person as well as Klopp the manager. Both are the same. While Brendan Rodgers was accused of being disingenuous, Klopp is, according to his captain Jordan Henderson, 'completely genuine'.

Shankly gave everybody a chance; staff as well as players were given the opportunity to prove themselves. Klopp did not rush to judgements either. He gave Simon Mignolet, the goalkeeper before Alisson Becker and Loris Karius, more opportunities to establish himself as Liverpool's number one than he probably deserved. After beating Cardiff, Mignolet was described by James Milner as 'probably the best professional I've ever played with'. The Belgian deserved credit for his attitude in training but Klopp had held long meetings with him, telling him that he was valued – that he would have no doubts about his ability if he had to call on him. Klopp described Mignolet as a number 1 and that made him the very best number 2 in the Premier League. When Mignolet heard this, he was delighted – though he was still desperate to be a number 1.

Shankly wanted talented, determined young footballers who were robust. 'If you don't live every minute of the day to keep fit and you don't think about the game all of the time, then really and truly you shouldn't be in the game,' he said. 'You're an imposter.' Klopp did not ignore injured players like Shankly and this, perhaps, is what separates them the most. Alex Oxlade-Chamberlain knew that Klopp cared when he suffered serious ligament damage to his knee. They would hold regular meetings about his progress, with Klopp offering emotional support, telling him how much he was valued and that Liverpool's future was bright – that he'd be a part of it. Klopp has faith in young people and he is caring. He is 'a friend – but not your best friend', as Christian Benteke found out when he was sold. When Klopp says 'no' he means it. When Mamadou Sakho flouted the rules by being late at the airport before a pre-season trip to America, he was eventually sold as well.

Klopp, like Shankly, is competing against teams with more money. Everton were the Mersey Millionaires in the 1960s. Tottenham and Arsenal were the glamour clubs of London. The size of Old Trafford meant Manchester United could pay out more in the years after rules around maximum-wage restrictions were lifted.

Liverpool's revenues increased because of Klopp's presence at the club, his charisma and achievements. This allowed Liverpool to compete more with Manchester City, United and Chelsea. Champions League progress generated the finance for transfer funds. Yet, all the time, Klopp was still building a team in the finest Liverpool tradition, one with a group of players you wouldn't have necessarily pinned together and claimed confidently they'd have a chance.

Shankly used Geoff Twentyman to scout players as low as the old Fourth Division. He could mould pig iron into gold. Liverpool's goalkeeper under Klopp is a world-record transfer but he has also once been short and fat. The right-back is a teenager from the academy, the left-back came from relegated Hull. There are three former Southampton players as well as one from Sunderland. Mohamed Salah carries the star status and the fee of Kenny Dalglish but he is also a Chelsea reject. The centre-forward in Roberto Firmino was not spotted by any of Brazil's top clubs and he arrived from Hoffenheim without anyone other than Klopp really understanding his best position.

Klopp, like Shankly, is able to see what others have not been able to. He has an advantage of understanding players more because he was once one himself. He understands people because he was not famous until he became a manager. He understands that if you give people hope, you have a chance of succeeding as a manager.

It was during a conversation with the German journalist Christoph Biermann, whose book focused on the importance of football to the industrial Ruhr region, where Klopp reflected on Borussia Dortmund's improbable victory over Malaga in 2012. It was 'one of those stories that will be told in twenty years' time,' he said. 'My motivation is to collect that kind of stuff, for people to tell and retell it.' Football, he believed, was a shared collection of stories, a shared history and identity.

The number of tales told about Klopp's ability to inspire has reached Shankly-esque proportions. In writing his book *Bring the Noise* Raphael Honigstein, the well-connected German writer, found there was simply too much information to include. One of the stories that did not make the final edit came from a director at the car firm Opel, who told him about the occasion when Klopp stood on a stage before 10,000 at an annual workers' rally. The talk developed into more of a performance and, by the end, the audience was chanting his name. Everyone believed him.

Huddersfield's resistance at Anfield lasted 15 seconds. Liverpool's lead came from a Naby Keïta goal, which he'd made possible by sprinting forward from the kick-off and pinching possession. Klopp appreciated Keïta's immediate determination and awareness: 'He made two or three really quick steps and he was there. I was surprised at how the Huddersfield player could not be surprised that there was a player around.'

Huddersfield had been relegated in March. They had taken just four points from the previous 66 available. A 5–0 Liverpool victory was hardly surprising but the intensity of the performance was encouraging. Records were set. Mohamed Salah was playing in his 100th Liverpool game and he became the quickest player in the club's history to reach 69 goals, ahead of the legendary Roger Hunt and Sam Raybould, more than 115 years before. Two goals each for Salah and Sadio Mané meant both were now battling it out for the Premier League's Golden Boot. Meanwhile, Alisson's clean sheet meant he had twenty for the season, equalling Pepe Reina's record in 2006 and 2009. Alex Oxlade-Chamberlain also made his comeback a year and two days after his last appearance. Liverpool had 91 points, eclipsing the total won by 105 of the 119 champions of English football when applying three points for a win to every season. City were two behind them again, but with a game in hand at Burnley two days later, an opponent they had beaten twice already this season by a scoreline of 5–0. All Liverpool could do was wait, hope and then win again. In terms of the Premier League title, there could only be one winner.

16. THE NEXT CAPTAIN

LIVERPOOL WERE DRAWING AT SOUTHAMPTON WHEN JÜRGEN KLOPP looked at Jordan Henderson and told him he was coming on. Liverpool's captain wasn't always a first-choice pick by Klopp, who rotated his midfield more than any other position. Rarely had a three played together in successive games. By the end of the 2018–19 campaign Klopp had tried twenty-nine combinations. There were two reasons for this. He expected each midfielder to defend and attack and this meant a supreme level of fitness. He had seen how the team suffered in Kiev when he did not have the options to make changes in the second half. After selling Philippe Coutinho five months earlier and replacing him with Alex Oxlade-Chamberlain, who was now injured, Klopp was low on numbers. He also recognized that Liverpool did not possess a number 10, a playmaker. By shuffling his selection regularly, opponents were unable to establish where the deeper central threat was really coming from.

In Sunderland, Kevin Ball was waiting to go on stage and do one of his after-dinner speeches as the tension began to rise on the south coast, 300 miles away. Henderson was placed in midfield. Though Trent Alexander-Arnold had supplied Naby Keïta's equalizer, he was withdrawn. Klopp decided James Milner's experience was needed at right-back. Ball recalled: 'I was asking people at the do, "What's the score?" I knew Liverpool were 1–0 down but when I found out they'd won 3–1 and Jordan had scored I was delighted.' He drove home listening to the radio. 'There was a phone-in and one caller said something like, "What a turnaround . . . and even Jordan Henderson scored." Now, that might have been the case but what gives people the right to come on and talk about a player who always gives his best for his team? He doesn't go out there to have a bad game. He goes out and does his job and does it exceptionally well.'

Ball acknowledged he was emotionally connected to the midfielder having been his coach for three seasons in Sunderland's youth system. Ball had been a footballer too, playing more than 400 games at the club where Henderson made his debut. Ball was known as 'Mr Sunderland' even though he was born in Hastings and racked up more than a century of appearances for Portsmouth before moving north in 1990, the year Henderson was born. Ball was immediately accepted by Sunderland supporters as one of their own because of his wholehearted approach, as well as his obvious up-and-at-them leadership qualities, which led to him becoming club captain. He was a working-class man representing a working-class club based in Roker, the area of the city immediately south from Fulwell, where Henderson grew up and was spotted playing for Fulwell Juniors.

Though Ball was loved by the fans, he could relate to what it was like being underappreciated. Managers didn't always take to him straight away and his ratings in the newspapers were not always that high. Henderson was viewed slightly differently but perhaps suffered from the same anxieties around acceptance. Brendan Rodgers was going to sell him before he made him his captain. Klopp was unsure at first, and Tottenham Hotspur wanted to sign him. Eventually, though, both coaches came to understand him, to love him. It turned out to be the fans Henderson struggled to win over the most.

'I played as a holding midfielder but I wasn't a patch on Jordan,' Ball reflected. 'I was given the job of man-marking Steve McManaman at Roker Park one season. I lost him for 30 seconds and he scored an unbelievable goal. He stuck it in the top corner. Even though I'd kept him quiet for the rest of the game I got a bollocking.' In the return game at Anfield later that campaign, Ball was asked again to 'keep McManaman quiet' – Liverpool's bandy-legged midfielder who in the late 1990s Sir Alex Ferguson identified as the team's greatest attacking threat. 'Stop McMana-man and you stop Liverpool,' was Ferguson's message. Peter Reid was in charge of Sunderland at the time, a manager who grew up supporting Liverpool but won two First Division championships with Everton. 'Gaffer said, "Don't leave him alone today . . ." He gave me the job again, so I couldn't have done that badly first time around. I warned Steve, "I'm sorry but I'm going to have to follow you around all day today – even if you go to the toilet." We drew 0–0 and I got a rating of four out of ten in the paper. The reporter wrote that I didn't do anything in the game, but I felt as though I'd helped stop their star performer.'

Though Ball was a dogged footballer he does not admire just the players who share the same characteristics as him. He cherishes individuality and creativity. He takes great pleasure from watching Henderson function in this Liverpool team. 'The way they move the ball so quickly, it doesn't allow the opponent to get close enough to stop them by making a tackle,' Ball said. 'Liverpool have pace and match-winners all over the park. But even teams with so many match-winners need players who understand the other side of the game – those who can read what is happening and then set the tone with the quickness of their thinking and passing.'

This is where he believes Henderson fits in as a 28-year-old footballer. A decade earlier, he'd been the star of Sunderland's youth system, where he was regarded as the creative hub of the teams he played for. He became a different player at senior level, where the game is more structured and managers have very specific expectations of players. As a teenager, according to Ball, Henderson was more spontaneous because he was able to do more of what he wanted. 'A first-team manager wants a player who understands his tactical responsibilities and to follow instructions without any recourse,' Ball said. 'Even though Jordan was a creative player in Sunderland's youth system, he was always willing to sacrifice his own game for the good of the team. At Liverpool and with England, managers have always selected him because he does what they want. He has sacrificed a lot of his game for the good of those around him. I know what else he can do because I've seen it.'

Ball recounted Henderson's artistry in a game where he picked his way out of a problem by fooling two opponents in one turn: 'I was gobsmacked, it was an unbelievable bit of skill. Initially I questioned whether he should have tried it but when players are gifted to that degree, you don't coach them at that age – you guide them.'

Ball first came across Henderson when he was 15. Ball was the Under-18s coach as well as the assistant academy manager: 'He was coming up to the time where players sign new scholarship forms. You knew he had the ability, you knew he had the desire, you knew he had the temperament, you knew he had the attitude. Now, he's like an Adonis – a man mountain. Opponents bounce off him, he's made himself very strong. When he was younger, though, we wondered whether he'd develop physically because he had quite a way to go. We decided he was so talented he was worth waiting for.'

On YouTube there is a video that Henderson would probably cringe at if he saw it now. As a 16-year-old, he takes the viewer on a tour of Sunderland's backstreets to the tune of Perry Como's 'Mama Loves Mambo' while demonstrating tricks, with one of his friends opening the sequence by kicking a ball onto the roof of a pub before checking his watch and anticipating precisely where the ball will fall then controlling it casually in an instant. When Henderson appears, he wears Sunderland's Lonsdale training gear in the middle of his street, with semi-detached houses in the background. By the time the video ends it is getting dark, a reflection of how long Henderson and his friends worked on it. 'This showed his love for the game,' Ball concluded. 'Only kids who love football would do that.'

Henderson's school was the other side of the River Wear from Fulwell – nearby was West Park, where he honed his skills as a Sunday-league footballer. Dave Robinson was his PE teacher at what is now called the Farringdon Community Academy, and he told the *Northern Echo* before the 2018 World Cup that he had kept in touch with him since graduating from the school. 'He always stood out in the team, but was happy to play anywhere to help his teammates and friends,' Robinson stressed. 'He just loved playing football and had this desire to constantly improve – and that has stayed with him. I had him in my Year 9, 10 and 11 teams. I could never fault his attitude. He just always wanted to learn. He always had something extra. His team won the league and cup Double at Under-16s. It was a lovely group to be the coach of and Jordan was such a key part of that. He might not have been the captain, because we used to give others the opportunity to grow into the role too, but he was always leading with his attitude.'

One of his first coaches at Sunderland was Elliott Dickman. Henderson was eight years old when he first signed forms with the club and, like Ball, it was his enthusiasm as a child that struck his coach the most. 'A love for the game, a passion for the game, dedicated to the game; if you've got the characteristics as a young player you do potentially have a future in the game,' Dickman said. 'You could see that football meant everything to Jordan. He wasn't casual like some of them can be.'

In Sunderland's Under-18s Ball considered him one of the pillars of a team that self-managed itself. The other leaders included Martyn Waghorn, who later earned different clubs more than £15 million in transfer fees, Jack Colback, who joined regional rivals Newcastle United and Conor Hourihane, whose development was slower but he did eventually become a full international with Ireland having impressed in Aston Villa's midfield. Ball could remember Henderson suggesting a change of direction when the players practised set-plays because he had recognized Sunderland earned a lot of free-kicks in the wide areas due to the trickery of their wingers. 'He wanted more variation,' Ball explained. 'He was the sort of lad who questioned the coaches but always in a progressive way. I like that because it showed he wanted to learn. If we did a possession session, he'd always want to get on the ball. If we did a shooting session, he'd always look to finish. If we did a running session, he'd always look to win it. That's not to say he'd always win it – but he'd always try and win it. By doing that he was always going to push himself to improve. If the other lads were better than him, he'd always try and catch up, and because he had the right attitude and capacity he'd end up going beyond them. His own determination drove others forward.'

One of the character traits Ball liked most was his thoughtfulness for teammates. When Sunderland reached the semi-finals of the FA Youth Cup in 2008, beating Liverpool *en route*, Henderson organized a meal for the squad at his house in Fulwell. It rankled with Ball that Sunderland never reached the final that year after a goal by Ryan Noble in the last minute of the second leg was ruled out, he believed incorrectly.

'To invite all the lads round and get them together as a teenager, you need to have the support of all your family, and Jordan had that,' remembered Ball, who also recalled the days off at the training ground when Henderson went in anyway, with other boys his age. 'I said, "What are you doing in?" And Jordan stepped forward saying, "We want to do a bit extra." The coaches had given them a day off because they thought the players needed it. I could have said, "Lads, you need to rest." But by doing that I was stopping them practising the game they love. You've got to trust them.'

Henderson, Ball concluded, was the sort of player who reacted better to constant communication. Ball would explain all of his decisions in full to him. When Ball left him out of a game to give him a break, Henderson was upset. 'He said, "I wanna play, I wanna play." I said, "I understand you want to play – I also understand you're going to have the hump with me but I don't mind that." I reminded him that lots of players had supported him along the way, and this was his opportunity to support them. He looked at me and said, "Yeah, you're right." There was just something about him – he got what being a footballer meant. He wasn't scared of sharing the glory.'

Ball admitted 'feeling lucky' to have worked with Henderson might sound like cliché but it was true to his memories. He was one of three captains at Under-18 level. 'A good captain will lead the team but a great captain can be led by others,' thought Ball, who wore the armband at Sunderland for more than a decade, but not at Fulham where Chris Coleman was already in position. Yet at Craven Cottage Ball still felt a sense of leadership responsibility. He went to Coleman straight away and told him that if he ever needed support, he'd back him up. 'Jordan was the same,' Ball said. 'He could point the way forward but if someone else was in control he'd support them all the way.'

It was a reserve-team friendly match in the summer of 2008 that perhaps defined Henderson's life. Sunderland were playing at Gateshead. The International Stadium is an athletics venue fifteen miles away from Sunderland. Beside the running track and a sand pit, Sunderland lost 2–0 to a side recently promoted into the top tier of non-league football, one coached by Ian Bogie, a former Newcastle midfielder.

Roy Keane, Sunderland's manager – the legendary Manchester United captain whose temper matched the ferocity of his play – was on the warpath. 'Roy was fuming with them,' Ball remembered. 'He felt like I did, when you play against local non-league opposition – with the utmost respect to them – even with a young team, you expect to win. You challenge them: "These boys are playing in the National League – they'd love to be where you are . . . put them in their place."'

Keane waited until Sunderland's players returned to the training ground. 'He gave them a right good shoe-in, saying it wasn't acceptable.' Keane proceeded to go around the dressing room asking each player whether they believed they were good enough to play in his first team. One player hesitated, and months later when he returned from a loan wondering whether his performances were enough for him to get a chance in Keane's side, he was told by Sunderland's staff that he'd blown it. 'He shouldn't have hesitated,' Ball believed. 'Roy thought, "Hmmn, I'm not sure about you."' When Keane challenged Henderson, who had played poorly that day, the 18-year-old responded, 'Yeah, I will.' 'Don't get me wrong, you're putting your *cojones* out there making that sort of statement to Roy Keane,' Ball thought. 'But it showed Jordan's confidence in himself.' The next day Henderson was selected in the squad for a first-team friendly against Ajax. 'Roy will have loved someone who said, "I will." He's then got to give him the opportunity to try.'

Though he finished a loan spell at Coventry prematurely because of injury, Henderson had made enough of an impression.

Steve Bruce had replaced Keane at Sunderland by the summer of 2009 and he appointed Eric Black as his assistant. Before that Black, who'd been in charge of Coventry, had recommended Henderson to Bruce in his previous position at Wigan. Bruce knew it would be very difficult to prise him away from the north-east and when he went there to manage himself he received more calls about Henderson's availability than any other player, mainly from clubs in the Championship looking for a loan deal.

'What grabbed me was his enthusiasm, [the fact that] he is 6 foot 2 inches, his running power, and then, of course, he can handle the ball. And when you have all of that, you have an outstanding chance,' Bruce said at the time. 'Of everyone who was here, he was the one who jumped out. It was pre-season, July 2009, and he had obviously worked extremely hard over the summer. He is a natural athlete, he is capable in games of getting right to the peak performance of anyone in the Premier League. Any midfield player, he is level with them at 19, and that is some going. The big thing is that we keep his feet on the ground.'

Bruce identified with his hunger: 'All Jordan cares about is football. He eats, sleeps and breathes it,' he later said. 'Long may that continue, but I have a feeling it will. He's never given anyone a moment's trouble and I wouldn't believe it if I heard he'd been caught up in something off the field.'

Bruce, who captained Manchester United before Keane, admitted he was unsure of Henderson's best position as a teenager and he used him as a right midfielder in what transpired to be the player's breakthrough game against Chelsea, even though Sunderland lost 3–1. Ball remembered: 'Ashley Cole was the best left-back in the world and Jordan's job was to go toe-to-toe with him. He was still a teenager, but he had the capacity to match him. He couldn't have had a tougher task. The game was at the Stadium of Light. It was packed to capacity and all of his family and friends were there. He didn't let them down.'

Inside twelve months, Bruce labelled Henderson as 'the brightest young prospect in the British game. At 20 years old, he's got the world at his feet, he's a fantastic footballer,' Bruce said. 'Jordan's got the lot. He covered 13 kilometres against Aston Villa without giving the ball away. He can tackle, he can pass, he can cross. He just needs to score a goal, but he can do that, he can hit the ball.' Bruce believed that £20 million was not enough to sign him. He warned that only if Real Madrid came in with a £30-million offer would he have a problem. Keeping Henderson was 'his biggest challenge'. If the biggest clubs did their homework, 'they'd all come calling'.

In June 2011 Jordan Henderson joined Liverpool for £16 million. He had played 79 games for Sunderland, scoring five goals. He was the first major summer signing of the Fenway Sports Group era. Immediately, this brought expectation – a situation not helped by the standard of Liverpool's other recruits. Charlie Adam was the next to be brought in and he lasted a season. Stewart Downing lasted two seasons. Sebastián Coates barely played. Meanwhile, Craig Bellamy was a short-term solution – but so was Kenny Dalglish, the legendary manager who left after eighteen months back in charge at the club. He had delivered Liverpool's last title in 1990, of course.

Before the start of the 2018–19 campaign the League Cup won in February 2012 under Dalglish had been Liverpool's last trophy. As Liverpool had struggled to rediscover its identity after the mess of Hicks and Gillett and the reign of Roy Hodgson as manager, Dalglish had brought old values back, helping the fans trust what was happening at Anfield again.

There was no coup to oust Dalglish but Liverpool's eighth-place finish was way off where Fenway wished to be, two places down on the year before which had involved the end of the disastrous Hicks and Gillett era as well as Hodgson's sacking. Dalglish's replacement was Brendan Rodgers, and his first season was a transitional period. Liverpool improved but only finished seventh. He had been unsure particularly of Jordan Henderson's abilities. Rodgers liked technical midfielders and Henderson did not quite fall into that bracket. His reputation suffered a knock on three levels. Firstly, because stylistically he did not appear to be in vogue, even with his own manager. Secondly, because Sir Alex Ferguson wrote in his autobiography that he had considered signing Henderson but chose not to because of his unusual gait. And thirdly, because it emerged that Rodgers was willing to trade him for Fulham's Clint Dempsey, an American international midfielder from Texas with an impressive goalscoring record.

He'd only been at Liverpool for fifteen months and yet it felt like nobody wanted him there. Still, Henderson wanted to stay, and he trained hard. This persuaded Rodgers to persevere with him. Rodgers admired his determination to prove people wrong as well as the way he interacted with his teammates. If he was down about his standing in the squad, it did not show. Rodgers would learn quickly that Liverpool is no place for a novice manager with dogma. He did not have the players or level of finance to deliver exactly the style of play he wanted. Rather than delivering a possession-based game, Liverpool became a counter-attacking force. The aim for 2013–14 was to get closer to the Champions League positions, but Liverpool finished second. Henderson had made himself a pivotal figure in the team, regularly playing on the right of an attacking midfield three or sometimes behind Luis Suárez – though not as a conventional number 10. Henderson ran, ran and ran, closing down opponents and giving the ball to Suárez as quickly as possible. Though Suárez won player of the year after scoring 31 league goals, Henderson's work-rate helped create space for him. Liverpool looked like champions when they beat Manchester City with a month of the season to go, but Henderson's red card late in that game put him out of Liverpool's next three matches. They won at Norwich but Liverpool were not quite as cohesive as they were with him in the side. They lost against Chelsea, where Steven Gerrard infamously slipped, and they subsequently missed his thrust. At Crystal Palace, where Liverpool blew a three-goal lead to draw, they missed his calm and his ability to play simple passes and keep the ball. It unravelled pretty quickly for Rodgers from there, and within fifteen months he'd been sacked as Liverpool's manager.

A measure of Henderson's new status was reflected in his appointment as club captain when Steven Gerrard departed for Los Angeles Galaxy in the summer of 2015 – but when Klopp came in his place was under threat again. Klopp wanted to sign a deep-lying midfielder to accompany Emre Can. Where did this leave Henderson? Like Rodgers, though, Klopp came to a realization: Henderson was a much better footballer than he first thought when he wondered whether he had the passing range to adjust to the new shape of the team – similar to Rodgers. Klopp saw in training how Henderson was quick to spot dangers, how quick he was to win possession back and to pass. Henderson could set the tone of the whole team performance from the base of Liverpool's midfield in a way Emre Can could not. Yet Klopp's fears also related to his availability. Henderson played just 17 league games in Klopp's first season due to a heel injury, and he would not make it off the bench when Liverpool lost the 2016 Europa League final to Sevilla in Basel.

A wider impression had formed of Henderson. On Twitter, a platform filled with supporters of whom the majority consume Liverpool coverage on television and rarely see what happens off the ball – where Henderson did so much – Liverpool's captain was unpopular. He was also a nearly man. By 2018 there had been near misses in all of the biggest competitions: a runner-up in the league; losers' medals in another League Cup final, an FA Cup final, a Champions league final, as well as that Europa League final; a World Cup semi-finalist.

Of all the pressures facing him, though, the challenge of replacing Gerrard as captain was the greatest. Henderson was supposed to lead like Gerrard, pass like Gerrard, tackle like Gerrard and score like Gerrard. Except, there is only one Gerrard, and Henderson is a different sort of midfielder. Where Gerrard was the direct point of creation, Henderson did the hard work so others could flourish.

'I've always said to him, "Don't forget, Jordan, you possess the ability and sometimes you might have to do something that makes people go, "Fucking 'ell," ' Kevin Ball said. Ball was on holiday in Spain when Henderson led Liverpool in the Champions League final against Real Madrid, the club Steve Bruce believed he was capable of representing: ' "But we're on holiday," my missus told me. "I don't care, we're watching the game." '

Liverpool would lose, of course, but the moment which made

the hairs stand up on the back of Ball's neck was the sight of his former youth player not looking at the trophy as he went to collect his runners-up medal: 'He walked straight past it. I'd seen that look so many times. It said to me, "I'm not taking you now but I will be back." That's the sort of lad Jordan's always been.'

April rolled into May. A Champions League semi-final for Liverpool with Barcelona. In the Camp Nou Jordan Henderson was left out of the side once again by Klopp. Klopp had explained his decision to him and he accepted it – he had no option but to. But this was not the sort of occasion any player wanted to miss. Trent Alexander-Arnold found himself in the same uncomfortable place, with Joe Gomez chosen at right-back despite not starting a game since Burnley in early December when he broke his leg. Gomez, it was thought, had stronger defensive qualities, and though Liverpool missed Alexander-Arnold's attacking threat, he remained unused.

At this point in the season, Henderson's omission was a surprise. Until the win at Southampton, Klopp had always selected him as a deeper-lying midfielder with the prime responsibility of protecting the back four while pressing the opponent higher up the pitch. This meant a lot of running. Fabinho's influence was growing in the same role, and Henderson was concerned that the Brazilian's development would see him spend the end of the campaign on the bench when it mattered. His other problem was data. Without Henderson on the pitch, Liverpool were a much more dangerous attacking side. Before the Southampton game, wins against Watford and Burnley had yielded nine goals – Henderson was a substitute. When he started – against Bayern Munich at home, and away fixtures at Manchester United and Everton – Liverpool failed to score. A deeper pattern reflected the same data: before Southampton Liverpool had scored three or more goals in 14 games but Henderson had started in just five of those. He had also started in four of the six games when they did not score. He had not scored himself either – or provided a single assist, creating just eight chances.

The rise of other players as well as the statistics led to a conversation. Henderson knocked on Klopp's door at Melwood and told him, 'Give me a chance higher up the pitch – I used to play there, I won't let you down.' It had not been amongst Klopp's thoughts, but he saw enough in a performance for England in Macedonia to think it might work. 'A mistake,' Klopp admitted later, for not thinking of the possibility sooner. Excellent performances in victories over Porto, Chelsea, Cardiff and Huddersfield followed. Henderson was able to play more freely on the right side of a midfield three and his aggression spread across the team. It worried him, though, that he finished the Huddersfield game five days before the Barcelona trip. It was a sign that the energy of other midfielders would be used in Catalonia.

Henderson, however, was needed much earlier than expected. Naby Keïta's season-ending injury meant an early introduction. Thanks to Jordi Alba's gorgeous cross and Suárez's movement and finish, it was 1–0 to Barcelona. Henderson soon sent in a similar delivery towards Sadio Mané, who scuffed a shot over the bar. It could have been 1–1. Liverpool would have had a priceless away goal; Henderson would have had a brilliant assist. Though other chances came their way and Liverpool's collective was greater than Barca's, the individualism of Messi swung the outcome his team's way. Messi would score his 600th Barcelona goal in a 3–0 win – Liverpool's heaviest defeat in eighteen months. They did not deserve to lose like this. When Messi turns it on, though, even the world's best can seem vulnerable. He is, after all, from another planet.

'Believe,' Jürgen Klopp told the Liverpool squad as they gathered in the meeting room of the Hope Street hotel on the morning of 7 May. 'We can still go through. You are giants – even if we don't score in the first 20 minutes, believe we can score in the 65th, 66th and 67th minute,' he told them. 'If we score just once then Anfield will be behind you.'

Dejan Lovren, the Croatian centre-back who knew he would only be a substitute following a season interrupted by injuries, was inspired by the speech. 'All the players were,' he said. Vincent Kompany's wonderful second-half goal against Leicester the night before had handed the incentive back to Manchester City in the title race and it meant Liverpool needed Brighton to do them a favour on the final day. Klopp asked his players whether any of them wanted to speak about City. It was an opportunity to get things off their chest but nobody came forward. 'Then,' said Lovren, 'the manager began to tell us that we could beat Barcelona.'

In the first leg Liverpool's match analysts had noticed how Barcelona took time to organize themselves when defending corners and free-kicks. This led to Ray Haughan, the long-serving players' liaison officer from the north-east, holding a discussion with Carl Lancaster, a coaching mentor at the academy in Kirkby who co-ordinated the ball-boys. Klopp had been frustrated with the time it had taken for the ball-boys to get the game going again in the quarter-finals against Porto and the perceived weakness in Barcelona meant reminders were handed out. The ball-boys were all junior players at Liverpool and were told this was their chance to play a part in Liverpool's performance. It certainly wasn't going to be a night off for them. If they wanted to eventually play for Liverpool, they had to watch, think and act quickly. This level of planning indicated Klopp's rallying call at the Hope Street hotel wasn't just blind faith. He really did feel Liverpool still had a chance.

It started like this: Lionel Messi racing towards the Kop. Andy Robertson and Fabinho chasing. Fabinho stuck out one of his long legs and won the ball, sending Messi sprawling. Robertson's momentum went with him and, in falling over Messi, he trampled over his left leg, leaving stud marks. Messi did not complain about that. But he did complain about Robertson cuffing him around the back of the head as possession shifted to another area of the pitch and the cameras switched their attentions. Messi had already been named as the world player of the year on four occasions, having won seven La Liga titles by the time Robertson made his debut as an amateur for Queen's Park. Messi had been introduced to Liverpool but he'd also been introduced to Glasgow and he was not happy, fronting Robertson. Liverpool had a corner but Jordan Henderson told Xherdan Shaqiri to wait as he ran back to the halfway line, telling Messi where to go. The touchpaper was lit.

In the press room, Jamie Carragher had felt that as long as Liverpool did not concede early they were capable of changing everything inside ten minutes. Considering how far Newcastle had taken Klopp's side three nights earlier where Divock Origi scored a winner late on to keep Liverpool's title race alive, considering too that neither Roberto Firmino nor Mohamed Salah were available through injury – 'two of the world's best strikers,' as Klopp called them – considering the number of goals Liverpool needed, and considering they could not really afford to let any in against an opponent which included arguably the greatest footballer of all time, what followed was incredible.

Henderson's individual story encapsulated the collective tale of Liverpool, his rise symbolizing the phoenix in the team. One–nil to Liverpool, it became, when the captain charged through midfield and got a shot away. He did not score but Origi did with the rebound. Anfield erupted. It fell silent when Henderson hit the floor. Half an hour had been played and he was clutching his knee, beating the ground. Klopp could not believe his luck. He looked to the heavens and cursed. Another injury to go with the one suffered by Alex Oxlade-Chamberlain twelve months earlier, Mohamed Salah in the Champions League final, Salah again at Newcastle – and Firmino before him. None of these were strains or the consequence of a lack of fitness. They were collisions and blows: pure football, pure bad luck. Improbably, Henderson rose slowly to his feet. It looked like the sort of moment where a player tries to run something off but then gives up. Henderson did not, though. By half-time he was still there. Liverpool were still there. It was 1–0, but only because of Alisson Becker's three saves. Liverpool were battering Barcelona but that meant gaps were left and, with the quality in Barcelona's midfield, it only took one pass to exploit them. The chances reminded of Liverpool's predicament: four goals to go through without conceding. It still seemed impossible.

Their chances decreased when Robertson did not return for the second half. Suárez had seen to him, kicking out at his calf as the Turkish referee looked the other way. He tried to carry on and hobbled around for ten minutes but anyone could see his discomfort. His exit was not a surprise, just another crushing blow to Liverpool's hopes.

And yet, they kept coming. In Barcelona Georginio Wijnaldum had been used as the centre-forward. A midfielder usually, Klopp wanted the Dutchman to screen the area between Barcelona's defence and midfield, winning possession quickly with the idea of feeding Salah or Sadio Mané. Klopp thought of Wijnaldum as being one of the most perceptive readers in his team of a game's flow, his knowledge enhanced by his upbringing in Holland where he played for two of the country's great clubs in Feyenoord and PSV Eindhoven. The 28-year-old had played in every position but in goal: as an attacking midfielder at Feyenoord, as a winger at PSV, then six different positions at Newcastle in his one season there, before anchoring Liverpool's midfield and playing as a centre-back. It sort of worked as a centre-forward in Barcelona and his performance there may have been enough to help get the better of lesser opponents, but this was Barcelona . . .

He was a substitute in the return leg at Anfield, and not happy about it. Klopp, though, had told him the decision was not a reflection of his ability, rather the circumstance. His last instruction before he left the dressing room? 'Attack the crosses, Gini.'

Henderson restarted the game. Ten minutes later, it was Liverpool 3–0 Barcelona. Both goals were Wijnaldum's. Both from crosses, the first fizzed brilliantly towards him by Trent Alexander-Arnold and the next by Xherdan Shaqiri – Salah's replacement. Wijnaldum had taken six touches in total, two of them goals. The foundations of the stadium were shaking, the noise off the scale. The first goal had given supporters belief it could happen. The second brought expectation that it was inevitable. An equalizer invited fear: that having come so far, it would be a catastrophe to lose it now. Somehow, Liverpool were now level in the tie, but they still knew just one Barcelona goal would leave them needing another two themselves.

No Liverpool players, however, were caught up by possibilities or implications. Fabinho was on a tightrope but he kept winning tackles. James Milner was a 33-year-old filling in at left-back for Robertson but he kept moving forward, joining Liverpool's attacks. Henderson was freer than everyone, blasting past Arturo Vidal and setting up another Liverpool attack. When Vidal, a Chilean international who had won eight domestic titles in a row having played also for Juventus and Bayern Munich, was removed after 75 minutes he could barely walk – he almost stumbled off the pitch. Philippe Coutinho had left by then, the midfielder whose sale to Barcelona funded Liverpool's signings of Van Dijk and Becker and, as it became much clearer who got the best deal out of that one, Henderson kept running, Liverpool's players kept tackling and Liverpool were massively on top – but it still needed one more goal.

Then, pandemonium. Alexander-Arnold had acted as a ball-boy during his time at the academy. There were pictures of him in the distance when Liverpool lost to Chelsea in 2014, the day Gerrard slipped and Suárez did not have it in him to inspire a Liverpool recovery. Five years later, Alexander-Arnold was facing one of his heroes. A 14-year-old ball-boy from Leeds followed his instructions, as they all had, helping a relentless Liverpool performance which never allowed Barcelona a break. Their defence was still arguing when Alexander-Arnold saw a gap. Klopp had told him and Xherdan Shaqiri to alternate between corner-takers and it was Shaqiri's turn. Alexander-Arnold was walking away when he saw Barcelona's players not paying attention, so he went off-grid, not following instructions. Though *Mundo Deportivo*, the Catalan daily, would label it 'the corner of shame', Origi's sweeping finish in front of the Kop was delivered like an awesome wave.

At the final whistle Henderson lay on the far side of the pitch near the Centenary Stand, collapsed, pole-axed, drained, elated, hands placed on his head. It was almost like the end had allowed his body to finally give way because he had given everything – just as his teammates had. Together, Wijnaldum and Milner, a man of granite, cried too. Milner, who had disguised the pass which allowed Shaqiri to serve Wijnaldum his second goal of the night, had booted the ball into the Kop when it was all over. His reaction was a mix of defiance, relief and achievement. Fabinho, meanwhile, also wept lightly as he sang 'You'll Never Walk Alone' with the rest of the Liverpool squad in front of the Kop moments later. The Brazilian was still learning English but he knew what the words meant. He could barely get them out as he sobbed lightly.

Salah was there now, wearing a t-shirt which said: NEVER GIVE UP. A Champions League final had been taken away from him eleven months earlier. He knew this was another chance. Even Klopp had his hands on his head. He had masterminded recoveries in football before but none that involved this margin against this standard of opposition. He swore live on television. He looked more drained than anyone. 'I feel,' Klopp tried to convince, 'fucking brilliant' – though he did not look it.

Back in the dressing room, Trent Alexander-Arnold breathed heavily, running his hands through his hair as he stared at the floor. A beaming Salah leaned over to Milner, who was now retired from international duty. 'Have you planned your holiday?' he asked. Milner, with his sodden shirt now draining on the floor, still could not find the words to respond.

Henderson floated through the mixed zone. He was still in pain. The doctor had told him to keep his knee moving and at half-time he'd taken painkillers and jabs to get him through the rest of the match. 'Give us everything you've got,' he told the medics. The adrenaline of the occasion and the will of the crowd would push him on. He could not really compute what had happened after that. The best night of his career, he called it. 'It was unbelievable. From start to finish I thought the lads were amazing. The atmosphere was amazing. It was just unbelievable. I think we proved quite a few people wrong tonight,' Henderson declared. 'We showed that if you never give up and you keep trying you can produce special things.'

He was surely now the most appropriate captain Liverpool could have had: a player written off, but never by his coaches; a leader of a team written off, but never by the fans – representing a city written off, but never by its people. Henderson was the ultimate outsider in a position of responsibility and authority. 'I have always wanted to prove people wrong and that will never change,' he admitted. 'I will continue to do that until I finish playing football.' Fortunes in football, he continued, could change quickly. He knew what Sunday meant, with Wolves coming to Anfield and Manchester City at Brighton. It was the defining weekend of the football season. It was his chance to become Liverpool's first title-winning captain since Alan Hansen. 'Imagine,' he pondered, though he would not, or maybe did not, have the strength to say any more.

17. IT'S ONLY PAIN

JÜRGEN KLOPP DID NOT CONSIDER WHAT HAPPENED AGAINST BARCE-
lona a miracle. The following night, he watched Tottenham recover
a 3–0 aggregate deficit to knock out Ajax in the other Champions
League semi-final on away goals. 'Big football performances,' he
called them. Arsenal would face Chelsea in the Europa League
final too, which meant English clubs were guaranteed to win both
major European competitions. Klopp thought about why this was
possible – never before had four English teams reached finals in the
same season. He analysed Tottenham's route to the final and
related to the struggle because Liverpool had fought hard as well.
'It's not about money,' he concluded. 'We went through because
of our desire, and Tottenham are the same.'

It was two days before Liverpool's final game of the Premier
League season. Their title pursuit had been remarkable, but so
had Manchester City's, a team that had won 13 league games in
a row without ever stretching further than a point ahead of Liverpool when both clubs had played the same number of games.
The Champions League had once felt like a consolation prize
for Liverpool, which was remarkable considering how desperate
they'd been to qualify for the competition after so many years
in the European wilderness. With Liverpool still needing an
unlikely slip from City in the final league game at Brighton, the
Champions League now felt like the club's most realistic chance
of silverware – though Klopp certainly did not see it as a consolation. He was trying to win it for the first time after two

losing finals. Barcelona was, he said, 'One of the best moments in football history, not only Liverpool.'

The statement appealed to a sense of Scouse exceptionalism but Klopp meant what he said and few could argue that he was wrong. He had delivered a rousing speech that helped make his players believe they could get past Barcelona, but he had given rousing speeches before and the outcome had not been so positive. This was different, he thought, because of a new maturity, with the average age of Liverpool's team ripening to just below 26. He called them 'mentality giants' and by that, he was referring to their 'readiness to deal with problems'. Though Klopp always had a plan and he always gave instructions, it didn't always work out, but the players accepted that and still had the assurance to stick to the plan regardless. The relationship between the players and their understanding of one another as human beings had helped Liverpool through what had seemed the impossible. Liverpool's players celebrated their victory over Barcelona. 'But there was never a moment when I had to tell them to calm down,' Klopp said. They were elated but drained so he gave them another day off on the Thursday because he could see they were tired and needed to think about something else. Georginio Wijnaldum, whose introduction as a substitute proved a significant moment, went back to Rotterdam and spent most of the day in a café with friends. The weather was warm on Merseyside and Alisson Becker had a barbecue at his home in Woolton.

In the dressing room after Barcelona Dejan Lovren had danced with Rhian Brewster, another substitute who was named on the bench because of all the other injuries in the Liverpool squad. Brewster was expected to replace Daniel Sturridge in the first-team squad over the summer to follow but it had been a testing fortnight for him after the death of his mum's cousin in London. She had gone missing twelve months earlier and her body was found at the end of April in a freezer. Klopp supported him, offering to give the 19-year-old time off if he needed it. Yet Brewster wanted to remain on Merseyside. He had been a part of most of the match-day squads throughout the second half of the season and he was included in all of the club's promotional videos for the 2019–20 campaign, which showed how much Klopp and Liverpool thought of him. Such was the hope, Mike Gordon watched his comeback match following a long injury lay-off through video link and phoned Klopp as soon as he scored to discuss his path. Now, he was moving across the dressing-room floor with Lovren confidently before placing himself next to Jordan Henderson, who could barely walk. The captain was sat slumped in the corner, his face flushed, almost as red as his shirt. Andy Robertson had got changed at half-time and he was hobbling around, telling anyone who asked, 'It's only pain.' Both Henderson and Robertson told Klopp straight away, 'I'll be ready for Sunday – it's only pain.'

Klopp retreated to a Melwood side room again, where he waited as Merseyside's football reporters shuffled down a corridor lined with prints of Roger Hunt and Ian St John on the walls. The interest and wider study around Liverpool's final game of the league season with Wolverhampton Wanderers at Anfield meant lots of what Klopp said next was lost in the match previews ahead of a game which had the potential to change Liverpool's history – even if that seemed unlikely considering City's relentlessness as they headed to Brighton, a team that was safe from relegation following a disappointing campaign.

Klopp has a knack of giving plenty of information and detail about the emotion involved in football. Even though he is reliably persuasive ahead of big matches, some of his more interesting arguments tend to get completely left out of newspapers where there's a limitation on space. On his arrival at Anfield he had speculated about his own future, asking whether people would still be so interested in him if he had not won a trophy inside four seasons. He looked back at the club he inherited to the one he now essentially ran. No major decision was passed without his consultation. If he asked for something, he usually got it. Fenway trusted him implicitly. He took pride in the development of the club, which to him was more important than the achievements of the team. 'If that leads to silverware then wonderful, but we cannot do more,' he said. 'If people judge me on not winning something in the past or winning something in the future, I cannot change that.'

He believed he had drawn a picture of what Liverpool was about through 'wonderful moments – wonderful moments spent together'. Whereas supporters had dreaded more games than they probably looked forward to between 2009 and 2015, they now could not wait for kick-off. It helped Klopp that in each of his seasons in charge the last game mattered, and this kept interest going in Liverpool as long as, if not longer than, any other club in the country. 'This is Liverpool, we say this is possible – this team, this club, this city makes it possible.' Perhaps Barcelona was worth more than silverware. 'If you struggle in a game, they hit the post and the bar but you win it, that's good for looking back and saying, "That year we won it and, oh, we were lucky." It's a nice story but it doesn't help with development. The job,' he added, 'is to develop as far and as high as possible so it gets more and more likely that you win silverware, and that's what we've done so far. Now we go to a final and we'll play it, learn from the past few years and see what we can do. Sunday is our last Premier League game, if we can win it, it's not in our hands what we get for that, but it doesn't make our season a little bit less good. It's just a different finish.'

Klopp defined his aim for Liverpool as 'being stable at the highest possible level – that's my wish'. It was not about the style of football his team delivered, though that did matter. He took most satisfaction from the first part of the season when Liverpool's players 'managed games', winning several 1–0. Those were the occasions where Liverpool's supporters demanded more football and the questions started about whether the team had lost some thrust. Klopp was associated with aggressive, heavy-metal football but he had realized that possession football allowed his team to rest and control what was happening. It was later on in the season when Liverpool switched on. 'Now,' he said, 'the boys know how to use the right tools in the right moments.'

Klopp recognized, however, that 'nobody sleeps in this business' – that Liverpool's competitors do not stand still. It had frustrated Manchester City from the top down that the media supposedly weren't quite as interested in their story as they were Liverpool's. Yet City should have been grateful for Liverpool's challenge. They had made the season interesting and, without their presence, the discussion may indeed have been all about City – but it might not have been the one their owners preferred, considering the number of investigations hanging over them.

At the start of the season Klopp had compared Liverpool to Rocky Balboa. Though Liverpool had the greater history, it was fighting to floor an opponent which had more resources, one which had used those resources to finish 25 points ahead the season before. History or not, Liverpool were the underdog in modern terms, and Klopp had narrowed that to just one in a campaign where every other team in the league lost ground. Klopp was asked about which Rocky he preferred. Balboa had been beaten by Apollo Creed in the first movie. 'Rocky IV,' Klopp said quickly. 'It was always Rocky IV.' Ivan Drago was Rocky's opponent in that movie. And he was eventually caught cheating.

For 83 seconds Liverpool were going to be champions. They had taken the lead against Wolves. Sadio Mané again. There had been an argument that the title was completely out of their hands, but by scoring first, City's players would know – the news would cascade from the terraces in Brighton and onto the pitch. Liverpool 1–0 Wolverhampton Wanderers. Brighton and Hove Albion (thanks to Glenn Murray) 1– 0 Manchester City. Liverpool on 97 points, City 95. Pandemonium inside Anfield again. In those moments, a Liverpudlian sitting near the press box, a Scouser to his bones, switched from being a confidently cynical seventy-something – the sort who holds court by telling stories from the side of his mouth like a 1930s Chicago mobster – and was reduced to a wreck, not moving but vibrating involuntarily. He could not control himself. Then City scored. Sergio Agüero. 1–1.

For a short while Anfield became a procession of a thousand funerals. There was still hope but a cold realization that an equalizer had come so soon, so instantly – Brighton could not resist them from here, a team flattened for confidence already. The following day Chris Hughton, their manager of four and a half years, would get the sack. This was a club flatlining with an owner worried about relegation. It finished Brighton 1–4 Manchester City. Liverpool 2–0 Wolves no longer seemed to matter. Mané had got his team's second, flicking in another Trent Alexander-Arnold cross (the right-back now had four assists in a week and twelve assists in the league all season, the most from a full-back in Premier League history). Liverpool had proved their valour but, although Anfield was defiantly rocking until the end, sober eyes were sunken with fatigue and disappointment. Klopp believed that had there been an award for the biggest jump in development, Liverpool would have got it. Liverpool, he insisted, had made the biggest step in the league. 'And there is more to come,' he insisted.

City's title had brought joy to supporters of other clubs, not least Everton, who were the first Premier League club to congratulate the champions on Twitter.

'Raheem Sterling, he's top of the league . . .

'You're gonna win f—k all . . .

'You nearly won the league . . .

'You f—ked it up . . .'

On and on the triumphant chants went that day, rarely mentioning the possibilities, of course, for the team those supporters in the away end at Anfield were actually following – a team who three weeks earlier at Wembley had a 2–0 advantage over Watford in their biggest game in decades and, well, 'f—ked it up.'

It would be like this for Liverpool until the first Saturday of June, at least, when Tottenham awaited in Madrid – reminders of what could have been even came from those who never in their lives had been in a position to dream as big as this and feel, for 83 seconds at least, that it was all coming their way.

It should eventually dawn that this is a Liverpool team which has only finished second to one of the best and most expensive squads in British history, having recorded the third-highest points total ever, while also reaching the Champions League final for the second season in a row. No Liverpool manager since Joe Fagan in 1984 had led convincing pursuits both in Europe's elite competition as well as the domestic championship.

Klopp was aware of the things his critics might say but he was also aware of the wider football landscape. 'People will tell us next season it is thirty years [since Liverpool last won the league], but they have bigger problems, to be honest,' he smiled. No second-placed team in any of the major European leagues had ever reached 97 points, and that should really worry the clubs thinking they can catch City.

But Klopp remained optimistic and bold. He called his team 'one of the best in Liverpool's history' and vowed that this was only the beginning – that City might not be able to resist them next time. His pride was genuine and, inwardly, he had taken more pleasure from the season than any of those in Germany when he led Borussia Dortmund to Bundesliga titles at the expense of Bayern Munich. Martin Quast, a football journalist and a friend of Klopp's since the early 1990s, had been invited into his office after the Barcelona game and had found Klopp happier than ever before. 'There was a deep contentment etched on his face, you could feel his pride and his sense of achievement,' Quast told Raphael Honigstein, another German journalist who knows Klopp well. 'I've never seen him this satisfied. Not even after winning the Double with Borussia Dortmund in 2012.'

'It is the first time we go for the title, not the only time,' Klopp vowed. Back on the Anfield pitch there was still one player to leave. Alexander-Arnold had invited his family to join him on the lap of honour and, long after the stadium had emptied, he practised crosses with his two brothers. Preparation for the next season had already started. But the current one was yet to end.

18. THE JOY OF SIX

JÜRGEN KLOPP WAS LEANING ON THE SEAT OF A GYM MACHINE AT MEL-wood which tested the flexibility and posture of athletes. Appropriate, perhaps, for an imposing straight-backed football manager whose reactions nevertheless throughout the course of his time at Liverpool had helped the team reach a second Champions League final.

He had seemed low after the final day of the league campaign. Though his messages were positive and the words powerful, there was little energy in their deliverance. 'I was rather done than down, it was a long season,' he reasoned, as his players got ready for a training session at Melwood in a dressing room nearby. For 'a minute or so' when Brighton scored to lead Manchester City, he had 'a bit of hope – we are human beings'. To him, the noise in the crowd at Anfield made it sound like Brighton were actually leading 4–0. He thought back to what City had done in the weeks before. 'The Burnley game was the moment' he saw the title drift away when Sergio Agüero's shot dribbled over the line. 'Then Kompany scores the goal against Leicester and you sit there and accept it. For me, it was done.'

The players were given five days off, and most of them went abroad to forget about the disappointment and prepare themselves for the next challenge: Tottenham Hotspur, three weekends later, in Madrid. Mohamed Salah went to a Greek island; Dejan Lovren returned home to Croatia; Trent Alexander-Arnold spent time in Saint-Tropez; while Divock Origi and Fabinho went separately with their girlfriends to Abu Dhabi. From his sun lounger,

Fabinho's voyage of self-recovery began with a book, C.S. Lewis's *The Problem of Pain*.

Six days at a training camp in Marbella followed, which Klopp treated as a mini pre-season. Klopp's attention to detail was reflected here. Most clubs across Europe had finished their seasons so options for potential opponents in warm-up games were thin, yet he still remained selective and listened to the advice of his first-team coach Pep Lijnders, picking out Benfica's B side because of similarities with Tottenham's style of play. Renato Paiva, the team's coach, agreed to do whatever Klopp asked of him and spent time ahead of the game analyzing how Tottenham would play in an attempt to mimic their approach tactically.

The suggestion that his record in finals had anything to do with his preparations annoyed Klopp and so, when he was asked whether Marbella had been different, he became prickly. 'Everything – we changed everything,' he snorted – largely because he'd never followed the same routine twice anyway, and was still trying to find the right combinations.

Three weeks was an unusually long stretch to wait but it did give Klopp the time to reflect on the progress of his team and build up their confidence again if it was needed. In the past, he'd always tried to present Liverpool in the role of the underdog, but now he wanted them to embrace being favourites against a team they had beaten twice in the league and finished 26 points ahead of. He believed this Liverpool side was stronger than any of those he'd managed in Germany – Borussia Dortmund were a 'brilliant, brilliant team', and they did win the Bundesliga twice, but they were younger than Liverpool and not as mature. It had been Liverpool's maturity over the course of a whole season which had impressed him the most, and he reminded them of that at the end of the trip to Marbella.

Klopp appreciated, however, that a final is something else, and no matter the events of the league campaign, Tottenham in Madrid would be different. The English public knew this more than the European public, he thought, because abroad they only look at the results and the placings in the table without seeing the bounces and bobbles of a season where 'Tottenham were fucking outstanding, to be honest'.

Like Klopp, Mauricio Pochettino has been admired for the way he's transformed Tottenham into one of the most consistently exciting sides to watch in Europe. And like Klopp, a big question mark hung over the Argentine because, after five years in charge, he'd won nothing. Pochettino said he'd never judge a manager on how many trophies he'd won, and Klopp agreed with him, though he accepted the conditions of his working environment for what they were. His 97 points in the league for Liverpool would only get the credit he thought was deserved if another team won the league with that total. 'We all have different circumstances,' he stressed. 'We have different teams, we have different clubs. We have to fight against different things . . . but nobody's *really* interested.' Sheffield United's Chris Wilder winning the League Managers' Association Manager of the Year was a good thing, he thought, because it showed that at least some people were looking at resources and how a team plays. Wilder would be a Premier League manager the following season having led the South Yorkshire club to second in the Championship, finishing above much richer competitors. 'Coaches, most of us, judge each other not on trophies,' he stressed. 'And not because most of us don't win, only because we know about the job.'

A year earlier in Kiev, Real Madrid were a lot more experienced in dealing with the occasion Klopp's players were facing, having won the competition for two seasons in a row and vying for a third title: 'For them it was very simple to deal with all the circumstances around the game.' Klopp thought about the twenty minutes after the warm-up where the players leave the pitch before they can enter it again: 'All the party is going on around and you are sitting in the dressing room. It is a lot of time to think.' Liverpool knew more about that process now – they also knew how mistakes and reactions to mistakes could define how things were remembered. 'But we don't feel halfway there because of that – we only feel positive. Let me say it like this,' Klopp stressed. 'It doesn't always mean that the better team will always win. Being the better team would help because it is a difficult game. But it is about scoring in the decisive moments, scoring in the right moments, conceding no goals. Stay in the game whatever happens, stay focused, stay concentrated – again and again and again. That is what we want.'

And that is exactly what he got.

In Madrid there were little signs that reflected the distance Liverpool had travelled over the previous ten years. The city is the birthplace of Fernando Torres, the centre-forward Liverpool supporters fell in love with before he abandoned them in the months after Fenway's takeover. Liverpool had sold Xabi Alonso to Real Madrid in the summer of 2009 (and Javier Mascherano to Barcelona by the time Torres had departed for Chelsea). Though Torres did not reach his Liverpool levels in London, the destination was confirmation of a shift: the money and success of another club had made this possible and Liverpool were now vulnerable in the English market and not just abroad. Had it been Luis Suárez's decision, he'd have gone to Arsenal in the summer of 2013. Two years later Raheem Sterling went to Manchester City. Liverpool were losing their best players to domestic rivals. Jürgen Klopp knew how difficult it was to maintain development when such figures are constantly being sold to those clubs who are competing to finish above you. Considering he'd signed Virgil van Dijk from under the noses of City and Alisson Becker, who could have gone to Chelsea, it felt like he'd reversed that pattern by the start of the 2018–19 season. Without those signings, would it really have been possible for Liverpool to reach Kiev, never mind Madrid?

The final was being played in Atlético Madrid's new Wanda Metropolitano stadium, way out to the east of the city – like the Santiago Bernabéu, round the other side of the centre from the old Vicente Calderón, located to the south of the city on the banks of the Manzanares river in the working-class Arganzuela district which is also known for its Mahou beer factory as well as its slaughterhouses. The Bernabéu, on the grand Paseo de la Castellana, was the setting for one of the most dispiriting nights in Liverpool's European history in 2014 when Brendan Rodgers named a weakened side in one of the world's great football arenas and lost easily, 1–0. He had taken the decision after seeing

Liverpool lose at Anfield to Real Madrid. A 3–0 scoreline did not reflect Real's dominance at all. Sterling, Steven Gerrard, Philippe Coutinho and Jordan Henderson were all 'rested' in the Bernabéu, according to Rodgers, because Liverpool had an important league game against Chelsea the following weekend, which they lost 2–1. To some of those not in the starting XI, it represented the night Rodgers not only lost faith in the players but the players lost faith in him.

Twelve months later Klopp had replaced Rodgers and his first game in charge was Tottenham in London. Mauricio Pochettino was in his second season in charge and though the hosts were clearly a more talented and organized team that afternoon, Klopp and Liverpool's will radiated and a goalless draw was fair. The day before, Klopp had received his first set-back as Liverpool manager after Danny Ings sustained an injury in training which would keep him out for nearly two years. Klopp was short on options and when he was asked by a journalist what he would do, he leaned over and asked, 'Do you remember Origi?' rolling the R across his tongue for emphasis. He had tried to sign the striker for Borussia Dortmund and clearly he rated him highly. Origi, though, had started his Liverpool career poorly in a struggling team and was without a goal in his first ten games. Thanks to Klopp's encouragement, he would finish the season having emerged as Liverpool's in-form striker before an ankle injury sustained in the Merseyside derby – a horrendous challenge from Ramiro Funes Mori – ruled him out of the Europa League final, where Liverpool lost miserably to Sevilla.

Origi's goals in 2018–19 had injected Liverpool's supporters with the belief that there was no such thing as the pursuit of the impossible. Any hangover from the league campaign had truly been washed away by the time they set off for Madrid, taking all sorts of mad routes to get there, before assembling at the Plaza Felipe II near the Goya metro stop. The square was transformed from a scruffy mess of lumpen concrete with a Corte Inglés as its centrepiece into a heaving mass of red humanity where an estimated 20,000 Liverpool supporters (there were meant to be 50,000 in total – despite there being just 17,000 tickets available, thanks to Uefa who kept more than half of the stadium's capacity for the sponsors) gathered to listen to a host of Scouse musicians do their stuff, with Jamie Webster headlining. If what happened at Shevchenko Park in Kiev twelve months earlier was incredible (it felt new, even though *Boss Nights* had been around for years) this was more dramatic – a true show of strength. In Kiev the crowd seemed smaller from the stage, because of all the trees, but here the river of red went on and on as far as the eye could see, along a narrow corridor of Madrid's city centre. The visual show of strength reminded what Liverpool had become, but it also indicated the potential for the club to become the biggest in the world. It now had the numbers who wanted it to win but also the financial landscape to take it whichever way. All it needed was trophies.

Bedlam. A child in a Liverpool shirt, no older than 13, is leaning forward at the front of the stand urging the referee to blow his whistle for the last time. The child's face is flushed, his eyes are widening. He wants it to all be over. He can see it coming. Tears are already streaming from his eyes. Then the moment arrives. He cries uncontrollably. Shaking with ecstasy. Grown men all around him tumble over seats not caring where they land, squeezing each other on the warm, damp concrete.

Trent Alexander-Arnold falls head first like he's been harpooned through the back. Virgil van Dijk, the tallest person in the Liverpool squad, loses control of his senses as he lies on the grass, and is helped to his feet by the smallest person, Xherdan Shaqiri – a substitute. Jordan Henderson embraces Jürgen Klopp in tears then embraces Adam Lallana, his best mate, in tears, before embracing his father Brian, in tears. Brian had cancer on his neck in 2014, when Liverpool nearly won the league, but decided not to tell his son because he did not want to distract him. Henderson held onto Brian for two minutes solid while the celebrations went on behind him. Klopp thumped his chest, hugging each one of his players: hugging Alisson – whispering something; hugging Trent – whispering something; hugging Joël Matip – whispering something; hugging Van Dijk – whispering something; hugging Andy Robertson – whispering something; hugging James Milner – whispering something; hugging

Fabinho – whispering something; hugging Gini Wijnaldum – whispering something; hugging Mohamed Salah – whispering something; hugging Roberto Firmino – whispering something; hugging Sadio Mané – whispering something; hugging Divock Origi – whispering something. Klopp gave longer hugs to those who didn't play for him. He had ensured they felt a part of it all for all of the season – 'That is why,' he insisted, 'it was possible for this club to come to Madrid.'

Trent spoke: a poor game, he was told. Liverpool didn't play well, *that* well, at all. He responded: 'None of us are even bothered about that. When we look back on tonight, we're not gonna think about it being a sluggish game. We're gonna think, "We've won the European Cup." ' He was asked about becoming a legend. 'I'm just a normal lad from Liverpool whose dream has just come true.' And then he smiled an exhausted smile.

All that matters is the information on the scoreboard: Tottenham Hotspur 0 Liverpool 2. There had been a penalty and a goal inside the first two minutes: Sadio Mané's cross, Moussa Sissoko's handball after just 22 seconds, complaints, then Mohamed Salah ramming the subsequent penalty kick past Hugo Lloris. Salah's expression was one of relief. Sissoko looked bereaved; Tottenham's players shell-shocked. Was it even a penalty? The ball was heading out of the box when it struck Sissoko's armpit but that sent it veering towards his ridiculously outstretched right arm and therefore potentially back into the danger area for defenders. Sissoko had been careless. Tottenham, unlucky. But it was a penalty – even if Liverpool had barely earned their lead.

As Klopp had predicted four days earlier, the outcome would be decided by mistakes or perceived injustices, and whoever dealt better with them. Liverpool had scored in a 'decisive moment', which did not allow Tottenham to settle even though there was so long to react. Liverpool conceded no goals, staying 'focused, concentrated again and again'. It emerged as one of the worst finals in football that anyone could remember, but Liverpool had served up so much drama throughout the season, their only duty now was to cross the line. 'People tend to remember greater performances when you lose,' Klopp had once thought.

From there Liverpool wasted time sensibly and increased Tottenham's frustration and impatience. Throw-ins and corners took an age. Free-kicks were pragmatic and sometimes awful, never ambitious but never reckless either. In the heat, Liverpool gave the ball away – Trent Alexander-Arnold's passing was way off but his defending was good, and others like him kept their calm. In the moments after his opening goal Jordan Henderson was telling Salah to focus on his defensive duties – to not forget to press and close the space. Salah and Mané's threat meant Tottenham's full-backs could not break forward and, in desperation, Pochettino brought more attackers on, pushing for an equalizer. 'Game management,' Klopp called it. 'No risks, no chance for mistakes.'

Alisson had tipped a brilliant Christian Eriksen free-kick around the post, his handling of tricky bouncing shots, superb. Klopp's substitutions were the right ones at the right times: Origi on for Roberto Firmino before the hour mark, and James Milner on for Georginio Wijnaldum a couple of minutes later. There was a comparison to be made between Klopp's and Pochettino's decisions here because Firmino had injured himself in training a month earlier and had missed four of the last five games while Tottenham's talismanic centre-forward Harry Kane had been out for two months, a spell which included the second leg of their momentous quarter-final against Manchester City, where three away goals sent them through.

Both managers could not resist starting them at the expense of strikers in Origi and Lucas Moura whose five goals between them had since sent their clubs to the final. While Klopp could see Firmino wasn't influencing the game as he normally would be, and removed him when it mattered, Pochettino pressed on with Kane, and Tottenham suffered as a consequence, lacking a firing focal point in attack.

In possession Origi was as unconvincing as any of his teammates but his positioning was excellent. Klopp had sent him on to make Eriksen think about his defensive duties instead of his attacking ones and this helped reduce the Dane's creative threat. Milner, meanwhile, slowed everything down. One corner kick took 90 seconds to take as he moved the ball in and out of the quadrant, forcing discussions with officials.

Klopp had turned Liverpool, a team known for its thrilling go-for-the-throat approach, into a weather-beaten finalist that appreciated now what it took to reach a summit. At a meeting in Marbella he'd told the players: 'We make this as horrible for them as it can be. They won't recognize us.' The players nodded. Each one knew they'd served up entertainment throughout the season and their only duty was to the Liverpool supporters who at this point only cared about winning having suffered so much disappointment in finals over the previous decade. Though Liverpool's players were clearly relaxed in Marbella there was a business-like manner in training, and the noise coming out of the camp was consistent: they were only thinking about winning. Entertainment was a bonus, but it did not really matter.

In the second half Tottenham were the more convincing team in possession but Liverpool were the better organized out of it. Tottenham's players looked tired but Liverpool's looked like they could go on for longer. Both Tottenham full-backs were on their haunches, knowing all of the substitutions had been made. It was no surprise when the clinching goal came from a flank. Kieran Trippier, a right-back who began his career in Manchester City's youth teams, had disappeared from view as Origi kept his composure to drag a low left-footed shot past Lloris and into the corner of the net. Another unlikely European champion in Joël Matip had engineered the opportunity, keeping the chance alive as the ball bounced around the box. Just four minutes remained and the roar at the Liverpool end of the stadium seemed to sweep across the pitch like a tidal wave hitting land.

Fifteen minutes later it was time to collect the cup. Salah could not take his eyes off it as he walked up. He could not stop smiling. He remembered where he had been and later referenced that journey from the village of Nagrig to Cairo, what happened in Kiev – the pain. 'I looked at the picture from last year before the game,' he admitted.

Henderson wanted Klopp and Milner to lift it with him but the manager and vice captain told him to go ahead. That said a lot about Henderson and a lot about Klopp and Milner. Henderson's face was an explosion when the cup went up: a fusion of joy, relief, frustration, pride and ownership. It was his trophy now. Van Dijk had become the symbol of the team but he saw Henderson as its leader: 'He is my captain,' he said. Steven Gerrard, up in the stands, knew he was no longer the last Liverpool captain to lead the team to silverware. He knew how all of this changes a player's life, how people view a player differently when there are images of him lifting the European Cup that last for ever. Everything else melts away, the mistakes of yesterday are forgotten and the mistakes to come get forgiven a lot quicker. It is Henderson's selflessness Gerrard admires the most, the midfielder who had the impossible task of succeeding him. 'He is someone who puts himself at the back of the queue because he looks after everyone first,' Gerrard thought. Now Henderson was at the front, the eyes of the world fixed directly on him. He is a European Cup-winning Liverpool captain, the fifth in the club's history (Emlyn Hughes lifted it twice).

A couple of hours later Alisson carried the trophy through the doors of a red-lit function room at the Eurostars Tower Hotel on the northern fringes of Madrid. A year earlier, the position he filled had been the weakness that had cost Liverpool dearly. Loris Karius had sent both Klopp and John Achterberg a text congratulating the pair after beating Barcelona, and Achterberg thought this was a reflection of the personality of the goalkeeper who ended up spending the season on loan in Turkey with Beşiktaş.

Achterberg rated Karius but realized the best solution for him was to get away from Liverpool and rediscover himself. The Dutch goalkeeping coach's introduction to Liverpool had been during the club's worst years, from 2009 to 2011, when the team plummeted from second in the league to the relegation zone, losing its best players. Achterberg was the only link on the staff, aside from the masseur Paul Small, back to that period. Brendan Rodgers liked the pair of them, so did Klopp. Yet criticism came for Achterberg from supporters after the popular Pepe Reina was sold and rumours surfaced about the Spaniard's views on the standard of coaching he was receiving. Simon Mignolet did not prove to be an improvement and Karius' Liverpool career ended in Kiev. Had Achterberg had his way Liverpool would have signed Marc-André ter Stegen from Borussia Mönchengladbach in the summer of 2013. Instead Rodgers went for Mignolet – and ter Stegen went to Barcelona a year later, becoming a European champion the year after that. It was around that time Achterberg first came across Alisson at Internacional following a conversation with the former Liverpool back-up goalkeeper, Doni. Achterberg has thousands of files on goalkeepers across the world and it was because of his recommendation that Kamil Grabara – a young Polish goalkeeper – became the first signing of the Klopp era. Achterberg liked what he saw in Alisson but considering Mignolet was so new to the club – and considering too that the Brazilian had not yet secured an EU passport through his German and Italian heritage – meant that his progress was monitored from a distance, until Liverpool played a pre-season friendly against AS Roma in St Louis the summer after Klopp's arrival. Klopp wanted a new first-team goalkeeper and he was impressed, and so Liverpool's scouts went regularly to Italy during the 2016–17 and 2017–18 seasons, following Alisson's progress through speaking to people who had access to training sessions. He mainly played in cup games for Roma in that first campaign.

Achterberg, like Henderson, had taken a lot of flak during his time at Anfield but he believed he was getting the best out of what he had to work with. Alisson's challenge was enormous because he was not just filling a key role in the team, he was having to pick up the pieces from Karius's disastrous end to the previous season. Perhaps the £66-million fee helped him in the end. Those early errors in the season ultimately were not punished by bad results and, because of the fee, many were willing to be more patient with him than they would have been had he seemed a cheap alternative like his predecessors.

Achterberg rarely speaks about his work. He is quiet and serious but nevertheless holds a Dutch sort of confidence when it comes to offering opinions. In the bowels of the Wanda Metropolitano in Madrid it would have been impossible to remove the grin from his face as he stood there with a gold winners' medal hanging around his neck. He thought about all those days at Melwood throughout the season where Alisson pushed himself to become better. He mixed talent and work ethic, becoming physically stronger. Achterberg helped him become fitter because he knew he'd have to play two or three games a week most weeks and that Mignolet would only feature in the domestic cup matches. It was about finding the right intensity between training and games. When outfield players were on recovery sessions, Alisson went at it even harder to try to keep the power in his legs as well as ensuring his reactions were sharp. Before Van Dijk's arrival and the introduction of Andy Robertson into the team, Liverpool's goalkeepers had a lot more to do, but now the challenge was different: 'Two shots to save a game,' Achterberg knew, 'is all he might have to do.'

For Achterberg, indeed, it was the way Alisson had nothing to do for 70 minutes against Spurs but then became busy that distinguished him. 'He's done it in a few games: Napoli to get to the knockout round, Barcelona to get to the final. We bought an expensive goalie but he paid it back with the trophy – he had a big hand in it anyway. The whole team worked their balls off the whole season.'

Achterberg – who spent the bulk of his playing career at Tranmere Rovers having been brought to the club by John Aldridge, a Liverpool legend – was insistent that he only helped Alisson with aspects of his tuition; information and guidance only being part of the game. He had not done anything particularly different with Reina, Mignolet or Karius, only tailored his methods to the demands of the manager he was working for: 'Decision-making you cannot teach, but also staying calm under high pressure is not to teach, it is natural. The training, you can prepare [for] what's going to happen in a game. But decision-making – when to come, when to stay, when to be calm and when to play – he showed that's all him. There are always things he can improve, but the level he has produced this season is probably one of the best in the world. He showed it today.'

Alisson, whose wife Natalia was back in Brazil expecting their second child, held beers in both hands for what seemed most of the morning that followed. On the dancefloor at around 6 a.m. Virgil van Dijk was drinking from a bottle of champagne. The British trio of Jordan Henderson, James Milner and Andy Robertson sat at a table out of the way, smiles on their faces – the sense of achievement slowly dawning on them. Daniel Sturridge, whose six years at the club would come to an end a few days later, shuffled his fingers across the decks, acting as DJ mostly playing hip-hop, obscure music few had ever heard of. Assisting him was John Gibbons from the *Anfield Wrap*, who was having the night of his life. Elsewhere Alex Oxlade-Chamberlain, whose serious knee injury against AS Roma sustained the year before (when Alisson was an opponent) had effectively ruled him out of two Champions League finals, challenged his popstar girlfriend Perrie Edwards to a dance-off.

In each of the finals Klopp had lost with Liverpool he had tried to be at the centre of the after-party, attempting to raise spirits. In Basel in 2016 he told his players 'this is just the beginning' and even though Milner and Henderson were the only surviving members from the squad that was selected that night, Klopp had proven himself good to his word. Here, there were no rousing speeches – no need for reassurances. Klopp posed for photographs with anyone who asked but otherwise seemed to melt into the background, allowing everyone else to share the glory. Liverpool's players, management, staff and owners all wore sunglasses as they left the hotel later that morning straight from the party which, but for a few tired players who managed to get an hour or two's sleep, did not end until the bus arrived to take them to Barajas airport.

The trophy was shared around on the flight home but Henderson had carried it onto the plane with him, posing for a photograph and using it as a foot stool. The assembly point on Merseyside would be at a police training centre on Mather Avenue in the south of the city. Many figured it would be at Melwood, and, Liverpool being a city of rumours, even more had gathered there. More than 250 accredited journalists, including writers from the US, Brazil and China, had arrived in Liverpool and Joe Anderson – the Everton-supporting mayor – estimated Madrid would be worth more than £150 million to the city in terms of tourism alone. 'I've talked a lot about the tourism and visitor economy and what it means for us – and Liverpool FC are the biggest contributors to that,' Anderson admitted. 'What they have done for the brand of this city on a global scale is incalculable. We would have paid a few million quid for that kind of advertising – it is fantastic for the city.'

'That kind of advertising' was a quarter of a million people lining the streets of Liverpool constituting images of incredible civic pride beamed around the world – images of something happening, something positive, something good; not something manufactured or trying to be anything other than what it was. It was the colour: the sheer redness of huge crowds, the cordite and the intensity of the noise. It was men who should know better but had been out all night in next to no clothing perched on top of cranes and cherry-pickers; groups of people traversing half-built and derelict buildings; kids hanging off traffic lights, speed cameras and road signs – all just to see their heroes return home. It was Georginio Wijnaldum, awestruck by the scenes from the top of the bus, dropping his phone but having it returned the next day. It was Alisson Becker drunk, crying. It was Jürgen Klopp pouring beer over Rhian Brewster's head then pretending it wasn't him – Klopp knows Brewster will be his next big star. It was Roberto Firmino dyeing his hair red and wearing Elton John glasses, thinking he's Rocketman. It was Klopp's wife Ulla perched on a bin outside the Liver Building so he could see her from his position aboard the bus. It was the sight of them waving lovingly at one another. It was the bus crawling back to Melwood hours later but taking a detour at James Milner's request to south Liverpool because he wanted to show the trophy to Andrew Devine, a 53-year-old victim of the Hillsborough disaster who's been wheelchair bound ever since. Devine wasn't expected to survive the day in 1989 but he fought on and lives with the support of his family and the help of twenty-four-hour professional care. Milner had met Devine at Melwood and thought the decent thing to do would be to share the greatest moments of his professional life with a supporter who never gave up.

The story of Liverpool's season would end that night in Formby at Klopp's home near the pinewoods. Liverpool's manager had invited Mike Gordon to stay – the person who'd done the most to bring him to the club; the person who picked up the phone and asked, 'Jürgen, would you like to become Liverpool's manager?' Gordon really wanted to be there because he felt it was appropriate to be with Jürgen and Ulla, who he saw as a team. After brandy, gin and tonics and takeaway food the pair slumped onto the couch in Klopp's living room, taking in the magnificence of the weekend, discussing the challenges ahead. 'I think we can do more,' Klopp said. 'Mike,' he stressed, rolling an ice cube around his liquor glass. 'I think this is only the beginning.'

LIVERPOOL RECORDS 2018–19
(in no particular order)

The 4–0 win over West Ham was their biggest opening-day league victory since winning 6–1 at Crystal Palace in 1994.

It was also their biggest opening-day league win at Anfield since the 5–1 victory over Wolves in 1932.

Alisson became only the fourth goalkeeper in Liverpool history to keep clean sheets in the first three league games of a Reds career.

Liverpool won the first seven games of a season in all competitions for the first time in the club's history.

They went 918 minutes without conceding a league goal at Anfield (last season and this) – their second-longest period ever.

Liverpool recorded their longest unbeaten run from the start of a Premier League season (20 games).

They went 21 league games unbeaten (the final game of the 2017–18 season and the first 20 of this one) – their longest ever unbeaten run in the Premier League era.

They were the last team in the top four divisions of English football to lose a league game this season.

Ki-Jana Hoever (aged 16 years, 354 days) became the youngest Liverpool player to appear in the FA Cup.

Liverpool reached a 19th European semi-final – a British record – and a ninth final, again a record for these islands.

When beating Watford at Anfield Liverpool recorded a first in the club's history – beating the same team by five or more goals in three successive home league games.

Liverpool remained undefeated in a fixture-record 19 Merseyside derbies (all competitions) and 17 in the league.

They are now unbeaten in eight successive league visits to Everton – a club record.

During the season James Milner extended his Premier League record by scoring in 52 games without ever losing (41 wins, 11 draws).

Mohamed Salah scored 39 goals in his first 50 league appearances – the second highest tally in the club's history from a player's first 50 games.

Mohamed Salah was quicker to 50 league goals (in 69 games) for Liverpool than any player in Liverpool history.

Salah also scored 69 goals in his first 100 games for Liverpool (in all competitions), more in a first century of games than any Reds player in history.

Naby Keïta's goal against Huddersfield was the second quickest in Liverpool history (15 seconds; the fastest was by Paul Walsh against West Ham in 1984 after 14 seconds).

Liverpool recorded their best points-per-game ratio in their top-flight history: 2.55 points per game.

Liverpool recorded a club record average home league attendance of 53,174, beating the 53,113 set in the 2016–17 season.

They also set a club record for the highest aggregate attendance in a single season at Anfield: 1,010,316, beating the 1,010,170 who watched them in 1972–73.

They recorded their second-highest points tally in a league season (97), only being beaten by the 98 (converted to three points for a win) accumulated in 1978–79.

Those 97 points have been bettered by only three teams in top-flight history (using three points for a win) – as well as Liverpool's own tally of 98 in 1978–79, Manchester City reached 100 in the 2017–18 season and 98 in 2018–19.

Liverpool went on an unbeaten run of 19 games in league and cup (ended by Barcelona) – their best since 1996.

Virgil van Dijk was awarded the PFA Players' Player of the Year Award – the first time since Kenny Dalglish (1983) and Ian Rush (1984) that Liverpool players had won it in successive years (Mo Salah won it in 2018).

Four players – Trent Alexander-Arnold, Virgil van Dijk, Andy Robertson and Sadio Mané – were named in the PFA Team of the Year, the most Liverpool have had in a team since 1989–90.

Liverpool went unbeaten at home for a second successive league season for the first time since 1979–80.

Liverpool equalled a club record by winning 13 away league games in a season – first set in 1904–05 then repeated in 2008–09.

They earned 44 points away from home – a new club record, beating the 43 won in 2008–09.

They conceded only 12 goals away from home in the league – the lowest total since shipping 12 in 1978–79 (and equal second best in their history).

The Reds went unbeaten at home in the league for a second successive season for the first time since 1979–80.

They only lost one away game in the league – their second-best return ever (they were unbeaten in the 1893–94 season).

The win over Barcelona saw them become only the third team in history to overturn a three-goal first-leg deficit in a European Cup semi-final.

Liverpool equalled a club record of 30 league victories in a season.

They became the first runners-up in English top-flight history not to lose to any of the teams that finished below them.

Virgil van Dijk was the first outfield player since Martin Škrtel in 2010–11 to start every Liverpool league game of a campaign. Mo Salah and keeper Alisson also played in all 38 – the first time since 2008–09 that three players were league ever-presents.

Alisson won the Golden Glove for keeping most clean sheets in the Premier League – 21.

His tally was the most by any Liverpool goalkeeper since Ray Clemence kept 28 clean sheets in 1978–79.

Liverpool conceded 22 goals in the league – a club record for the Premier League era.

Mo Salah and Sadio Mané scored 22 Premier League goals to share the Golden Boot along with Arsenal's Pierre-Emerick Aubameyang.

Liverpool scored 55 home league goals – their best in a season since 58 in a 21-game campaign of 1985–86.

At home Liverpool won 17 league games – their best since 19 in the 21-game season of 1978–79.

ACKNOWLEDGEMENTS

Without David Luxton's support, this project would never have happened. I would also like to thank his colleague Rebecca Winfield. At Transworld, Henry Vines showed faith not only in me but also in Liverpool, and Henry is a Middlesbrough supporter. Ian Preece did a fine job as an editor, keeping me on track in the short timeframe we had. I am appreciative of the advice taken from Ian Herbert and the guidance and information of Jeremy Docteur and Matthew O'Connor. To Ged Rea, Andy Kelly, Raphael Honigstein, Andrea Ruberti, Richard van Elsacker, Phil Buckingham and Paul Ashcroft, thank you. Neil Jones, David Lynch, James Pearce and Ian Doyle (sometimes) made fine travelling companions this season. I am sorry for Naples but it worked out well in the end. Tim Abraham, what a man you are – the steak in San Sebastián and then the greeting in Entre Santos from you, Andrew, Heywood, Phil Blundell and Jon Cook (who still doesn't have a lanyard) will always be remembered. Nice one to Tony Barrett, Carra, Mike Gordon and the *Indy* lads: Ed Malyon, Miguel Delaney, Jack Pitt-Brooke and Mark Critchley. And, of course, to my best mate and best man, Mark, as well as Ian, Howie, Andy, Matt, Jay and Billy, even if some of them are Blues. There is my dad, Peter, and my wife, Rosalind, of course. Without their backing, I would never have been in Madrid.

ABOUT THE AUTHOR

Simon Hughes is a journalist and author. He covers Merseyside football for the *Independent* and has written for the *Daily Telegraph* and the *Sunday Telegraph*. His book *Red Machine* won the Antonio Ghirelli Prize for Italian Soccer Foreign Book of the Year 2014. His other titles include *Secret Diary of a Liverpool Scout*, *Men in White Suits* and *Ring of Fire*. He lives in Liverpool.